Food Culture in
Mexico

Food Culture in
Mexico

JANET LONG-SOLÍS AND LUIS ALBERTO VARGAS

Food Culture around the World

Ken Albala, Series Editor

GREENWOOD PRESS
Westport, Connecticut · London

Library of Congress Cataloging-in-Publication Data

Long, Janet (Long Towell)
 Food culture in mexico / Janet Long-Solís and Luis Alberto Vargas.
  p. cm. — (Food culture around the world, ISSN 1545–2638)
 Includes bibliographical references and index.
 ISBN 0–313–32431–X (alk. paper)
 1. Food habits—Mexico. 2. Food preferences—Mexico. 3. Dinners and dining—
Mexico. 4. Cookery, Mexican. 5. Mexico—Social life and customs. 6. Nutrition—
Mexico. I. Vargas, Luis Alberto. II. Title. III. Series.
GT2853.M6L66 2005
394.1'2'0972—dc22   2004025907

British Library Cataloguing in Publication Data is available.

Library of Congress Catalog Card Number: 2004025907
ISBN: 0–313–32431–X
ISSN: 1545–2638

First published in 2005

Greenwood Press, 88 Post Road West, Westport, CT 06881
An imprint of Greenwood Publishing Group, Inc.
www.greenwood.com

Printed in the United States of America

The paper used in this book complies with the
Permanent Paper Standard issued by the National
Information Standards Organization (Z39.48–1984).

10 9 8 7 6 5 4 3 2

The publisher has done its best to make sure the instructions and/or recipes in this book
are correct. However, users should apply judgment and experience when preparing recipes,
especially parents and teachers working with young people. The publisher accepts no responsibility for the outcome of any recipe included in this volume.

Contents

Series Foreword *by Ken Albala*   vii

Acknowledgments   ix

Introduction   xiii

Timeline   xvii

1. Historical Overview   1

2. Major Foods and Ingredients   31

3. Cooking   63

4. Typical Meals   83

5. Regional and Cultural Differences   97

6. Eating Out   123

7. Special Occasions   139

8. Diet and Health   163

Glossary   181

Resource Guide   185

Index   191

Series Foreword

The appearance of the Food Culture around the World series marks a definitive stage in the maturation of Food Studies as a discipline to reach a wider audience of students, general readers, and foodies alike. In comprehensive interdisciplinary reference volumes, each on the food culture of a country or region for which information is most in demand, a remarkable team of experts from around the world offers a deeper understanding and appreciation of the role of food in shaping human culture for a whole new generation. I am honored to have been associated with this project as series editor.

Each volume follows a series format, with a timeline of food-related dates and narrative chapters entitled Introduction, Historical Overview, Major Foods and Ingredients, Cooking, Typical Meals, Eating Out, Special Occasions, and Diet and Health. Each also includes a glossary, resource guide, bibliography, and illustrations.

Finding or growing food has of course been the major preoccupation of our species throughout history, but how various peoples around the world learn to exploit their natural resources, come to esteem or shun specific foods and develop unique cuisines reveals much more about what it is to be human. There is perhaps no better way to understand a culture, its values, preoccupations and fears, than by examining its attitudes toward food. Food provides the daily sustenance around which families and communities bond. It provides the material basis for rituals through which people celebrate the passage of life stages and their connection to divinity. Food preferences also serve to separate individuals and groups from each other, and as one of the most powerful factors in the construction of identity, we physically, emotionally and spiritually become what we eat.

By studying the foodways of people different from ourselves we also grow to understand and tolerate the rich diversity of practices around the world. What seems strange or frightening among other people becomes perfectly rational when set in context. It is my hope that readers will gain from these volumes not only an aesthetic appreciation for the glories of the many culinary traditions described, but also ultimately a more profound respect for the peoples who devised them. Whether it is eating New Year's dumplings in China, folding tamales with friends in Mexico or going out to a famous Michelin-starred restaurant in France, understanding these food traditions helps us to understand the people themselves.

As globalization proceeds apace in the twenty-first century it is also more important than ever to preserve unique local and regional traditions. In many cases these books describe ways of eating that have already begun to disappear or have been seriously transformed by modernity. To know how and why these losses occur today also enables us to decide what traditions, whether from our own heritage or that of others, we wish to keep alive. These books are thus not only about the food and culture of peoples around the world, but also about ourselves and who we hope to be.

Ken Albala
University of the Pacific

Acknowledgments

Many people have inadvertently helped in the formation of this book during the many years I have lived in Mexico. Friends and family members who have shared their tables and knowledge about local food traditions throughout the years; an incredible mother-in-law, from whom I learned about all things Mexican; and friends who work in the food industry as cooks, chefs, caterers, restaurant owners, teachers, food writers, and market vendors have all shared their views and personal ideas about Mexican food customs with me on innumerable occasions. I am grateful for their patience and generosity.

Weekend excursions to provincial Mexico with friends or family, to visit sixteenth-century convents and archeological sites and at the same time look for restaurants well known for their good food and service, have been great fun and provided many cultural and gastronomical pleasures.

The book has also benefited from the many discussions about Mexican food with other anthropologists and archaeologists at the National University, where, in recent years, food-related subjects have become legitimate topics of academic research. Unlike France, Italy, England, and the United States, which have a long tradition in food studies, until the past decade, Mexican universities tended to regard food as a superficial subject, inadequate for serious investigation. Today, anthropologists, sociologists, nutritionists, historians, physicians, and biologists are involved in researching food topics from their own disciplinary approaches and have made important contributions to our pool of knowledge on Mexican food traditions.

I am also indebted to the Instituto de Investigaciones Históricas at the Universidad Nacional Autónoma de México, for granting me a year's sabbatical leave and allowing me to concentrate exclusively on the manuscript of this book.

A word of special thanks is due to the series editor, Ken Albala, and the acquisitions editor, Wendi Schnaufer, from Greenwood Press, who have been perceptive judges and, at the same time, generous about not enforcing promised, but unmet, deadlines. It has been a pleasure to work with Luis Alberto Vargas, coauthor of this volume, who is an unending source of information on Mexican food habits and customs. I must also thank graduate students Verónica Isabel Torres Cadena and María de la Luz del Valle, who have generously allowed me to glean information from their unpublished theses. Many of the recipes included in the book are variations on recipes contained in the cookbooks listed in the Resource Guide at the end of the book under the title "Mexican Cookbooks in English." Their publications have been an inspiration throughout the endeavor. Finally, a very special thanks to Greenwood Press for sponsoring this book on Mexican food traditions.

Janet Long-Solís

This book is part of an ambitious adventure in exploring the anthropology and history of Mexican foodways, a journey that Janet Long-Solís and I have shared for many years. She is the real author of this book. Her ability to cope with my English and give coherence to my disperse ideas has not been an easy task. Thus, my first words of thanks are for her.

As do many of us with long-lasting marriages, I have to acknowledge the understanding and patience of those close to me. My wife, Leticia, has been a close collaborator in our joint research, which is part of the background of this book. Equally important has been the relationship with colleagues at the Institute of Anthropological Research (Instituto de Investigaciones Antropológicas) at the National University and the Grupo Mexicano de Antropología de la Alimentación, which is a branch of the International Commission on the Anthropology of Food. Special thanks go to all of our friends who have participated in the program *Historical Journeys through Mexican Cuisines* (*Recorridos históricos por las cocinas mexicanas*), where in addition to learning from the students, we have been able to re-create, taste, and enjoy recipes from all periods of Mexican history. It is hoped that the readers of this book will be able to visit Mexico to explore these tastes and textures and enhance their appreciation of Mexican food.

Finally, I must add my thanks to Ken, Wendi, and the staff of Greenwood Press, who guided us in this endeavor.

Luis Alberto Vargas

Introduction

The Mexican food tradition began more than 5,000 years ago. By 3500 B.C., the most important foods in the Mexican diet, namely corn, beans, squash, tomatillos, and chile peppers, had been domesticated and were being cultivated by Mesoamerican farmers. Over the years, this basic diet has served the Mexican people well. It has provided them with wholesome food; a nutritious diet; and sufficient energy to live, work, and reproduce, as well as to maintain good health. This book attempts to explain why, after five centuries, the diet is still being adhered to by a large part of the population.

A historical panorama of food traditions is presented in chapter 1, beginning with pre-Hispanic foods, taking into consideration both the foods of New Spain (the colonial Spanish name for Mexico) and the century of independence, and finally describing the many changes in eating habits that took place in the twentieth century.

The Mexican diet, as we know it today, was established in the sixteenth century, after European foods and plants were introduced by the Spaniards. The combination of the new food products and those already being used in the native Mexican diet produced a more varied and nutritious food tradition. The diet of New Spain showed little variation during the 300 years of Spanish domination, because food novelties had to come directly from or by way of Spain. Spain attempted to limit entrance into Spanish America to Hispanic subjects, on the pretext that people from other countries might contaminate the Indian cultures. When Mexico gained independence from Spain in 1821, the country's borders were opened to new foods, new influences, and new commercial contacts with other European countries and the United States.

The principal foods and ingredients used in the Mexican diet are reviewed in chapter 2, along with cultural and historical information on the preparation of Mexican food.

The role played by the cook, cooking utensils, and cooking techniques are the subjects of chapter 3. Information is presented on the use of ancient stone and clay utensils up to modern microwave ovens. Throughout Mexican history, cooking has been considered women's work. The role of professional chefs today may be played by either men or women; however, women are still expected to take charge of preparing the daily food in the home.

Typical Mexican meals are reviewed in chapter 4, taking into consideration whether the meal is eaten in a rural or urban setting, the age group involved, the social and economic level of those considered, and the different geographic regions of the country.

Chapter 5 examines Mexico's "many cuisines" with regard to their regional and cultural differences. Many factors play a role in describing regional foods. Natural resources, climate, the diets of ethnic groups in the area, and even the type of local chile peppers must all be taken into account when describing regional diets.

Chapter 6 covers eating outside the home, one of Mexicans' favorite pastimes. Mexican women are increasingly joining the labor force and have less time to prepare complicated meals. Millions of Mexicans patronize street-food stands, which are conveniently located and reasonably priced. Those who would rather eat seated at a table frequent the many *taquerías*, *torterías*, *fondas*, cafés, and restaurants that abound in urban areas.

Mexicans have many opportunities to celebrate throughout the year, because the Mexican calendar is rife with official, unofficial, and religious holidays, which are usually community celebrations where everyone is encouraged to participate. Rite-of-passage ceremonies are more private, family-oriented occasions, usually for friends, neighbors, and family members. Food is an important feature of all festive occasions. A few of the 10,000 fiestas registered in Mexico are described in chapter 7.

The final chapter deals with diet and health and includes official data on malnutrition, anemia, obesity, and many of the chronic diseases associated with these illnesses. The Mexican government has helped alleviate nutritional problems over the years by implementing multiple government-sponsored programs. Obesity is the most serious health problem in Mexico at this time and is proving to be more difficult to treat than either malnutrition or anemia. The Mexican Health Ministry encourages people to eat a more healthy diet by consulting the food guide sponsored by them called *The Plate of Good Eating*, which stresses the consumption of fruits, vegetables, and whole grains.

As to why Mexico's basic diet has persisted for over five centuries, the answer may lie in the fact that corn, beans, squash, and chile peppers make up a conglomerate of components that together form a nutritional equilibrium. This interdependence strengthens and helps their survival as a group. If one of the food products is missing, the equilibrium is destroyed and the nutritional value of the others is compromised. Together, they provide the necessary ingredients for physiological development and the preservation of good health. For example, the proteins contained in corn are incomplete because they lack lysine and tryptophan, amino acids necessary for forming a complete protein. Beans, however, are rich in these two amino acids, and when corn and beans are consumed together, they make up a complete protein. Squash and chile peppers contain vitamins and minerals necessary for a healthy diet. Chile peppers provide additional benefits such as variety, color, and pungency to an otherwise monotonous diet. Peppers are also known to incite the appetite, increase saliva, and stimulate gastric juices. Each of the components in the basic diet has a role to play in forming and maintaining the complex equilibrium.

Timeline

ca. 35,000 B.C.	Humans are estimated to have arrived in North America by way of the Bering Strait.
ca. 35,000–7000 B.C.	Food procured by hunters and gatherers.
ca. 7500–5000 B.C.	Beginning of plant domestication in Mesoamerica.
ca. 5000–4000 B.C.	Grinding stones (*metates*) and mortars and pestles (*molcajetes*) used for grinding seeds and grains.
ca. 2500–1500 B.C.	Olmec civilization flourishes on the Gulf Coast and extends its influence into central and southern Mexico.
ca. 1800–300 B.C.	Clay vessels used for cooking are found.
ca. 1500–1000 B.C.	Clay vessels used for serving food are found.
ca. 600 B.C.–800 A.D.	The Mayans develop a complex civilization and a unique food tradition.
ca. 150 B.C.–750 A.D.	Teotihuacán (most important city in Mesoamerica during the Classic phase) flourishes in central Mexico.
ca. 0–500 A.D.	First evidence of clay griddles for cooking tortillas and toasting seeds.
ca. 1000–1500	Clay sieves for straining *nixtamal* appear in archaeological sites.
1325	Tenochtitlán settled by Aztecs in Lake Texcoco in central Mexico.

1492	Italian explorer Christopher Columbus arrives in the Caribbean.
May 1493	Columbus presents first American plants to the king and queen of Spain at the court of Barcelona.
November 1493	Second voyage of Columbus to New World, bringing European domesticated animals, plants, seeds, and cooking utensils.
1519	Hernán Cortés and other Spanish conquistadores arrive on Gulf coast of Mexico, near modern-day Veracruz.
1519–39	European animals; foods and plants; cooking techniques; and utensils, including wood-burning ovens, introduced into New Spain and Mexico by Spaniards.
August 13, 1521	Spaniards conquer Tenochtitlán.
1521	Philippine Islands "discovered" by Fernando de Magallanes (Magellan), Portuguese sailor in the service of the Spanish crown, claimed by both Spain and Portugal by papal bull.
1523	Franciscan missionaries arrive to establish Catholic Church in New Spain.
1535	Don Antonio de Mendoza, first viceroy in New Spain, initiates the elaborate banquets for which the viceroys became famous. The Viceregal Palace serves as an important link for introducing new food trends into New Spain.
1538	Famous banquet offered by Viceroy Antonio de Mendoza to celebrate the peace treaty of Aguasmuertas signed by the kings of Spain and France.
1545	Yucatán finally conquered by the Spaniards.
1545–48	Serious plague in New Spain causes a crisis in the food-distribution system. Spaniards take control over the markets from Indian merchants.
1550	Second half of sixteenth century sees an increase in the construction of large convents and monasteries. Convent gardens are important in the adaptation of European plants; convent kitchens make important contributions to Mexican cuisine.
1564	Miguel López de Legazpi, a Spanish explorer, sails from the port of Acapulco and takes possession of the Philip-

	pine Islands in the name of King Philip II of Spain. The Manila Galleon sails once or twice a year between Acapulco and Manila for 250 years, enabling an exchange of food products between the two cities.
1590	Publication of Bernardino de Sahagún's *Historia General de las Cosas de la Nueva España* (The General History of the Things of New Spain) (*Florentine Codex*). The book contains important information on the Aztec diet, plant cultivation, and food preparation.
1651	Publication of the first version of Francisco Hernández' *Historia de las plantas de Nueva España* (History of the Plants of New Spain), written at the end of the sixteenth century.
June 8, 1692	Beginning of the most serious revolt in the history of New Spain, caused by a food shortage, when the masses rebel and set fire to the National Palace.
1810–21	The War of Independence, ending 300 years of Spanish domination.
1821	Mexico opens its borders to new diplomats, merchants, and travelers, who bring new influences in food and merchandise.
1831	Publication of first cookbooks in Mexico: *Novísimo arte de cocina* (The New Art of Cooking), written by Simón Blanquel, and *El cocinero mejicano* (The Mexican Cook), by Mariano Rivera.
1837	First concession granted by the Mexican government to build the railroad system, which facilitates transportation of food products to markets. At the end of the nineteenth century, immigrant Chinese railroad workers introduce Chinese food into the country.
July 26, 1859	First patent issued for a *nixtamal* mill to grind corn, liberating millions of Mexican women from spending an average of five or six hours a day grinding corn on the *metate*.
1864–67	During the short reign of Maximilian and Carlota, Austrian emperors of Mexico, they introduce French cuisine and table service to upper-class Mexicans.
1899	First patent issued for a mechanical tortilla press, enabling women to produce more tortillas, in less time, with less work.

1910–20   Mexican Revolution mobilizes the rural population and brings about important demographic changes in the country.

1949   First *masa harina*, or *nixtamal*, flour factory set up in the state of Nuevo León.

1950s   Intense migration from countryside to urban Mexico. High rate of population growth strains the political system, forcing the government to subsidize basic food products.

1953   Osterizer blender comes on the market, which frees Mexican cooks from the labor-intensive grinding of ingredients in the *molcajete* for use in the preparation of soups and sauces, mainstays in the Mexican diet.

1984   Mexico joins the General Agreement of Tariffs and Trade (GATT).

1994   North American Free Trade Agreement (NAFTA) signed on January 1, effectively opening Mexican markets to the importation of foodstuffs and electric domestic implements. This trade agreement is still in effect.

1

Historical Overview

Mexican cooking began with the arrival of humans in Mexico some 35,000 years ago. Early humans crossed over the Bering Strait from Asia to the American continent as early as 70,000 years ago by following the big-game herds and by gathering wild plants, seeds, and roots to complement their diet. At this point in time, the water level in the Bering Strait was low enough for them to travel between the two continents on foot.

Gradually humans migrated southward, hunting, gathering, and completing their diet with small game, birds, insects, and reptiles. They knew and used basic technological skills such as fire making, flint chipping and the basic knowledge of procuring food, shelter, and clothing. Knives and scrapers were made of chipped flint, while projectile points and awls were created from bones. They may have used some sort of grinding stone to prepare seeds and roots and knew how to weave baskets, mats, carrying nets, bags, and ropes, and they were also capable of making sandals. Faunal remains of the game herds include evidence of the extinct peccary, bison, turtle, giant land tortoise, glyptodon, wild horse, camel, and mammoth. Human-made tools were found associated with the animals as proof that the animals were butchered and eaten. Marks, scratches, and cuts found on many of the bones give further proof of this.

When the big game herds began to become extinct due to climate change and overhunting, ancient humans had to concentrate more on gathering wild plants and seeds and on hunting and trapping smaller game such as deer, rabbits, gophers, rats, turtles, and birds. Hunting became less important as a means of procuring food, and the gathering of seeds, fruits, and roots increased. Early man was well acquainted with all aspects of plant resources, such as the seasons when the plants produced fruit, when they were ripe, and in what areas they were most abundant. They also knew which plants were poisonous and which were nutritious enough to provide them the necessary energy to maintain their health, grow, and reproduce.

Ancient caves and archaeological sites contain remains of early humans' diet in the form of oak acorns, pine nuts, maguey leaves, gourds, and mesquite. Seeds and roots were ground on stone slabs or in mortars and pestles to convert them into flour and make them edible. Food was prepared in many ways, such as roasting meat and toasting seeds.

PRE-HISPANIC CUISINE

Mesoamerica is the term used by archaeologists to describe the region of high cultural achievement, with certain diagnostic cultural traits, that includes much of present-day Mexico and extends as far south as northern Costa Rica in Central America. The area can be divided into several large areas whose climate, geography, and natural resources later played a role in determining the type of diet developed in each region. The tropical area of southern Veracruz and western Tabasco was inhabited by the Olmecs in the Pre-Classic Period. Beginning about 1500 B.C., the Olmec culture emerged as an important element in southern Mexico. Some archaeologists refer to them as the mother culture of ancient Mexico, because many elements of this highly advanced culture are found in later societies. Nothing is known of the origins of the culture; they merely emerged as an extremely advanced culture and built ceremonial centers on a massive scale, which indicates a complex and centralized society.

The Maya culture in southern Mexico and the Yucatán peninsula extended as far south as El Salvador in Central America. This civilization flourished during the early centuries of the first millennium A.D. The Mayas developed a sophisticated system of writing and various counting and calendrical systems that employed the concept of zero. They built great ceremonial centers such as Palenque, Tikal, Uxmal, and Copán in Honduras. Oaxaca, in southern Mexico, was the center of the Zapotec and Mixtec civilizations and built cities with complex architecture like Monte Albán and Mitla.

Teotihuacán, located at the northeastern edge of the Valley of Mexico, began about the time of Christ and developed into the most important city in all of Mesoamerica. Its political, economic, and cultural influence was felt from as far north as the American Southwest and at least as far south as Guatemala. Its leadership was extended by long-distance trade rather than conquest, possibly by colonization in some cases, and by the collection of tribute. This enormous urban center was unique in North America during its time. The great city was sacked and burned by invading groups from the north about 750 A.D. Some years later the Toltecs made their appearance on the Mesoamerican stage and established their capital at Tula, in the modern state of Hidalgo. The Toltec empire grew quickly and extended its influence to northern Mexico and to the Maya center of Chichén Itzá in the Yucatán peninsula.

In the fourteenth century A.D., the Aztecs arrived in the central Valley of Mexico, where they established their city of Tenochtitlán, where Mexico City is located today. In less than 200 years they built the most powerful empire in Mesoamerica. They demonstrated their supremacy over their conquered neighbors by demanding tribute from them, and held "flower wars" for the purpose of obtaining victims for human sacrifice. The Aztecs, also called the Mexica, spoke a language called Náhuatl. Their social order was a strict hierarchy of classes, including the ruler (*tlatoani*), the priesthood, the nobility, the military, certain classes of merchants, commoners, and slaves. This complex and powerful society was in power when the Spaniards arrived in Veracruz in 1519.

THE AZTEC DIET

Central Mexico, where the Aztecs were situated, is a temperate, semi-arid zone where agriculture was practiced extensively. The principal source of the Aztec food supply came from the *chinampa* system, established in the freshwater lakes of Chalco and Xochimilco, in the southern part of the city. They are commonly called "floating gardens," but they do not actually float, as they are held in place by the deep roots of willow trees that serve as anchors. *Chinampas* can best be described as deeply rooted artificial islands, composed of reeds and water lilies and covered with silt. They were among the most fertile gardens of the New World and were extremely productive agriculturally, which assured ample supplies of staple foods. Here the Aztecs grew corn, squash, beans, chile peppers, tomatoes, amaranth, and many other vegetables and flowers. Seminomadic groups inhabited the desert areas of northern Mexico, where agriculture could not be practiced and people still relied on hunting and gathering methods for some of their sustenance.

Starting around 8000 B.C., the Mexican climate became considerably warmer and more arid; big game became scarce, and hunting and gathering groups were forced to find more efficient methods of procuring their food. Hunting became less important as a means of survival, and more attention was placed upon exploiting vegetal resources.

People gathered their food on a seasonal basis: during the spring, families had to spread out over a large area in order to find enough food; in summer, rains were plentiful and food was abundant, allowing extended families to gather together in large camps and search for food as a community; in autumn, families dispersed again to collect the ripening fruits; and in winter, activities included the hunting of available animals and the small-scale gathering of whatever foods could be found. Gatherers began concentrating on collecting nutritious edible plants such as squash; chile peppers; avocados; corn; amaranth (*Amarantus* sp.), a cereal plant used mainly for its tiny seeds; beans; and *zapotes* (for example, *Diospyros ebenaster*), a tropical fruit. These are some of the first plant remains found in early archaeological sites.[1]

People who lived on the coasts or near rivers and lakes took advantage of available aquatic resources such as shellfish, fish, and birds that visited the area. On the coasts of Veracruz and Chiapas, clams, oysters, crabs, turtles, and shrimp were consumed in such quantities that large mounds of discarded shells, or *shell middens*, have been found that reached as high as 35 feet.

The development of agriculture in Mesoamerica was not an overnight discovery; rather, it took thousands of years and advanced very slowly. Gatherers were well informed about the growing process of plants, how to select large or sweet fruits, and how to plant the seeds from them. They were also able to select those plant traits they wanted to reproduce in each species, in this way achieving genetic changes in their crops. Many plants, such as wild corn and beans, lost their ability to reproduce in the wild upon domestication and must rely upon humans' help in order to reproduce. Squash plants were first cultivated to be used as a recipient or vessel for storing seeds, water, or food. This is one of the oldest food plants in Mexico, whose presence dates back to 7500 B.C. in the valley of Oaxaca.[2] Chile peppers, beans, and corn followed in succession, and by 3500 B.C., this group of plants, which still makes up Mexico's basic diet, had been domesticated and was being cultivated.

Domesticated plants have several selected advantages over wild ones. They generally have larger fruits and seeds that stay on the plant for a longer period of time, show more visible variation, are better tasting, and are less likely to be poisonous. Agriculture allowed pre-Hispanic humans to settle in small villages or hamlets on a permanent basis and forage in surrounding areas. At this time, cultivated plants made up less than half of the diet; the remaining half comprised wild plants, small game, and aquatic resources. New plants, like green tomatoes, peanuts, lima beans, guavas, amaranth, *zapotes*, *jícamas* (*Pachyrhizus erosus*), sweet potatoes (*Ipomea batatas*), and yucca (*Manihot esculenta*), and turkeys began to be cultivated sometime between 200 B.C. and 700 A.D. The additional food resources permitted an increase in the population.

Food was of great importance in pre-Hispanic Mexico. It was a source of energy and a means to placate hunger and had religious, symbolic, and artistic uses as well. It was the most common offering to the gods during rituals and played an important role in the fiesta system. Religion determined which foods could be eaten, which were to be offered to the gods, and which foods had to be abstained from. The Aztecs, in addition to being good farmers and hunters, also obtained food in the form of tribute from groups that had come under their control through warfare. Goods obtained in this way played an important role in the economy.

A system of measuring time was essential to organize agricultural activities, fiestas, and other daily events. The calendar determined when plants were to be sown, when rituals were to be held, and when specific gods were to be worshipped. Each god made his appearance during a particular month and was given offerings during that time period. A specific period of time was dedicated to the rain god Tlaloc, when he was said to shower the earth with his benefits. Another period was dedicated to Xipe Totec, the god of springtime, who turned the countryside green and made the flowers bloom, or to the corn goddess, Xilonen, who was in charge of ensuring a good corn crop. The god's presence was regulated by the calendar, which also stipulated when the soil was to be prepared for planting, when the seeds were to be sown, and when the harvest was to begin.[3]

The year was basically divided into two seasons: the rainy season and the dry season. These were divided into 18 months of 20 days each, plus 5 ill-fated days left over at the end to complete the yearly cycle. It was considered bad luck to be born on one of the five extra days of the cycle. Each month a special meal or a particular food was prepared in honor of the god who was celebrated during that month. The food was related to a particular subsistence activity.

The first month of the Aztec calendar, called Atlacahualco, corresponded approximately to the month of March in the Gregorian calendar. During this month, farming activities were initiated in Highland Mexico.

The land was cleared of brush and weeds, set afire, and burned to prepare the soil for the first rains of the season. The first fiesta of the year was celebrated in honor of the rain gods, the Tlaloques, to solicit a good farming year and sufficient rains to produce a good harvest. During this month, Maya groups in Yucatán also carried out a ceremony to ask for rain. Four young men dressed as the rain god Chac stood in the four corners of a patio with jugs of water that were used to put out the flames in four hearths, in this way symbolizing the end of the dry season and the beginning of the agricultural cycle.

The second month was dedicated to Xipe Totec, god of springtime and of the renewal of plants. Warriors and priests dressed in the skins of sacrificial victims during the 20 days of the month. Ears of corn that had been hanging from rooftops since the last harvest were shelled and blessed before they were planted. Some of the corn was used to make special twisted tortillas called *cocolli*, and a type of raw corn turnover called *uilocpalli*. These foods were made to celebrate the event.

The first rains generally began in April, a month dedicated to Tozozontli, when people gathered in the fields to symbolically plant the first seeds, although the actual sowing was not performed until the rains began during the next month. They offered incense, liquid rubber, and food to the gods of the fields. Later they pulled up those plants that had sprouted and started to grow and offered them to Tlaloc, along with small loaves made of amaranth seeds mixed with honey. To the corn god Cinteotl, they offered five small baskets of tortillas and roasted frogs, because they believed that frogs invoked the rain with their croaking.[4]

After this ritual, the actual sowing of corn took place. In this ceremony, priests led the farmers on their way to the fields and consulted the calendar to see which was the best day to plant. The rainy season began fully in May. The Maya celebrated this by breaking large jugs full of beverages in honor of the rain gods, the Chacs, and asked their help in protecting the corn crop from weeds and animals that could damage it.

The corn harvest began in October, when the rainy season ended. Months before, the stored provisions were usually depleted, and people looked forward to the first fruits of the season with great anticipation. Nobles and important officials who had large granaries of corn were obliged to offer fiestas for the poor in order for them to subsist until the new harvest could be gathered. Food was an important part of the fiesta. People were given as many tamales as they could hold in their hands, as well as a beverage made of a type of sage called *chía*, corn, and water and a semiliquid form of gruel known as *atole*, made with corn dough and water.

Another motive for offering a fiesta fell to the long-distance merchants, called the *pochtecas*, who traded in luxury goods for the *tlatoani* and the Aztec nobility. Long-distance trading was difficult and dangerous, but the rewards for a successful trading expedition were great. The merchants had to wait for a lucky day on the calendar and perform special ceremonies, such as offering blood, paper, incense, and quail to the gods of the roads and to Xiuhtecutli, god of fire. If the trading expedition was successful, the merchant waited for a special calendar day to return to Tenochtitlán. He arrived at night, dressed in rags to avoid attracting undue attention to his success, and began the preparation for an elaborate banquet, which he offered to Yacatecuhtli, god of the *pochtecas*. A special dish was prepared for this banquet made of corn and fowl, called *totoatolli*. They also served meat turnovers and drank chocolate flavored with vanilla. At the end of the banquet, the host gave the guests small bowls full of cacao beans and special sticks to stir the chocolate. When a merchant became rich through many trading expeditions, he was expected to offer an elaborate banquet to show his wealth. This fiesta, accompanied by singers, dancers, musicians, and an abundance of rich food, lasted several days and nights, and the celebrating continued until all the food was consumed. It was considered in bad taste to offer a banquet where the food was finished in less than two days. Throughout the fiesta, the merchant entertained his guests with stories of his experiences on the road.

The "ceremony of the first fruits" was held to celebrate the goddess of corn, Xilonen, and the fact that the cornfields were now almost ready to provide sustenance for the people. The goddess was offered tender ears of corn and tortillas made of fresh corn along with garlands of corn ears and green chiles that were hung around her neck. This food had to be consumed during the ceremony.

Before the arrival of the Europeans in the sixteenth century, the basic Mesoamerican diet had a common substratum, although it varied between areas due to plant resources, latitudes, climate, and cultural and ethnic differences. There were certain characteristics, such as a reliance on beans, maize, squash, and chile peppers, that were common to most cultural groups. The turkey and the dog, fattened especially for eating, were the only domestic animals available as good sources of protein. Additional protein was obtained through the hunting of small game and the use of lake resources, such as frogs, waterfowl, fish, salamanders, and a large variety of insects and insect eggs. Algae (*Spirulina geitlerii*), called *tecuitlatl* by the Aztecs, was another good source of protein and was widely used by the inhabitants of the Valley of Mexico. Fruits, such as the wild plum, cherimoya (*Anona cherimolia*), chokecherry, crab apple, blackberry, guava, *zapotes* of various colors, avocado, and mamey (*Calocarpum mamosum*) were available on a seasonal and regional basis.

The most common beverages of pre-Hispanic Mexico were the fermented juice of the agave plant, called *pulque*; a refreshing beverage made of a cornmeal base, called *atole*; and several drinks made with chocolate, which was the favored drink of the nobility. These beverages provided additional sources of calories, protein, vitamins, and minerals.

Pre-Hispanic banquets can best be represented by the lavish feasts prepared daily for Montezuma II (1466–1520), who was the leader (*tlatoani*) in power when the Spaniards arrived in Mexico. Montezuma was a fragile man with an air of mysticism surrounding him. He was a light eater and barely tasted the many dishes prepared for him in the palace kitchen.

His daily meals were rituals, celebrated with reverence and dignity, and were served in an undesignated room in the Royal Palace. No one was allowed to speak in a loud voice or make noise while Montezuma was eating. He separated himself from the rest of the court with a gold-painted wooden screen in order to avoid being seen while eating. He sat on a small leather cushion in front of a low table covered with a delicate white cotton tablecloth and used napkins made of the same material.

Before the banquet began, four young maidens spilled water from a pitcher used by Montezuma for washing his hands. The towels used to dry his hands were used only once and then destroyed. Four elderly nobles stood at attention during the meal and made quiet conversation with him while he ate, or gave him advice on state matters. Montezuma often shared morsels of his food with them.

According to several accounts, servants prepared 30 different dishes for his table every day, as well as over 1,000 extra dishes to feed his royal staff. Food such as spicy meat stews, made with turkey, venison, rabbit, wild fowl, or fish, was kept warm over small clay braziers, and was accompanied by vegetables and salsas made with a variety of chile peppers. Two young maidens prepared and served him tortillas from a dish covered with a white napkin. After the main dishes, the four maidens served fruit and small jugs of cacao or chocolate, which Montezuma enjoyed drinking at the end of each meal. On special occasions, dwarfs and hunchbacks performed acrobatics and sang or danced for the *tlatoani*. After the ceremony, the elder statesmen left Montezuma alone to relax and smoke a pipe of tobacco mixed with sweet gum, or *liquidambar*.[5]

The pre-Hispanic diet is considered to have been sufficient in proteins, vitamins, and calories through the consumption of fruits, vegetables, grains, insects, and small game. The diet was adequate enough to maintain good health and protect the population against infectious disease, although one must keep in mind that there were periods of food scarcity and severe hunger.

In spite of the efficient use of food resources, the inhabitants of pre-Hispanic Mexico were constantly under the threat of hunger. Hunger often followed battles between neighboring groups, the loss of a harvest due to insects or animals, or droughts that sometimes lasted for several years and could destroy whole civilizations. The *Annals of Cuautitlán* describes the great hunger in the city of Tula, which lasted seven years and ended only when the Toltecs began practicing human sacrifice.[6]

Another time of severe hunger was under the reign of Montezuma Ilhuicamina (1440–69), when four consecutive years of drought depleted all the foodstuffs stored, even in the royal warehouse (*petlacalli*). Seeing how his people were suffering from hunger, the Aztec king gave them permission to sell themselves or their children into slavery in exchange for food. Some families migrated to the coast of the Gulf of Mexico. Many proud noble Aztecs were sold and turned into slaves. In the fifth year, heavy rains fell and farmers were able to harvest a good crop of corn. Montezuma Ilhuicamina rescued those nobles who had sold themselves into slavery and allowed them to return to Tenochtitlán.

The last great hunger in Aztec Mexico was caused by the Spaniards and their allies, who surrounded and laid siege to Tenochtitlán in 1521 when they conquered the city. The conquistador Bernal Díaz del Castillo wrote that the Spaniards also suffered from hunger during this great battle and barely subsisted by eating tortillas, wild greens, chokecherries, and prickly pears from cactus plants.[7]

THE FOOD OF THE MAYA

The basis of the Maya diet was also corn, both in liquid form as a type of gruel called *pozol* and as a solid in the form of tortillas and tamales. The importance of the tortilla in the Maya diet is somewhat controversial, because no pre-Hispanic tortilla griddles have been found in most Mayan excavations. This has lead some archaeologists to propose the hypothesis that the Maya were more consumers of tamales than tortillas. Nonetheless, sixteenth-century reports indicate that the Maya made bread (tortillas) in many ways, which were described as "good and healthy," but warned they were not good eaten cold. Griddles were present in archaeological sites on the east coast of Yucatán, in Copán, Honduras, and in the highlands of Guatemala.

One of the Maya rituals performed by Mayan kings and queens at every event of political or religious importance was bloodletting. This type of sacrifice, when the leaders sacrificed their own blood, was also carried out to celebrate the planting of crops. On these occasions, the rulers pierced their bodies; the queen generally pierced her tongue, while the king performed the same act upon the superfluous part of his penis to allow the blood to flow. They then inserted a piece of rope in the opening to keep the wound open and allowed the blood to seep down the rope into a bowl filled with cloth paper until the paper became saturated with blood. It was then burned in a brazier, creating large clouds of swirling black smoke, where the gods, who were expected to sanction a good corn harvest, could be discerned. The royalty prepared for the ceremony some days before by fasting, performing acts of massive blood loss and deprivation, and were culturally conditioned to expect a hallucinatory experience. Through such vision, the Maya came directly into contact with the gods, whose help they solicited. The Spaniards were shocked by this sacrificial ceremony and discouraged it as idolatrous worship.

Much of the information on the Maya diet comes from the book *Relación de las cosas de Yucatán* (An Account of the Things of Yucatan), written by the Franciscan bishop of Yucatán, Diego de Landa, in the late sixteenth century.[8] Landa is a much maligned figure in Mexican history, as he incinerated 27 Maya painted books and thus destroyed valuable information on Maya culture and religion. On the other hand, he recorded a Maya alphabet that has provided important clues in the recent decipherment of Maya writing and left a detailed account of the daily life of the Maya.

Landa noted that corn served the Maya as both food and drink. Of the three Maya meals eaten daily, two comprised corn drinks made of corn dough. In the morning one of the drinks, *pozol*, was taken warm with ground chile peppers the top. The midday meal was also in the form of *pozol*, and consisted of the leftovers of the morning meal, to which cool water was added to make a refreshing drink. The evening meal comprised a stew, if meat was available; if not, chile-pepper sauce and vegetables, such as black beans, sufficed for the evening repast. Some authors include tortillas in the evening meal. Food was also a common tributary item.

Meat, fish, and fowl were high-status articles in the Maya diet. They formed part of the elite diet and were mainly consumed on holidays or during special banquets. On these occasions, they prepared turkey; venison; tortillas; black beans; and some form of greens, such as *chaya* (*Jatropha aconitifolia*). The bones of several animal species have appeared in archaeological sites—for example, in the postclassical site of Mayapán, bones from the white-tailed deer, the peccary, the iguana, the dog, and the ocellated turkey were found. Other animals used included the spider monkey, howler monkey, tapir, manatee, armadillo, rabbit, dove, partridge, duck, curassow, chachalaca, horned guan, and crested guan.

Seafood was also high-status nourishment reserved for the tables of the elite. Bones or shells of oysters, conches, crabs, turtles, and iguanas have been found in shell middens in Cozumel. Snails, frogs, snook, and other fish bones have been found in other sites in the Maya area. Seafood could be salted, smoked, sun-dried, or roasted, depending upon the type of fish or shellfish prepared.

The Maya were excellent orchard keepers and kept many fruit-bearing trees. Pineapple, papaya, mamey, chicozapotes (Manilkara zapota), and many species of the annona were received by the Spaniards as gifts from the Maya when they arrived. The ramón tree (Brosimun alicastrum) was plentiful in Yucatán. It is a high-yielding tree whose seeds are higher in protein than corn and beans and contains the amino acid tryptophan, which is absent in corn. It was considered a famine plant and was consumed by the Maya when there was a scarcity of corn.

Yucatán was as excellent place for producing honey. The honey the Maya produced was white, of good quality, and used to sweeten some corn drinks, such as atole and posolli, and to make a ritual beverage called balché. The latter was prepared from the bark of the balché tree (Lonchocorpus longistylus).

Bishop Landa noted that some ceremonies required the consumption of great quantities of alcohol and that Maya men were hard drinkers. The favored drink of the Maya elite was chocolate, which was consumed hot or cold and could be mixed with honey, chile peppers, a red paste made from Bixa orellana seeds called achiote, or water.

Root crops were important in the Maya diet. Yucca, sweet potatoes, jícama, and a tuber called the macal (Xanthosoma nigrum) were cultivated in house gardens or gathered wild in the forest. These were high-calorie foods and important items in the diet when corn products were scarce due to crop failures.

One of the most important items of Mayan produce was the small black bean, called buul, usually prepared with epazote (Chenopodium ambrosioides) and served with a chile-pepper sauce. The usual method of preparation was to boil them in water in which toasted chile peppers had been steeped. Greens in Maya cuisines included shoots of chayote (Sechium edule), chipilín (Crotolaria sp.), and chaya, which must be cooked to be ed-

ible. Squash was a common ingredient in the Maya diet, both as a vegetable and for the seeds, which could be roasted, ground, or eaten raw.
They were also mixed with ground chile peppers and used as a relish or a
sauce. A special drink was made of ground, toasted squash seeds and
ground beans.

Pumpkin-Seed Dip (*Sikil P'ak*)

- 1 cup toasted pumpkin seeds, finely ground
- 1 large tomato, roasted on the griddle and peeled
- 2 fresh jalapeño chile peppers, roasted on the griddle
- 2 tablespoons fresh coriander, finely chopped
- 2 tablespoons onions, finely chopped
- salt and lemon juice to taste

Cover tomato with water in saucepan, bring to a boil, reduce heat, and simmer
for 12 minutes. Drain. Place tomato and chile peppers in a blender and purée
until smooth. Pour into a small bowl and stir in the ground pumpkin seeds, coriander, onion, and salt. Let mixture stand for 30 minutes. Just before serving, add
the lemon juice. If it is too thick to spread, stir in a little water.

The Maya were very efficient at exploiting the resources available to
them. Their diet was varied and sufficient, but probably not abundant,
during certain seasons of the year. At other times, hunger reigned when
their crops were destroyed due to drought, locust plagues, or the eruption
of nearby volcanoes. There were severe droughts and hunger in the Maya
area also. The books of *Chilam Balam* contain several references to the
predictions of the priests, warning of the years of drought and hunger that
could be expected in the future.[9]

Landa mentions times of severe hunger brought on by the destruction
of crops, trees, and animals by hurricanes, when the food warehouses were
depleted and the population had to subsist on the bark and roots of trees.
By the time the Europeans arrived in Maya territory, their days of glory
were long past. There was no centralized governing organization control-
ling the group of small city-states in the Yucatán, and they were more difficult to conquer than the Aztecs, who were ruled by a centralized
government under one family. Kanek, the last independent chieftain of
Tayasal, did not surrender until 1697, and the caste wars carried out during the middle of the nineteenth century showed the pent-up resentment
of the Maya toward European domination.

FOOD IN NEW SPAIN

Mexican food as we know it today had its origins in the sixteenth century. The introduction of European plants and food products by the Spanish conquerors were combined with local foods and gave birth to a new cuisine. This interchange not only included the introduction of new foods, but also entailed the reception of new cooking utensils and new techniques of food preparation. European foods that made a strong impact upon the Mexican diet in the sixteenth century and can still be observed in the Mexican food tradition today can be reduced to six major items: wheat; meat and its derivatives, such as milk, cheese, and eggs; sugar; citrus fruits; new vegetables, such as onions and garlic; and the herbs parsley and coriander.

During the colonial period, when Mexico was known as New Spain, the Mexican diet underwent few changes after the initial modifications in the sixteenth century. The Spanish crown was protective of its new colonies and tried to control immigration into the country by awarding permits exclusively to its own subjects, under the pretext that people and influences from other countries could contaminate the Indians. During their 300-year rule, culinary novelties had to be introduced by way of Spain, even though they may have originated in other European countries. When Mexico gained its independence from Spain in the nineteenth century, it was free to establish its own contacts with other countries, and the influence of other European countries and the United States can then be noted in the diet.

The Spanish conquistadores and explorers brought with them a culture that was essentially medieval in character. The Italian Renaissance was late in reaching Spain, and many medieval customs were still being practiced there at the end of the fifteenth century. These values, customs, and ideas were continued in New Spain during the early years after the conquest. The Spanish food tradition introduced into Mexico by the Spaniards was essentially that of the medieval Spanish kitchen, with a strong Arab influence, because many of the conquistadores were from southern Spain. The Arab influence can still be noted in the Mexican food tradition today in the importance given to rice, sweets, candied fruits, and an abundance of spices in the diet. Some popular foods are still known by their Arab names: *alfajores* is a Mexican sweet, and *albondigas* is the term for meatballs.

Early chroniclers who wrote of their experiences in the New World were surprised to see how sparsely the Indians ate, and observed that many of the recently arrived conquistadores ate more in one day than an entire Indian family with several children ate in a week.

Spaniards ate to placate their hunger, but they also used food as an excuse to participate in a celebration and share food with friends and companions. For pretentious hosts it offered an opportunity to impress their guests with their generosity, wealth, and high social position. Sometimes they ate and drank until they were satiated or until there was no food or drink left. This was the case in the famous banquet offered by the first viceroy, Antonio de Mendoza, and Hernán Cortés to commemorate the peace treaty of Aguasmuertas, signed by the French and Spanish governments in 1538. This banquet has passed into history as a colossal extravagance of food and drink due to the impressive number of dishes served, the wines offered, and the behavior of the participants, as described by Bernal Díaz del Castillo, who was present at the feast.[10]

The banquet began with two or three types of salad, followed by various kinds of broths with vegetables. In succession came roast kid with parsley, roast ham, quail, and dove pies, as well as turkey, stuffed chicken, and pickled partridge and quail. The number of dishes filled to the brim with meat stews seemed to have no end: a parade of lamb, pork, beef, and sausage stews decorated with turnips, cabbage, and chickpeas followed one after another. Roast turkeys and chickens were brought to the table with silver feet and beaks, while roast ducks were served with golden beaks. The tables were decorated with hog heads, deer heads, and calf heads. The amount of meat served gives us an idea of the Spaniards' appreciation of meat. It was impossible to taste all of the dishes served; many were not even touched, but helped give a lavish atmosphere to the meal, which was the impression the hosts wanted to convey. As a grand finale, large turnovers of live rabbits, quail, and doves were brought to the table. When they were opened, the rabbits jumped out and began running all over the table, while the birds took to flight around the room, reminiscent of medieval European banquets. The guests consumed great quantities of wine as well as a drink called pulque, made from the sap of the century plant, and a type of sweet wine called *aloja*, much appreciated by the Arabs. The cutlery was solid silver, with a servant standing guard at each place setting to make sure that the guest did not take the table silver with him when he retired. On two occasions, the table linens were changed to initiate a new food course.

Meanwhile, in the courtyard below, the servants, mulattoes, blacks, and Indians roasted entire young steers stuffed with chickens, quail, doves, bacon, and strings of a type of Spanish sausage called chorizo. Everyone ate and drank to excess. At the end of the banquet, the guests, completely inebriated, rolled down the stairs and under the tables. The ladies became sick from so much food and drink and had to excuse themselves from the table. The Indians, accustomed to their usual moderation in food consumption, were shocked at such behavior. The banquet was more like a raucous medieval European feast than a quiet commemoration of a peace treaty celebrated in distant New Spain.

Food Distribution in New Spain

The conquistadores were astonished by the size of the great market in Tlatelolco and the number of products sold there and declared it larger than any market they had ever seen in Spain. They were also impressed by the discipline and order that was enforced in the market and left many descriptions of the market that we can still read with fascination.

Initially, the arrival of the Spaniards did not generate important changes in the organization of the market. As long as there was no scarcity of provisions in the city, the Spaniards decided to leave the commerce in the hands of the Indians and permit them to continue their usual manner of exchange. There was a necessary adjustment in the type of products sold in the market according to the necessities of the new clientele in the marketplace. The role played by the long-distance traders, who brought goods for the emperor and nobility from as far away as Chiapas, in the south, became less important, and the need to buy luxury goods such as fine feathers, precious stones, and products made of gold and silver disappeared. The itinerant traders began dealing in flowers and fruits that they brought from the tropics to sell in urban markets or for religious fiestas.

The Spaniards tried to follow the same tax system established by the Mexicas: during the first years, tribute paid by the Indians to the *encomenderos* (grantees who were entitled to receive tribute and labor from the Indians delegated to them) played an important role in the food supply of the city. Tribute was paid *in specie* and included corn, fowl, eggs, fruits, vegetables, fish, honey, and chocolate. With the increase in the Spanish population and the decrease in that of the Indians, tribute became insufficient as a means of supplying the city, and by the middle of the sixteenth century the system had begun to fall apart.

The means of exchange in the market was modified with the introduction of Spanish coins that had a fixed value with respect to cacao beans, small pieces of cotton cloth called *quachtlis*, and transparent duck feathers filled with gold that were used for important commercial transactions in Aztec markets. In 1555, a Spanish real was equivalent to 140 cacao beans. The small pieces of cotton cloth and duck feathers disappeared from the exchange system, but the cacao beans continued in use during the entire colonial period, and shopkeepers were obliged to accept them as money.

In order to regulate sales in the markets, Spanish weights and measures were introduced. Because the corn tribute was paid in a Spanish measure called a *fanega,* the Indians quickly became accustomed to the rest of the Iberian measures that served to weigh seeds as well as liquids. Market days were adjusted to the Christian calendar and became weekly markets instead of being held once every month or every twenty days, as marked by the pre-Hispanic calendar.

The Spaniards respected the Indian organization of the commerce system until the great plague of *cocoliztli* in 1545–48, which reduced the Indian population drastically and was the cause of the first serious food-supply crisis in Mexico City. After these years of food scarcity, the Spaniards began to take measures to assure the food supply, such as the order that all towns in a radius of 20 leagues around Mexico City had to deliver 100 turkeys, 400 chickens, and 2,800 eggs, plus firewood and forage for the animals on a weekly basis. Indian markets outside Mexico City were only allowed to sell tortillas, corn flour, tamales, and local fruit. Authorities forbade the direct interchange in the markets of Indian communities if the transactions affected the food supply of the urban markets. By the end of the sixteenth century, the public markets and commerce in general was in the control of the Spanish authorities.

In the markets one could find Spanish products sold along with Indian fruits and vegetables. This combination improved the local diet, providing a more varied menu. After the 1520s, meat became plentiful and cheap on the market, which surprised visiting Spaniards who were accustomed to the scarcity and high price of meat on the European market. The English traveler Robert Thompson arrived in Mexico during the middle of the sixteenth century and was surprised to see that one-fourth of a steer, or all that a slave could carry, was worth five reals, which was indeed cheap if one compared it with the beef prices in Spain.[11]

Up until the middle of the sixteenth century, the only public market in Mexico City was located in the main plaza. This was the best market in New Spain, where nearly all the commercial activities of the Spaniards was located. Years later, the market extended to almost completely fill the central plaza (*zócalo*), which always looked dirty and disheveled due to the market stands overflowing with fruits and vegetables, the animals brought in from surrounding areas daily, and the lack of hygiene. In 1777, the Spanish writer Juan de Viera described it as a miniature city, whose streets were formed by the flimsy stands and baskets of the market sellers, set up according to the product they sold.[12] In the Portal de los Mercaderes (the merchant's arcade), all types of candied fruit, marmalades, cookies, and high-quality fruit were offered. Viera describes a street of food stands where cooks prepared food for the many buyers and sellers who came to deal in the plaza or for visiting tourists who ate breakfast, lunch, and dinner there due to a lack of hotels and restaurants in the city.

The Role of the Catholic Church

Franciscan friars who began to arrive in New Spain in 1523 were invaluable to the Spanish crown in helping them to establish their position in the New World. They were able to gain the confidence of the Indians through their humility and sensibility toward Indian cultures. Together with the Dominican and Agustínian orders, which arrived in later years, they carried out the difficult evangelization of New Spain.

During the early years after the conquest, many convents and monasteries were founded by the Catholic Church, which expanded rapidly in the second half of the sixteenth century. The convents included a church, rooms for the priests, and additional areas such as orchards and gardens. Convents also served as centers of learning new agricultural techniques, and they carried out important irrigation systems in the sixteenth century. The orchards were generally planted in the back patio, where friars planted rows of medicinal plants, fruit trees, and vegetables. When the European plants had adapted to the new climate and soil, the friars encouraged local Spaniards to sow the same plants outside the convent so the Indians would learn to cultivate and eat them. The convents served as experimental stations for the adaptation of the new crops. There was a continual exchange of plants and plant knowledge between convents both in Mexico as well in as other Latin American church groups.

Strict rules of behavior were established in the convents to enable the priests and nuns to live in a communal pattern in their convents without undue friction. The refectory or dining hall was one of the spaces where everyday habits were strictly controlled, because the consumption and sharing of food was considered a way of expressing communal union.

The daily menu in the nunneries varied according to the religious order and the members of the convent; in none of them was food abundant or prepared in an elaborate fashion. In those convents restricted to daughters

Refectory of the Barefoot Carmelite Convent. Anonymous painter, seventeenth century, Museo Nacional del Virreinato. Courtesy of CONACULTA-INAH-MEX. Reproduction authorized by the Instituto Nacional de Antropología e Historia.

of Spaniards (*criolla*), like those of Santa Brígida, each nun received daily a bowl of broth; a pound of lamb, which was divided between lunch and dinner; and desserts and fruits of the season. On fasting days, fish or eggs took the place of lamb. In the convents of Indian nuns, such as the Convent of Corpus Christi or Our Lady of Guadalupe, the food consisted of products made from corn and beans, to conform to the basic Indian diet. There were other convents, such as that of San Felipe de Jesus, where the nuns were required to fast all day, every day, and only ate a normal diet on Sundays or on Christmas.

Daily food was scarce and simply prepared. Fasting and penitence were important means of reaching the purification of the soul, and the refectory was a good place to practice personal humility. Returning the oranges, lemons, salt, and salsa to the kitchen in exactly the same form as they arrived at the table was considered a manifestation of great spirituality.[13]

Festive food was more elaborate in the convents and monasteries. In the celebrations of the foundation of new orders, fiestas lasted three or four days, during which time they offered masses, special ceremonies, and processions through the streets of the city. During the Christmas season, the convents celebrated the *posadas*, fiestas celebrated on the nine days before Christmas, with music and theater, when they ate candy, desserts, and many sweets prepared by the nuns themselves in the convent kitchen. The viceroy and his wife, the archbishop, patrons or sponsors of the convent, and family members of the nuns attended these celebrations.

Convents were the most important producers of sweets and desserts in New Spain. They reproduced recipes brought from Spain by members of the same order, or they invented new recipes using tropical fruits and local flavors. Many convents had their own special culinary specialties and became famous for them. Some were specialists in candy and marmalades, others in cookies, syrups, and caramels. They also catered food for elaborate luncheons and dinners. Some were specialists in imitating all sorts of savory dishes using sweets. To the surprise of the guests, almond paste could be transformed into an object that looked identical to a turkey leg.

An important route for the diffusion of the convent recipes was through the young girls of good families being educated in the convents. Besides reading, writing, and religious doctrine, many convents also offered classes in sewing, embroidering, painting, and cooking to the future housewives of New Spain. Some of the most famous recipes of New Spain came out of the convent kitchens. Traditional dishes like *mole poblano*, *chiles en nogada*, *rompope*, and many kinds of sweets were invented by the nuns and have since become festive dishes in Mexico.

Food in the Monasteries

The frugality and humility that characterized the diet of the Franciscan friars that arrived in 1523 was lost over the years when the enthusiasm for converting the Indians lost its fervor. In later years, the religious friars learned to enjoy the abundance that life in the monasteries offered them.

The Irish friar Thomas Gage, who visited New Spain on his way to become a missionary in the Philippines, was a keen observer of gastronomic customs in the monasteries and left us a rich description of monastery life in New Spain in the seventeenth century. He spent six months in the monastery of San Jacinto in San Angel, where he enjoyed all kinds of fish and meat as well as sweets and marmalades that were given to the monastery by the faithful. Gage comments that he was constantly hungry and that the immense variety of delicious food found in the kitchen was not enough to satisfy his appetite. He attributed this to the belief that local foods were not as nutritious as European foods. Two or three hours after eating a substantial meal that included three or four dishes of lamb, beef, veal, kid, turkeys, and other fowl, he declared that "we were so hungry we could hardly stand up and almost fainted." The only remedy was to recuperate with a cup of hot chocolate, some bread, and a bit of jam.[14] When Gage was told of the harsh living conditions awaiting him in the Philippines, he quickly changed his mind and decided that life must be easier in Chiapas and Guatemala, whereupon he modified his itinerary and journeyed south.

In some monasteries, the friars ate five times a day: when they woke up in the mornings, they enjoyed a cup of hot chocolate and sweet bread before they got out of bed. At nine o'clock they ate a breakfast that consisted of white rice, lamb or pork, and fried beans. At noon they ate their main meal, which consisted of a bowl of broth, one or two stews of meat and vegetables, fruit, and tea. At three o'clock in the afternoon, they drank another cup of chocolate, and between eight and nine o'clock at night they had a supper of roast meat, salad, and hot chocolate. The nuns in the convents could never imagine eating in such an elaborate fashion.

Sometimes the priests offered sumptuous banquets, completely out of fashion with the sacrifice and discipline associated with monastery life. Juan de Ortega y Montañés was serving as bishop of Michoacán in 1696 when he was named a temporary viceroy after the count of Galves left the position, until a new viceroy could be appointed. In a matter of days, the bishop forgot about all monastic austerity and became haughty and arrogant, given to living the good life and celebrating pompous ceremonies.

Antonio de Robles, the chronicler of Mexico City, left a detailed description of a luncheon offered by Bishop Ortega y Montañés on January 12, 1702, attended by members of the Real Audiencia and other important people of the times, under the strictest rules of protocol.[15] During the luncheon, 30 dishes were served, divided into 10 types of meat, 10 types of fish, and 10 different desserts. Other authors insist that 50 different dishes were served. A large selection of wines and ice creams completed the menu. After the luncheon, a finger bowl with a small towel perfumed with orange blossoms was placed before each guest.

The viceroy-bishop offered banquets in the Royal Palace every day, with the table luxuriously set with fine china brought by the Manila Galleon, fine crystal, and delicate linens embroidered by the nuns in the convents. This sharp change, too sudden for a bishop, made him lose all good sense and equanimity in his behavior and caused scandal and concern among the faithful in eighteenth-century Mexico City.

Foreign Influences in the Diet

The Philippines were conquered by the Spanish, sailing from Acapulco, Mexico, in 1562. This enabled the establishment of a trade route between the two countries that was to last 250 years. During this period, at least one and sometimes two ships known as the Manila Galleon, or the *Nao de China*, sailed between Acapulco and Manila every year. Several new food products were introduced to Mexico through this route, including a variety of spices such as cinnamon, nutmeg, and cloves. Black pepper traveled directly from Asia instead of taking the long route through Europe. The cultivation of mangoes arrived from Ceylon and Malaysia, tamarind pods arrived from India, and many other products were to have a lasting effect upon Mexican cooking. Africa contributed millet, sorghum, the African calabash or squash, horsebeans, and ginger. The latter products have had little effect upon the Mexican diet.

The Viceroy's Table

Spanish viceroys represented the king of Spain in Mexico and lived with the elegance and luxury that corresponded to their status in the New World. Many new ideas, clothing fashions, customs, and culinary novelties were brought by the viceroys and their staffs to New Spain. The viceroy was replaced every three years, so there was a constant introduction of novelties.

The Viceregal Palace served as a point of contact between European and Mexican societies. The influence of French cuisine first arrived in Mexico during the eighteenth century, introduced by Viceroy Francisco de Croix. The Marqués de Croix was born in Flanders and was a well-known gourmet and connoisseur of French food. Among his staff, he included an entire team of chefs and kitchen staff who were well trained in the art of French cooking and the decoration of dishes and proper table service in the French style. Dishes served were referred to by their French names, and the marqués became well known for the fine French food served at his table. He considered it important to serve an elegant table in a refined atmosphere and followed the strictest of protocol. During the time he was viceroy, the habits of the aristocracy in New Spain took on a French veneer, and French-style garden parties and picnics became popular. The French influence did not affect the great mass of the Mexican population, who clung to their own food habits.

The elaborate banquets offered by the viceroys in the Viceregal Palace have gone down in history for their extravagance. Numerous dishes were served, and all official banquets were accompanied by background music and some form of entertainment. The strictest protocol was observed at all official functions, and the place assigned to each guest was closely noted for its social significance.

It is not easy to describe the diet of New Spain as pertaining to only one eating tradition, as there were many different social and cultural levels among the population. Despite the abundance and variety of new foods on the market, the Indian population continued eating their traditional diet, based on corn, beans, and chile peppers. Urban Indians slowly began incorporating some European products in their diets, such as wheat bread and meat, but refused to give up their traditional food habits.

Those born in New Spain of Spanish parents (criollos) and those of mixed Indian and European descent (mestizos) were accustomed to both European and Mexican food flavors from childhood and became the promoters of the new cuisine. The cooks in open-air markets began blending the two food traditions by selling food that combined products from both continents, such as quesadillas, made with Indian tortillas and European cheese and served with chile peppers and green tomato sauce, or small, round tortillas called sopes, prepared with pork bits and complemented with a spicy chile sauce. Chicken-filled tacos and many other finger foods (antojitos) were also popular and represented a combination of the two culinary traditions. Indian cooks in the great houses of Mexico City or on the ranches (haciendas) and Catholic convents began adding corn and beans to Spanish-style stews and ollas. European fruits and vegetables shared space in the market stands with local products such as purslane (quelites) and chile peppers. This combination of foods from both worlds provided Mexico with a more varied and nutritious diet.

Products of European origin were considered to be more prestigious and nutritious than local Mexican products. Wheat bread, meat, olive oil, wine, sugar, distilled liquor, spices, nuts, olives, and capers were imported from Spain and later produced locally for the tables of the Spanish and Creole population. Meat and meat-based dishes were the preferred foods of the ruling class. The Spaniards preferred wheat bread to tortillas and considered the latter an inferior food. Wheat, in the form of the consecrated host, played an important role in the liturgy of the Roman Catholic Church and was considered a necessity by ecclesiastical authorities. Wine arrived from Spain during the early years after the conquest, along with various distilled beverages. Wine was principally destined for the tables of the local Spaniards for use in banquets and in the rites of the Catholic Church. Olive oil was brought to New Spain carrying a well-established prestige as a symbol of peace, hope, and abundance. It was essentially used as a substitute for animal fat during periods of religious fasting and as a fuel to ignite church lamps. Initially, Spanish products were expensive, scarce, and difficult to acquire, due to the problems and expense of transporting them from Spanish ports. This helped increase their status and prestige in New Spain.

The social lives of the criollos in New Spain constituted a fiesta without end. Mexican historians describe them as spending most of their time organizing games, charades, dances, parties, bullfights, fiestas, banquets, and theatrical presentations. All activities were carried out in an atmosphere of luxury and ostentation, where etiquette, style, and manners were of the utmost importance. Food and drink played an important role in the festivities as elements of ostentation and social status. Elaborate banquets and menus of official receptions indicate that the number of dishes served was often more important than the quality of the food. The arrival of a new viceroy in New Spain was commemorated by elaborate festivities; the enthronement of Spanish kings and the births and baptisms of royal princes or princesses served as opportunities to organize receptions, where food and drink played an important role.

New Spain: A Country of Contrasts

One of the characteristics of New Spain that most impressed foreign visitors was the contrast between the opulence enjoyed by a small number of the population and the extreme poverty of the masses. After visiting Mexico in 1803, the German scientist Alexander von Humboldt called Mexico "a country of inequality" and wrote that in no other country had he seen such a disproportionate distribution of riches and culture.[16] Others divided the country into "those who had everything" and "those who had nothing." Those who had everything in eighteenth-century Spain were the Spaniards—owners of commercial enterprises and warehouses, and who filled all the official government positions—and the Creoles, owners of the great haciendas and the gold and silver mines. Those who had nothing were the Indians, mestizos, mulattoes, and blacks, who threatened the security of the city and the government itself in times of unrest.

The principal cause of insecurity in New Spain was a lack of sufficient food for the whole population. Despite the variety of foods from both worlds, on the market, many foodstuffs were out of the reach of the marginal classes. There were various causes for the hunger that affected the population: some authors blame it on the lack of organization in the distribution of wheat and corn; others blame the lack of food on agricultural crises, the loss of harvests, and the epidemics and plagues that affected the country during the three centuries of colonial rule. No doubt hunger was caused by a combination of all these and other factors as well, because agricultural crises, hunger, and epidemics tend to walk hand in hand.

The government took several measures to try to prevent food scarcity, such as the establishment of organizations to regulate, distribute, and control the price of wheat and corn; programs of public works to create sources of jobs; and the distribution of free food in hospices and churches during periods of hunger. The years 1624 and 1692 were marked by hunger, causing social unrest that put the position of the government in danger. In the riots that followed the food crisis of 1692, the public attacked and set fire to the National Palace, the Municipal Council of the Spaniards (las casas del Cabildo), and the market stands that filled the main square. As these buildings went up in flames, the enraged public circled the plaza crying, "Death to the viceroy," "Death to the magistrate [corregidor]," and "Long live pulque." The riot ended only when the people finished rampaging and destroying the stores surrounding the plaza. The viceroy, count of Galves, quickly took a series of measures to restore the food supply in the city and forbid the entrance and sale of pulque, on which he lay the full blame for the riots.

The lower classes were the first ones to be affected by a scarcity of corn and by an increase in its cost, because it was their major food. At the same time, an increase in corn prices affected the price of wheat, meat, and other foods in such a way that the loss of the corn harvest affected the entire population, not just the Indians. Epidemics reduced the population in the cities and affected the poor people first because their defenses were low due to a lack of food.

The same disproportion in culture and goods that had so impressed von Humboldt when he arrived in Mexico was reflected in the eating patterns of the different levels of society. The Indians, in general, continued with their tradition of eating lightly. In spite of all the new products introduced by the Spaniards, they never abandoned their basic diet of corn, beans, and chile peppers.

THE CENTURY OF INDEPENDENCE

The commotion and turmoil of the nineteenth century ushered in an independent Mexico after 300 years of Spanish domination, a strong demographic mobilization of the population, and new influences in Mexican food. Many social changes took place after Mexico obtained its independence from Spain. When they were able to break the Spanish domination, Mexican frontiers became open to other influences and direct contacts with other countries. Mexico during the first years after the War of Independence has been described as an agitated river, where French tailors, merchants, shoemakers, and pharmacy owners; German merchants; and English businessmen came to fish.[17] The nineteenth century is considered by some historians to represent the second discovery of Mexico, this time not by conquistadores and missionaries but by businessmen, adventurers, and diplomats.

When the new government took power, the Spaniards were expelled from the country, and Spanish food products were prohibited from being imported. France, Germany, and England quickly filled this vacuum and began sending products to the new market. Germany sent gin, rice, codfish, beer, cookies, and canned vegetables. France contributed oil, vinegar, olives, wines, cheese, grapes, rum, pickled meat and fish, liquor, and many other products. Among the contributions of England were whiskey, rice, cinnamon, beer, butter, cookies, black pepper, and tea. During the first half of the century, it was the European countries that dominated the market, but after the middle of the century, the market fell into the hands of English and North American merchants, the latter taking advantage of the long frontier between the United States and Mexico.

What was the reaction of the Mexican public regarding Spanish products after the rupture between the two countries? Some foods that had been prestigious merely by being the preferred foods of the ruling class lost their favored status. Others were able to conserve their prestige as products of status because formal luncheons and dinners continued to serve their usual Spanish-style food.

Historians describe a mini–culinary revolution during this period when a spirit of nationalism and pride prevailed in the preparation and consumption of typically Mexican food. This was part of a conscious effort, encouraged by intellectuals and government officials, to promote a new national identity. In spite of their efforts to praise and exalt native dishes, cookbooks published in the nineteenth century contain mostly French and Spanish recipes, which creates some doubt as to their success in encouraging the consumption of popular food.

New food products, influences, and immigrants arrived from Europe and the United States after Mexico broke its binding ties with Spain. All of these left their influence on the Mexican diet in different degrees. One of the results of the opening up of the country to outside influences was the arrival of many foreign travelers, who left their impressions about Mexican food in written form. Mexican food and culinary traditions attracted the attention of these travelers because it was so distant from their own food culture. Many of the sources of information on nineteenth-century food come from this literature. Travelers were impressed by the dependence of Mexicans on corn and by the great quantity of chile peppers consumed by the people.

The most influential foreign cuisine during the nineteenth century was French haute cuisine, introduced by the Austrian archduke Maximilian and his wife, Carlota, who arrived in Mexico in 1864 to establish the Second Empire. This short-lived adventure lasted only three years; however, French influence at state dinners and official receptions continued throughout the presidency of Porfirio Díaz (1876–1911), until his government was overthrown by rebel forces in 1911. French cuisine replaced the heavy Spanish colonial food that had been served at official functions for over 350 years. Menus of banquets served in the National Palace during this period were printed in French but always accompanied by details of pre-Hispanic design to give them a local flavor. Don Porfirio Díaz's table was said to be as elegant as that of any European king, decorated with Limoges china, Vieux Paris porcelain, and Christofle tableware, ordered and brought to Mexico by Emperor Maximilian during his short-lived and ill-fated empire.

THE TWENTIETH CENTURY

The first decades of the twentieth century were marked by revolution and upheaval, when people were more concerned with getting enough food to eat rather than the nutritional or gastronomic state of their diets.

In the years following the Mexican Revolution, during the 1920s and 1930s, government officials tried to balance agricultural and industrial modernization with agrarian and labor reforms, based on the new constitution of 1917. In order to accomplish this, they attempted to promote a new national identity by incorporating the rural sector into the new regime through a massive program of rural schools, oriented toward teaching the Spanish language and Mexican patriotism. Thirty-some years of revolutionary struggle contributed to the growth of national unity.

There have been more profound changes in the Mexican food system and eating habits in the last 50 or 60 years than in the preceding 400 years. The second half of the twentieth century saw essential changes in the Mexican diet and in food distribution and preparation. Many factors analyzed in this book have contributed to the changes.

The technological improvement in cooking aids has eased the heavy burden on Mexican cooks and made their lives much easier. Of these improvements, the most important consisted in the invention of the corn-grinding mill to make *nixtamal*. This machine was first invented during the second half of the nineteenth century, but was not placed on the market and accessible for popular consumption until the twentieth century. Tortilla-making machines were also a nineteenth-century invention, but were not part of the Mexican domestic kitchen until the twentieth century. They were not easily accepted by the public for many decades. Women cooks in the neighborhood of Tláhuac continued to pat out their tortillas by hand until well into the 1980s. The last step in the industrialization of the tortilla arrived with the invention of dehydrated tortilla flour called *masa harina* in 1949. When mixed with water, the flour can be used to produce pliable tortillas. These inventions made significant changes in the lives of Mexican housewives, who were liberated from many hours dedicated to making tortillas and could use the time to pursue commercial interests in the marketplace, much to the chagrin of Mexican husbands, who worried about how their wives would spend their new-found leisure time.

Another labor-saving device that has become very popular in Mexican kitchens is the electric blender. Soups and sauces make up an important part of the daily menu, whose ingredients formerly had to be carefully ground in a mortar and pestle. The first Osterizer blender came on the market in 1954 and was almost immediately popular. Mexican husbands did not seem to mind the extra time this would afford their wives. Middle-class households have also adopted the food processor as a more powerful implement for grinding ingredients. Most households still have a mortar and pestle, which may be used for special sauces or to prepare food for special occasions. By the middle of the century, many other energy-saving electrical appliances became common implements in Mexican kitchens.

The 1950s also saw an increase in migration from rural to urban Mexico. The population in Mexico doubled from 16 million in 1934 to 32 million in 1958. This placed a heavy strain on the agricultural system, which soon affected the middle class. Farmers left the countryside en masse in hopes of finding work in urban areas, but soon realized that the number of available jobs was much smaller than the number of country people flowing to the cities. Poverty remained widespread, and the population growth placed a strain on urban services, which were incapable of keeping up with the demand.

Migrating groups brought their regional food habits with them to the cities. When they could not find employment, many of them set up small street stands (*fondas*) and served food from their part of the country. An increase in the income per capita of the population was reflected in their diets, in spite of the fluctuations in the country's economy and multiple peso devaluations.

Many of the communication barriers were broken at the end of the nineteenth century when isolated haciendas and new plantations were connected to markets via the railroad system. During the middle of the twentieth century, an extensive highway system was constructed that connected many rural areas to city markets. This was very important for the commercialization and distribution of produce in isolated parts of the country that heretofore had not had access to markets, and much of their produce was left to rot in the fields because local prices did not even merit its harvest.

Beginning in the 1930s, transnational food companies arrived to set up business in Mexico. The Swiss company Nestlé, which initially produced canned milk, made important changes in the reorganization and modernization of the milk industry. In later years, their production included milk-chocolate tablets and dehydrated coffee (Nescafé), which replaced hot chocolate as the favorite beverage of the masses. During the 1950s, many foreign companies, such as McCormick, arrived in Mexico to collaborate with Mexican businessmen in setting up new food production companies. The local soft-drink industry also combined their products with licenses of foreign companies. Orange Crush, Coca-Cola, Pepsi, and many other companies set up factories in Mexico beginning in 1928 and are now some of the most important industries in the country. Soft drinks are an important part of the Mexican workers' diet. Much short-term energy is attained through the sugar and fructose contained in soft drinks.

New and improved methods of marketing food took advantage of the improvement in the communications system, particularly in television, to foment the sale of novelty food products on the market. U.S. techniques of offering samples of a new product, along with instructions on its preparation, are also common methods used in upscale supermarkets.

The migration of undocumented workers to the United States and Canada, who return with modified food habits, is another factor contributing to changes in the Mexican diet. However, it must be said that most return from their foreign experiences with a new appreciation of their own local foods.

The North American Free Trade Agreement (NAFTA) signed with Canada and the United States on January 1, 1994, effectively opened Mexican borders and markets to the importation of foreign foodstuffs and electrical domestic products. This has created considerable discourse in Mexico, particularly on the part of rural food producers and factory owners, who did not have to face serious competition before this time and could operate under inefficient conditions and still make a profit. For the consumer, it has been a windfall in the marketplace, where high-quality products at accessible prices have changed the panorama of food purchasing.

All of these factors, as well as many others, have contributed to what one could almost call a revolution in food habits in Mexico during the past 50 years.

NOTES

1. C. Earle Smith, Jr., "Plant Remains," in *The Prehistory of the Tehuacán Valley*, vol. 1, *Environment and Subsistence*, ed. Douglas S. Byers (Austin: University of Texas Press, 1967), 225–26.

2. Kent V. Flannery, "Los orígenes de la agricultura en México: Las teorías y la evidencia," in *Historia de la agricultura: Época Prehispánica-Siglo XVI*, ed. T. Rojas Rabiela and W. T. Sanders (Mexico City: Instituto Nacional de Antropología e História, 1985), 237–65.

3. Yoko Sugiura and Fernán González de la Vara, *La cocina mexicana a través de los siglos*, vol. 1, *México Antiguo* (Mexico City: Editorial Clío, 1996), 19–25.

4. Ibid., 21–32.

5. Bernal Díaz del Castillo, *Historia verdadera de la conquista de Nueva España* (Mexico City: Editorial Porrúa, 1980), 166–68.

6. *Anales de Cuauhtitlán*, in *Códice Chimalpopoca*, ed. Primo Feliciano Velázquez (Mexico City: Imprenta Universitaria, 1975), 3–68.

7. Díaz del Castillo, *Historia verdadera*, 248.

8. Diego de Landa, *Relación de las cosas de Yucatán* (Mexico City: Editorial Porrúa, 1978), 36–37.

9. Alfredo Barrera Vásquez and Silvia Rendón, trans., *El libro de los libros del Chilam Balam* (Mexico City: Fondo de Cultura Economica, 1963).

10. Díaz del Castillo, *Historia verdadera*, 544–48.

11. William Mayer, *Early Travelers in Mexico, 1534–1816* (Mexico City: Edtl. Cultura, 1961), 12.

12. Juan de Viera, *Breve y compendiosa narración de la ciudad de Mexico, 1777* (Buenos Aires: Edtl. Guarania, 1952), 20.

13. Rosalva Loreto López, "Prácticas alimenticias en los conventos de mujeres en la Puebla del siglo XVIII," in *Conquista y comida: Consecuencias del encuentro de dos mundos*, ed. Janet Long (Mexico City: Universidad Nacional Autónoma de México, 1996), 494–95.

14. Thomas Gage, *Nuevo reconocimiento de las Indias Occidentales* (Mexico City: Fondo de Cultura Economica, 1982), 130.

15. Antonio de Robles, *Diario de sucesos notables, 1665–1703*, vol. 3 (Mexico City: Editorial Porrúa, 1946), 193–94.

16. Alexander von Humboldt, *Tablas geográficas politicas del reino de Nueva España y correspondencia mexicana* (Mexico City: Direccion General de Estadistica, 1970), 47.

17. Luis González y González, *Historia mínima de Mexico* (Mexico City: El Colegio de Mexico, 1973), 103.

2

Major Foods and Ingredients

The invasion of food plants and products that followed the arrival of the Spanish conquistadores changed the Mexican diet forever. The combination of local food products with those introduced by the Spaniards launched nutritional changes that surpassed anything that had yet been seen. While much of the world fought against food shortages and famines, Mexico, with its growing supply of foods, was able to produce a surplus of grains and meat by the middle of the sixteenth century.[1]

The Spaniards quickly set about adapting European plants and animals to local conditions in an attempt to turn the country into a virtual New Spain. The three most important food items introduced that have had a long-lasting influence on the Mexican diet are meat and its derivatives, such as milk, cheese, butter, and eggs; wheat, which gave rise to the important bread industry in Mexico; and finally sugar, used today in alcohol, desserts, candy, and above all in soft drinks. Rice; citrus fruits; certain vegetables, such as onions and garlic; and Mediterranean herbs like parsley, coriander, and oregano also have had a marked effect upon the Mexican diet.

The list of ingredients that follows is divided into two categories: (1) Mesoamerican plants and animals, listed by their importance in the diet, and (2) food products of European origin. Additional cultural and social information about the food product is included when appropriate.

MESOAMERICAN PRODUCTS

The Triad of Mexican Agriculture

Corn, beans, and squash form what is sometimes called the triad of native Mexican agriculture. The three crops originated and were domesticated in Mexico during pre-Hispanic times. They constituted the basic foods in the ancient Mexican diet and make up the most important ingredients in the modern diet as well. Throughout history, the combination of these three food products has provided Mexicans with a diet sufficient in nutrition to allow them to maintain their health and provide enough energy for everyday living. Any of the three consumed alone would not have given them the necessary nutrients. Corn is deficient in lysine and tryptophan, amino acids indispensable for forming the set of proteins needed by the human body. Beans are rich in these two amino acids, and when corn and beans are consumed together, they provide elements to form a complete protein. Squash, tomatoes, and chile peppers are an important contribution to the Mexican diet as providers of vitamins and minerals.

Early farmers developed a unique method of farming by intercropping the three plants in the same field, which allowed them to produce more food from a single plot of ground. This method of farming is still being used in modern Mexico in small subsistence fields. Climbing beans and squash use cornstalks for support, which allows their fruit to ripen off the ground and, at the same time, protects it from excess water and predatory animals. Beans provide an additional advantage when planted alongside corn, as this plant is a well-known reducer of nitrogen in the soil, and beans have the ability to fix this chemical in the soil through certain bacteria located in the root nodules of the bean plant.

Corn

It is common for many food systems to be dominated by a particular food item that is closely identified with the culture and can be considered vital to the group's well being. In Mexico, this role is played by corn (*Zea mays* L.). It is the most important as well as the most respected food crop in the Mexican diet and is considered sacred by indigenous peoples. There is a common belief among the population that human beings and corn share the same essence and that their destinies are closely connected. The corn plant is believed to be analogous to the life stages of a human being.

The transformation from corn seed to young plant; the flowering of the plant and the production of tender, green ears; and finally the fully ripe ear of corn can be related to humans' passage through life.[2] It plays an important role in agricultural rituals, fiestas, and ceremonies, sometimes as an offering to solicit a good crop; in others, it is offered in appreciation for a plentiful harvest.

Corn, or maize, as it is known in Mexico, is an ancient plant in Mesoamerica. Corn is a generic term for a staple grain that has been applied to many grains throughout history. In Náhuatl, the language spoken by the Aztecs, corn was known as *centli*. *Maíz* is a term derived from the Caribbean language Taíno and was introduced into Mexico by the Spaniards when they arrived.

The ancestor of corn is believed to be a wild, weedy grass called *teosinte* (*Zea* spp.), which can still be found growing wild in some parts of the country. The Aztecs knew this variety of corn as *teozintli*, or "corn of the gods." The plant appeared in Mesoamerica sometime between 7,000 and 10,000 years ago, and by around 3500 B.C. it had undergone the process of domestication and was being cultivated by Mexican farmers. Plant domestication is a very slow process, and it was no doubt enjoyed as a wild or protected plant long before it was fully domesticated. Through the process of domestication, the plant lost its natural ability to reproduce by itself and must depend upon man's intervention for propagation. The protective corn husk that encloses the ear of corn does not allow the seeds to disperse freely, and the husk must be opened and the seed kernels separated from the cob in order to develop into a new plant.

The earliest archaeological evidence for corn was found in the domestic refuse of caves in the Tehuacán Valley in the state of Puebla, in central Mexico, and dates from around 5000 B.C.[3] Very small corncobs, ranging from two to three inches long, with four to eight rows of kernels covered with long glumes, were excavated from cave deposits in the site. The tiny eight-rowed ears were gradually transformed into early cultivated corn, which evolved into the corn known and eaten today. Corn is so important in the Mexican diet that no meal can be considered a proper meal without it. Aztec women breathed on corn kernels before placing them in a pot to cook so they would not be afraid of the fire. Even today, Mexican myths are filled with warnings for those who do not show the proper respect for corn. If it is not treated properly, its spirit may depart, leaving the people miserable and hungry. Another accepted belief is that burning a tortilla on the griddle will cause bad luck.

Corn products are eaten by Mexicans at all three meals, and as snacks between meals as well. In some parts of the country, adult workers consume approximately one pound of corn daily, which provides 80 percent of food-energy calories. It is a better source of energy than other cereals due to its high fat content and has always served as a good source of complex carbohydrates in the Mexican diet. Ground cornmeal has 1,789 calories per pound. It contains about 4.5 percent good fat, is high in linoleic and oleic fatty acids, and contains approximately 10 percent protein. It is often consumed with beans and chile-pepper salsa, which contribute protein, lysine, vitamins, and minerals to the diet.

Following an ancient tradition, cooks try to make use of all parts of the corn plant. Green corn leaves, as well as corn sheaths or husks, are used for wrapping tamales. Corncobs are sometimes ground and added to corn flour to increase the supply of cornmeal and are also used as fuel for cooking. Another use for corncobs is as an artifact for shelling corn by tying them together in an upright position and scraping the dried ears of corn over the surface to remove the corn kernels.

There are many ways of preparing corn. It can be boiled, toasted, roasted, ground into a fine corn flour, or used as whole kernels and added to a variety of stews. The most common use of corn in present-day Mexico is in the form of tortillas and tamales.

The Nutritional Value of Corn

When the Spaniards arrived in Mexico, they were intrigued by the dependence of the local population upon corn and corn products. They considered corn an inferior crop and hesitated to substitute their wheat bread for corn tortillas, unless they had no other option. In reality, corn offers many advantages over wheat. It produces more calories in less space, in less time, and with less manpower than wheat. It adapts to a variety of climates, soils, and altitudes, and can be used as animal fodder and as food for human consumption. Along with wheat, rice, and potatoes, it is considered one of the four most important crops on the world market.

The nutritional value of corn became a controversial topic in the early twentieth century when Senator Francisco Bulnes published a book attributing Mexico's backwardness to a combination of Iberian conservatism and Indian debility. He blamed native Mexicans' weakness on their diet and proclaimed that corn had been the eternal pacifier of America's indigenous races and the foundation of their refusal to become "civilized." He believed that "the race of wheat" was the only progressive one and that salvation lay in the adoption of European culture and the consumption of wheat bread. The members of Don Porfirio Díaz's cabinet found this argument appealing, because many considered the Indian to be one of the barriers to Mexican development.[4]

For nearly half a century, this topic was debated by Mexican leaders, who were looking for a way to incorporate the Indians into the national community and the market economy. When the diet was finally analyzed by the National Institute of Nutrition in 1940, they found wheat and corn equally nutritious and their caloric intake quite similar.

A roll of white bread, called a *bolillo*, contains 76 calories, while a corn tortilla is calculated to have 64 calories. After these investigations, the tortilla could no longer be blamed for the poverty and underdevelopment of the Indian cultures. The Mexican government then wisely began a program to supplement corn with vegetables, salads, and fruits rather than trying to replace it with wheat products. Ironically enough, corn farmers were incorporated into the national economy through the commodification of corn, when it changed from a subsistence crop to a market commodity.

Atole

Atole is a type of gruel thickened with *masa,* sweetened with sugar and flavored with any kind of crushed fruit, such as strawberries or pineapple, and seasoned with chile pepper. When it is flavored with chocolate, it is called *champurrado*. It is a popular accompaniment for tamales and is considered a remedy for digestive problems as well.

Corn Beverages

Corn also serves as a base for several beverages, such as *chicha,* made with germinated corn and brought to a boil; *chilote,* made with corn kernels, sugar cane, and honey; and *tanchuera,* a Yucatecan beverage made with corn kernels, anise, and chocolate. Other beverages are *tesgüino,* a fermented corn drink from northern Mexico; *nequatolli,* a beverage of *atole* with honey; *tascalate,* made with chocolate mixed with water and ground tortillas; *tejate,* made with chocolate, water, and toasted corn; *yorique,* prepared with corn, cactus paddles (*nopales*), and apple vinegar; and many others.

Huitlacoche

Corn fungus (*Ustilago maydis*) is known in English by the degrading term *corn smut*. It is essentially a fungus that forms on the ears of corn when the kernels become swollen and deformed and are covered with a silvery-grey skin. The inside of the fungus is black and juicy and sometimes goes by the name of *cuitlacoche* as well as *huitlacoche*. In recent years it has become an element in Mexican haute cuisine, in the form of *crepas de huitlacoche*, as a substitute for pâté in filet of beef Wellington, and in many other refined dishes. It is also used in tacos or as a vegetable. It is much appreciated in Highland Mexico, where, due to its high price, it has become a luxury item in the marketplace. *Huitlacoche* can be found on the market during the rainy season.

Tamales

Whereas tortillas accompany meals and are eaten on a daily basis, tamales are considered festive foods, made for special occasions. First Communion breakfasts, children's parties, and weddings are popular occasions to serve tamales. They are also prepared to be placed on the altar on All Saints' Day, for special meals during Holy Week, or as a light Sunday-evening meal.

Street seller of popular snack, Mexico City. © TRIP/M. Barlow.

Tamales are prepared with the same corn dough (*masa*) used for tortillas, which is then beaten with lard and stuffed with a diversity of fillings. It is steamed in a corn husk (*totomoxtle*), a banana leaf cut into a square, a *chaya* leaf, or any of a variety of large green leaves that serve as a wrapping for the tamale and at the same time add flavor to the dish. Tamales are prepared by spreading corn dough inside a corn husk, adding chile-pepper sauce, chicken or pork, and sometimes beans. They are then tightly folded up like small gifts, to prevent water from seeping in while they are in the steaming pot. Sweet tamales (*tamales dulces*) are favorites of children. These are prepared with raisins or other fruits, and the *masa* is colored with pale pink food coloring. There is an enormous variety of tamales being prepared and sold in tamale outlets today. Many regions of the country, such as Oaxaca and Chiapas, include a large variety of tamales in their food traditions.

Tortillas

Tortillas are indispensable in the Mexican cuisine. These are small disks made of corn dough (*masa*), about five or six inches in diameter, and are sometimes compared to American corn pancakes. Their preparation begins with nixtamalized corn dough (further described in chapter 3), which can now be bought in a tortilla shop (*tortillería*) as ready-made *masa* or by mixing tortilla corn flour with water.

Tortillas can be made or purchased in a variety of colors, depending upon the color of corn used and the ingredients added to the dough. White or yellow tortillas are the most common tortillas eaten on a daily basis. Blue tortillas, made with blue corn, are considered a delicacy and are widely available. Red tortillas are prepared from red corn, while pink tortillas contain added ground chile powder. After preparation, the tortilla can then be eaten as a complement to a meal, by itself with a sprinkling of salt to add flavor, rolled around a meat or vegetable filling to form a taco, or used as a base for a variety of finger foods. Tortillas serve as a convenient implement, as they can take the place of a plate or a spoon, reducing serving dishes to a minimum. This is important in street-food stands, where an assembly-line pattern is often set up. One seller can set up shop with a basket of warm tortillas, and the buyer, after purchasing his tortilla, can pass on to the next stand with open tortilla in hand and purchase a good-sized dollop of beans, stew (*guisado*) heated on a small brazier, or a spoonful of salsa to fill his tortilla. The tortilla is then rolled with the ends tucked in somewhat like a small envelope, to avoid losing the filling, whereby it can be eaten without the use of a plate or cutlery.

There are many varieties and shapes of tortillas served as finger foods, or *antojitos*. *Sopes, garnachas, picadas*, chalupas, *panuchos*, and many others are prepared with small round tortillas with pinched edges to form a low ridge, so the sauce or filling will not overflow the tortilla. These can be filled with a variety of fillings such as refried beans, shredded chicken, or pork with salsa, and crumbled aged cheese or simply a chile-pepper sauce with chopped onion, aged cheese, and sour cream. With *tlacoyos, huaraches*, gorditas, quesadillas, *envueltos, dobladas*, flautas, *memelas, peneques*, tostadas, and *molotes*, the variety of tortilla-based dishes are in-finite.

Quesadillas Mexicanas

- 6 tortillas
- 1/4 pound grated Oaxaca cheese
- 1 small onion, chopped
- 1 teaspoon dried epazote
- 1 small avocado, sliced
- vegetable oil

Place small amounts of cheese, onion, and epazote on one half of the tortilla. Arrange avocado slices on top and fold the tortilla in half. Toast the tortilla on a griddle until the cheese melts. Serve with hot sauce.

Beans

Mexico, along with Brazil, Paraguay, and Nicaragua, constitute the principal consumers of beans in the Americas. The consumption of beans in Mexico is the highest in the world. Four species of beans are important in Mexico and other Latin American countries: *Phaseolus vulgaris* (the common bean), *P. lunatus* (the lima bean), *P. coccineus* (the climbing bean), and *P. acutifolius* (the scarlet-runner bean). Some 50 other bean varieties can be found as wild or semidomesticated plants.[5] In Mexico, beans can be produced throughout the country, while the states of Zacatecas and Durango are the most important producers of the crop. The country produces over 968 million tons of beans annually; nevertheless, during some years, the consumption is higher than the production, making it necessary for Mexico to import beans from other countries.

Beans have been an important ingredient in the Mexican diet through-out history. They are considered one of the earliest plants to be domesticated in ancient times. Dried beans have been excavated from the most ancient archaeological sites in Mexico, such as Tehuacán; Puebla; and Ocampo, Tamaulipas.

Beans are a good complement to corn in the diet, as they contain the amino acids tryptophan and lysine, which are lacking in corn, and when consumed together, provide the necessary protein requirements. Thirty percent of the protein in the diet in rural Mexico comes from the consumption of beans. Beans are an important source of complex carbohydrates and are also high in magnesium, calcium, potassium, and folic acid. They are also a good source of fiber and are considered an aid to the digestive system. Today, they are consumed in all social levels and along with corn form the basic food of millions of Mexicans.

There are more than 20 varieties of beans on the Mexican market. They are commonly known by the public by the color of the seeds, their shapes, or the region where they are grown. Their demand on the market is determined by their size, shape, color, appearance, storage qualities, cooking facility, quality, and flavor. Beans are sold in a variety of colors, such as black, pink, white, and beige (*bayo*). Spotted (*pinto*) and mottled (*moteado*) beans are also distinguished, as are particular shapes, such as goat's-eye beans and peanut-shaped beans. The choice of a certain color or shape of bean is determined by regional preference. Pinto beans (called *flor de mayo*), pink beans (called *catarino* beans), goat's-eye beans, and peanut-shaped beans are popular in the Bajío region of central Mexico. Mexicans from northern Mexico prefer pinto or *bayo* beans, while in Veracruz and Yucatán, consumers prefer small black turtle beans. Navy beans (*ayocotes*) are a favorite in Highland Mexico, where all kinds of beans are popular. Fava beans (*habas*) are also popular in several parts of the country.

Quick-cooking beans called *instantaneos* have become popular in recent decades. These are dried beans ground into a flour that are packaged and sold in the supermarket. They are easily and quickly prepared by adding a small amount of water and frying as refried beans, a technique that was not used until the Spaniards arrived, bringing with them lard for frying.

Squash

Squash may be the oldest food plant domesticated in pre-Hispanic Mexico. Seeds of squash (*Cucurbita pepo*) dating from between 8750 and 6670 B.C. have been found in the Güilá Naquitz Cave in the Valley of Oaxaca.[6] Evidence of its domestication before 6670 B.C. has also been found. This species of squash still holds a prominent place in Oaxacan cuisine.

Acorn squash, summer squash, and zucchini are varieties of *Cucurbita pepo*, as are some (but not all) pumpkins. The nomenclature of plants is a fascinating and confusing topic. For example, "pumpkins," which are native to Mexico, are now called "Spanish squash" or "*la calabaza de Castilla*," where they were completely unknown before the discovery of North America.

Squash has had many uses throughout history. Initially, humans took advantage of its round shape and used it as a receptacle or container for liquids and to store dried grains. Wild squash are very small, with almost no pulp. After the squash passed through the process of domestication, the plant began to produce large specimens.

Zucchini with Pork (*Calabazitas con Puerco*)

- 1-1/2 lbs. pork loin
- 10 tomatillos
- 5 zucchini, sliced
- 2 cloves garlic
- 3 sprigs coriander
- cooking oil
- salt
- 1 small green chile pepper

Cook the zucchini in a small amount of water. Put the pork loin in a casserole with one cup water and cook until the water has evaporated and the meat begins to brown in its own grease. Boil the tomatillos and the chile pepper and place them in the blender with the garlic cloves and the coriander. Blend all ingredients well. Sauté this mixture, adding salt, and cook until it is well seasoned. Pour over cooked pork loin along with cooked zucchini and let cook a few minutes more. Serve with white rice.

The seeds are the most nutritious part of the plant, as they contain potassium, magnesium, copper, and zinc, as well as 35–55 percent oil and 30–35 percent protein by weight. Squash leaves are rich in calcium, and the growing tips are good sources of iron as well as vitamins B and C. Squash, especially those with deep yellow or orange flesh, is rich in carotenes, the precursors of vitamin A.

Squash is a complement to the diet of corn and beans and often prepared in stews, succotash, pumpkin and squash-flower soups, and as sauces. Stuffed squash is a popular item on Mexican menus. The beautiful yellow blossoms of the squash plant give color and flavor to stews, soups, and salads, and can also be stuffed, battered, and fried, or used as a filling for tortillas and quesadillas. Yucatecan cooking makes ample use of toasted ground squash seeds to prepare a popular dish called *papadzules* or a paste made of ground squash seeds called *sikil*. Squash seeds have a delicious nutty flavor and are popular snacks throughout the world.

Amaranth

Although amaranth was an important food product in pre-Hispanic Mexico, its present use is principally in the preparation of a popular candy called *alegría*, translated as "joy" or "happiness." It contains a higher level of protein than corn, and its calories and carbohydrates are equivalent to those of corn. The grain contains 16–18 percent protein, compared with 14 percent or less for wheat and other grains. Its protein has a good balance of amino acids. It is rich in lysine, the amino acid that corn lacks, which means that it could substitute for beans as a good companion for corn and is often planted simultaneously with it. It has a shorter growing cycle than corn and ripens earlier, so the harvests do not overlap. Amaranth leaves are high in protein and contain important amounts of vitamin A. It has other qualities as well, because it is resistant to both drought and freezing weather.

The seeds, flowers, stems, and leaves of the amaranth plant are used in the Mexican diet. The leaves are sometimes added to soups, stews, and moles, or as an addition to scrambled eggs. Amaranth leaves are also prepared as a cooked vegetable or used fresh in salads. Ice creams, desserts, candy, and beverages are made with the popped seeds of the amaranth plant. Seeds ground into flour are used in soups, *atoles*, cookies, and amaranth *masa*.

To make *alegrías*, amaranth grains are toasted, popped on a griddle, and mixed with syrup to form a sticky mass. The dough is then kneaded and pressed into round molds some three inches in diameter, which are later packaged and sold by itinerant vendors on the streets of Mexico City, following the late summer harvest. The seeds are also ground into fine flour, mixed with sugar, and shaped into paper-thin disks that are folded in half and sold on the street or in specialized candy shops. These disks resemble the communion wafer used in the Catholic mass.

Avocados

Avocados come from a tree of the *Lauracea* family, which is native to Mexico. It bears a fruit with a leathery skin; a large seed; and soft, buttery flesh. Avocados have thick green skin or paper-thin black skin, which has a strong flavor of anise. The skin of the black avocado can be ground up and mixed with the avocado sauce for more flavor. The Hass avocado, a dark, knobby-skinned fruit with a wonderful flavor of hazelnuts and anise, is a popular choice on the market. Avocado leaves are commonly used in south central Mexico to add extra flavor to rice or beans. These can be used fresh or dried and are usually lightly toasted on the griddle, when they give off a wonderful fragrance, before being added to the dish. They can be used as a substitute for *hoja santa* (*Piper sanctum*) in tamales or as a special flavoring for Oaxaca-style beans.

Cactus Paddles

Cactus paddles (*nopales*) are the flat-jointed leaves or joints of opuntia cacti, which are cultivated as a green vegetable throughout Mexico. They are sometimes called prickly pears due to the spines or thorns on the flat sides of the paddles. They resemble okra in that they exude a slimy substance when cooked, which must be washed off in cold running water. The paddles have spines that must be shaved off with a sharp knife before cooking. Spineless cactus paddles can now be purchased in upscale supermarkets in Mexico City. Cactus paddles may be diced and sautéed, steamed, or boiled. In the latter case, they are diced and then placed in a saucepan with a garlic clove, onion, salt, baking soda, and water to cover. The mixture is brought to a boil and simmered for 10 minutes or until the cactus is soft enough to pierce with a fork. They are then drained, washed, and set aside to be incorporated into the recipe. They are popular as ingredients in salads, stews, tacos, and scrambled eggs, or served by themselves, cooked in a tomato and green chile-pepper sauce.

Nopales are produced in large quantities in the arid parts of Mexico and are much in demand on the market. The fruit of the opuntia cactus, called *tunas* in Mexico, is a refreshing red or green fruit with many tiny seeds. *Nopales* are rich in vitamin C and calcium. Canned *nopalitos*, packed in brine, can be used as an acceptable substitute for fresh *nopales*.

Chayote

A pear-shaped member of the squash family, chayote is also known as the vegetable pear. It is native to Mexico, where three varieties can be found: (1) small green pears, (2) dark-green ones with porcupine-like spines, and (3) creamy-white ones. It has a mild, cucumber-like flavor, pale green flesh, and a large seed, which many consider a delicacy. Chay-

Edible cactus in the Mercado de la Merced, Mexico City. © TRIP/J. Highet.

otes can be boiled and made into a salad, breaded, and sautéed or stuffed with a well-seasoned mixture to add extra flavoring.

Chocolate

Chocolate was a luxury food in pre-Hispanic Mexico, accessible only to the nobility. It was given the name *Theobroma cacao* by the Swedish botanist Linnaeus in 1753. Its place of origin is thought to be an area between the Amazon and Orinoco rivers in South America. It diffused very early to Mesoamerica, and was used by the Olmec and Maya cultures since ancient times. The word *cacao* comes from the Maya word *kakaw*. The Maya, in turn, passed it on to the Aztecs, who gave it the nomenclature of *chocolatl*, which can be translated as chocolate and water. The Aztecs

Aztec woman preparing a foamy chocolate beverage. From the Códice Tudela. Courtesy of Museo
de America.

drank it as a refreshing cold drink, to which corn kernels, ground chile
peppers, vanilla beans, or honey could be added. The English word
"chocolate" is derived from the Náhuatl term *chocolatl*. Today the word
cacao is used to refer to the tree and its products before processing, while
chocolate refers to any manufactured cacao product. Chocolate contains
the alkaloids theobromine, caffeine, and phenylethylamine. The latter is
a source of energy and influences the nervous system. Chocolate has a
high fat content and less than 10 percent by weight is protein and starch.
The Spaniards modified the preparation of chocolate by adding milk and
sugar.

   Chocolate is a widely used ingredient in Mexican cooking. In some
parts of the country, such as Chiapas, Oaxaca, and Michoacán, special

chocolate is still being ground on a *metate*, which produces a rough-textured product that is then shaped into small storable cakes, tablets, or round balls to be used in the making of hot chocolate, for baking, or for other desserts. Chocolate ground on the *metate* is sometimes ground together with almonds and sugar. Cinnamon or vanilla are other popular additions. Hot chocolate is sometimes considered a children's drink, but it is a common accompaniment for tamales, when it is consumed by people of all ages. Chocolate tablets constitute a common offering placed on the altar during the All Saints' Day celebration. It is also a part of family gatherings, funerals, marriage ceremonies, and New Year's Eve celebrations.

The industrialization of chocolate in Mexico began during the middle of the nineteenth century. It is now produced as a solid or powdered baking ingredient, used to prepare popular dishes such as mole or as a fine candy made of dark chocolate, or mixed with milk to produce milk chocolate. White chocolate is cacao butter and is used both as a baking ingredient as well as in fine candies.

Beverages made of chocolate are popular in Oaxaca, Chiapas, and Tabasco. *Tejate* is a popular refreshing drink in Oaxaca made of corn *masa*, ground together with toasted mamey seeds and cacao. It is served cold with a bit of sugar water and produces a thick foam when beaten with a chocolate mill or *molinillo*. *Pozol* is a beverage from Chiapas and Tabasco made of strained *masa de nixtamal* mixed with cacao and water, without sweetening. *Tascalate* is made with a mixture of ground corn, *achiote*, and chocolate powder dissolved in water or milk. A*tolechampurrado* is made by mixing *atole* with tablets of chocolate at the time of cooking. It is then beaten with a *molinillo*, sweetened, and left to boil. *Chocolateatole*, popular in Oaxaca, is prepared with corn *atole* and cacao powder and beaten into a thick foam.

Jícama

The *jícama* is a tuber native to Mexico and South America. It resembles a huge brown radish, with thin, patchy skin. It is also called a yam bean. It is juicy and crisp with white flesh and a radish-like texture. Some people compare its taste and texture with that of a water chestnut.

It is often eaten as a raw snack, peeled, thinly sliced, and seasoned with ground chile pepper, a bit of salt, and a squirt of lime juice. It can also be grated or sliced and used in salads or appetizers. It is found on a year-round basis in markets throughout the country, especially in the Yucatán.

Peppers

Chile peppers are one of the most important items in the Mexican diet. More than any other ingredient, peppers identify Mexican food, both nationally and internationally. When asked to describe Mexican food, most foreigners will make a reference to its pungency.

Chile peppers are a New World plant and belong to the genus *Capsicum*. They were unknown in other continents before the discovery of the Americas at the end of the fifteenth century. There are no references to peppers prior to the sixteenth century in ancient languages such as Greek, Sanskrit, or ancient Chinese. It has preserved its ancient Náhuatl nomenclature of *chilli* in many parts of the world.

The genus contains 5 domesticated species and some 22 wild species of peppers known today. Botanists hold that the genus *Capsicum* originated in South America and arrived in Mesoamerica thousands of years ago as a wild plant (*Capsicum annuum*, var. *aviculare*), popularly known as *chile piquín*. They probably traveled by natural means, such as the wind or water currents, or they may have been transported by birds. This species was domesticated in Mexico and later given the taxonomic term of *Capsicum annuum*. All domesticated peppers in Mexico, with the exception of the habanero (*Capsicum chinense*), manzano (*Capsicum pubescens*), and Tabasco (*Capsicum frutescens*), belong to the species *C. annuum*. It is the most important commercial species of chile peppers in the world.

Chile peppers have been part of the Mexican diet for at least 7,000 years. One might even speculate on the duration of Mexico's basic diet, made up of corn, beans, and squash, without the flavor, pungency, and variety proportioned by the chile pepper. The diet would have been much more monotonous. Peppers not only provide the vitamins A and C in the diet, they are also a stimulant to the appetite and increase the presence of saliva in the mouth. They had many uses in pre-Hispanic Mexico. Their main use was in the diet, but they also served as a tributary product, a medicine, and a weapon.

Peppers are consumed by all social levels in Mexico and thus can be considered a common denominator between social classes and one of the cultural traits that is said to identify Mexicans. Some historians have observed that peppers are as necessary to Mexicans as salt is to Europeans. Chile peppers have now become a product in demand on the international market. With the mass migration of undocumented Mexican workers to the United States and the popularity Mexican food is enjoying in American restaurants, chile peppers have become a popular item in demand on both the American and Mexican markets.

Plantains

Plantains are larger and contain more starch than the typical banana. They resemble long, curved bananas and have thick skins that are green in the unripe stage but acquire dull, black skins when fully ripe and soft. Their most common method of preparation is by slicing them into vertical slices and frying them. They are often used to garnish white rice, when it is served as a "dry soup." They are never eaten raw. They go by the name of *plátano macho* in Mexico and are considered a vegetable rather than a fruit. They must be very ripe, juicy, and sweet to add flavor to Mexican dishes.

Tomatoes and Tomatillos

The word *tomato* is confusing in central Mexico, where the word, by itself, is used to refer to husk tomatoes or tomatillos, of the genus *Physalis*. The red tomato is known as *jitomate* in Highland Mexican Spanish, to differentiate it from the tomatillo. Its present-day nomenclature comes from the Náhuatl *xitomatl* and is believed to mean "peeled or skinned tomato," from the Náhuatl word *xipehua*, which denotes "to peel, skin, or flay." This may be a reference to the calyx that covers the fruit of the tomatillo and is lacking in the red tomato. Tomatillos are more ancient and were more commonly used in pre-Hispanic Mexico than red tomatoes. When Mesoamericans came across the red-fruited tomato, they may have noted its general similarity to the husk tomato and referred to it by a similar name, *xitomatl*, to differentiate it from the tomatillo. Sixteenth-century Spanish writers did not distinguish between the red and green tomatoes and translated both as *tomate*; thus it is impossible to know to which fruit they were referring.

The red tomato belongs to the genus *Lycopersicon*. It is a relatively small genus within the large and diverse family *Solanacea*. The genus is currently thought to consist of the cultivated tomato, *Lycopersicon esculentum*, and seven closely related wild *Lycopersicon* species, all of which are native to northwestern South America. There is no archaeological evidence that tomatoes were used by ancient South American cultures.

No plant remains have appeared in site excavations, and there is no word for tomato in ancient Andean languages. This may indicate that, although the tomato existed as a wild species in the Andean region, it was never utilized by pre-Hispanic populations.

The theory of the origin of the tomato is strikingly parallel in many ways to that of the chile pepper, of the genus *Capsicum*. The wild species of both are South American in origin. They reached Mesoamerica at an early date, probably by natural means, and there found a favorable ecological niche, were domesticated, and eventually gave rise, respectively, to the cultivated plants *L. esculentum* and *Capsicum annuum*.

The tomato contains significant amounts of vitamins A and C, although probably less than the general public has been led to believe. Its importance as a provider of these vitamins depends more on the quantity consumed than on the amount of vitamins in each fruit. Its vivid color, the fact that it can be used as both a raw and cooked vegetable, and its ability to blend easily with other ingredients has made the tomato a popular food item and an important vegetable on the Mexican market. The tomato's most important use throughout history has been as an ingredient in Mexican salsa, and it is served with countless dishes to add color and flavor to meats, tortillas, and beans.

Tomatoes have played an important role in genetic research programs that have contributed to its improvement. The tomato has many characteristics that make it an ideal subject for plant research. It has the ability to produce and prosper in a variety of climates and has a short life cycle that, under a well-managed program, permits it to produce three generations per year. Tomatoes produce high seed yields, important in genetic research programs. A self-pollinating mechanism practically eliminates crossing, although plants can be crossed under controlled conditions. All of these qualities have enabled rapid progress in the improvement of the tomato in the past decades.

Tomatoes are a versatile plant and can be grown in most parts of Mexico. As early as the 1920s, tomato production began in northwestern Mexico to satisfy the demands of the American market. Today, the industrial production of the crop is concentrated in the state of Sinaloa and surrounding areas.

Tomatillos are native to central Mexico, where they have a significantly longer tradition of dietary usage than the red tomato. They are the favorite tomato in the Indian diet, where they are used mainly for making *salsa verde*.

Green Chile Sauce (*Salsa Verde*)
- 12 fresh or canned tomatillos
- 2 serrano chile peppers
- 3 cups boiling water
- 1 onion, chopped
- 1 clove garlic

- 1 tablespoon fresh coriander, chopped
- salt to taste

Cook the tomatillos and chiles in water until soft. (Do not cook the tomatillos if they are canned.) Drain and reserve liquid. Combine tomatillos, chiles, onion, garlic, coriander, and salt in food processor. Process briefly with some of the reserved liquid until thin, but not smooth. Serve in a sauce bowl.

Tropical Fruits

Many tropical and semitropical fruits from Latin America were not diffused to Europe because they could not grow and produce in European climates and latitudes. Some fruits, such as the pineapple and the papaya, were taken to Hawaii and have become important commercial products there. The guava can also be found in Southeast Asian and Indian markets.

Most tropical fruits are best eaten by themselves as fresh produce. They are also used to prepare refreshing beverages, ice creams, sherbets, marmalades, mousses, salads, trifles (called *antes* in Mexico), puddings, and other desserts. Some are also added to savory dishes and are commonly used to decorate serving platters. Sliced fruit with a sprinkling of ground chile pepper and lime is a favorite item sold at street food stands. Pineapple was given the Spanish name *piña*, because the conquistadores believed it looked like a pine cone.

Much of the pineapple (*Ananas sativus*) production in Mexico is processed by the canning industry as sliced or diced fruit or as canned or packaged pineapple juice. It can occasionally be purchased as frozen fruit; however, with the exception of orange juice, the frozen-fruit industry is not as yet well developed in Mexico.

The large, brightly colored fruit called papaya (*Carica papaya*) is rich in vitamins A and C, and its seeds are also processed into a meat tenderizer. It is believed to have originated in Central America, between southern Mexico and Nicaragua, and grows easily in a warm and humid climate. It is an extremely prolific plant and can produce 100 or more fruits per year. The flowers and fruits of the female tree form directly on the tree trunk. It has shiny, black seeds that make a beautiful contrast with the deep yellow or orange color of the fruit. In recent decades, a new variety of papaya, crossed with the mamey and called *papaya maradol*, has become popular in Mexico. The color of its pulp is a deep orange color, and its flavor is quite different from the typical papaya. It is most popular as a fresh fruit, sliced or diced, with a bit of lemon juice added, but can also be prepared in a variety of desserts, salads, and beverages.

The *Anona* family includes both the *guanábana*, soursop (*Anona muricata*), and custard apple (*cherimoya*). Both are medium or large sized with a rough-textured pericarp and a soft, white, creamy pulp that disintegrates in the mouth when eaten. Both fruits have shiny black seeds and a strong aroma. The *guanábana* has spines, somewhat like a pineapple. The *zapote* family of fruit includes the mamey, the sapodilla (*chicozapote*), and several varieties of *zapote* distinguished by the color of their pulp. *Chicle*, or chewing gum, was originally processed from the sap of the *chicozapote* tree. The Aztecs grouped these three fruits together under the name *tzapotl*. The black *zapote* is actually green with black pulp and is used for making a popular dessert called *enzapotada*, prepared by mixing *zapote* pulp with orange juice. This makes a light and refreshing dessert.

The cactus plant produces two fruits popular in the Mexican diet. The prickly-pear fruit, called *tuna* (*Opuntia* spp.), and the fruit of the *Hylocereus pitahaya*, known by the name of *pitahaya*, can be found on the market at the end of rainy season and well into autumn. They are both refreshing fruits with a high water content and an abundance of black seeds, which is a deterrent to their popularity on the international market. The pulp of the *pitahaya* ripens into a beautiful deep vermilion tone that makes beautiful ices or sherbets when it is used for that purpose.

The fruit of the guava tree, called *guayaba* (*Psidium*), is quite well known on the international market, as it can be shipped easily when harvested in its green stage. It is also produced in Southeast Asia. It is very high in vitamin C, much higher than citrus fruit, and has an abundance of seeds. The Aztec gave it the name of *xalcocotl*, or "sandy fruit," because of its high seed content. More than 150 species of guava from tropical and subtropical America have been classified.

Turkey

Turkeys were one of the six animals domesticated by the Aztecs. The others were the Muscovy duck, the dog, the rabbit, the bee, and the cochineal insect. The domesticated dog formed part of the pre-Hispanic diet on special occasions. The turkey, *Meleagris gallopavo*, played an important role in the diet and appear to have been very plentiful. In the urban market of Tepeyacac, 8,000 birds were supposedly sold every five days, year round. Turkeys were prepared in moles, using red, yellow, or black chiles to vary the flavor. In the banquets of the Aztec nobles, a whole turkey was sometimes covered with *masa* and cooked in a barbecue pit. This dish had the complicated name of *totolnacaquimilli*. Turkey was also served in a sauce of *pipián*, made with red chile peppers, tomatillos, and ground squash seeds.

The tom turkey was called *huexolotl* in Náhuatl. From this term comes the present-day term of *guajolote* in Mexican Spanish. The Spaniards gave it the nomenclature of *pavo*, because they found a certain similarity with the Asian peacock, also called *pavo*. When the turkey was taken to Europe, it substituted for the stringy peacock on the banquet table, because it provided more meat.

The most renowned turkey dish today is *mole poblano de guajolote*, prepared in a rich, dark sauce, prepared with ground chocolate and three types of dried, toasted chiles. No fiesta is complete without this rich and colorful dish. It is quite an effort to prepare, when it is done from scratch, grinding all the ingredients on the *metate*. Today, many women with limited time and effort buy the ingredients ready-made in a paste, add turkey broth and turkey pieces to simmer, and top it with sesame seeds, and it is ready to serve.

Nowhere in Mexico are turkey-based dishes as much appreciated as in the Yucatán, where a species of wild turkey called *Meleagris ocellata* can still be hunted. This turkey has proved to be very difficult to domesticate. Soused turkey (*pavo en escabeche oriental*), cold spiced turkey (*pavo en frío*), turkey served with black sauce called *chilmole*, or turkey in almond sauce (*pavo en salsa de almendras*) are a few of the ways to prepare turkey in the Yucatecan cuisine. Whole turkeys are cooked in *atole* today in the highland Maya villages of Guatemala for special festivals, such as confraternity celebrations (*fiestas de cofradías*).

Turkey in Almond Sauce (*Pavo en Salsa de Almendras*)

- 2 turkey thighs
- 3/4 cup blanched almonds
- 1/2 teaspoon oregano (Mexican preferred)
- 1/2 teaspoon whole black peppercorns
- 2 onions, roasted, peeled, and chopped
- 3 fresh *xcatic chiles* or banana chiles, roasted, peeled, and chopped
- 1 head of garlic, roasted, peeled, and chopped
- 2 tablespoons white vinegar
- 3-1/2 cups water

- vegetable oil, for frying
- 1 large banana, peeled and cut into 1/2-inch rounds

Place almonds, oregano, and peppercorns in a spice grinder and process to a fine powder. Place the powder, half the onions, chile, garlic, vinegar, and 1/2 cup water in blender and purée until mixture is the consistency of a smooth paste. Spread half the almond mixture over turkey pieces and marinate for 2 hours. Pour about an inch of oil in a heavy skilled and heat until very hot. Sauté turkey pieces lightly, being careful that almond mixture does not burn.

Remove turkey and set aside to drain off any remaining oil. Pour off excess oil and add remaining garlic, onions, and chiles to the pan with the turkey pieces. Add about 3 cups of water, cover, and simmer until turkey is done, about 45 minutes. Remove turkey and keep warm. Stir remaining almond paste into the sauce and simmer to thicken. To serve, place turkey on a serving platter, top with additional almond sauce, arrange the banana around the turkey, and serve.

THE ARRIVAL OF EUROPEAN FOOD PRODUCTS

Spaniards and their plants and animals promoted great nutritional changes in the Mexican diet. European grains and animals were only part of the new foods that quickly became part of the diet of New Spain. By the end of the sixteenth century, Mexico produced and consumed a combination of pre-Hispanic and European food products.

Citrus Fruits

Citrus fruits play an important role in Mexican food traditions. Sweet and sour oranges, grapefruits, tangerines, sweet and sour lemons, and limes arrived in Mexico soon after the conquest and adapted easily to the Mexican soil and climate. The conquistador Bernal Díaz del Castillo claims the honor of planting the first orange trees in the state of Veracruz on his initial trip between the port of Veracruz and Tenochtitlán (Mexico City). Veracruz is now one of the most important citrus-producing areas of the country.

In many countries, salt and pepper shakers commonly form part of the everyday table setting. In Mexico, limes, cut into wedges and placed on a small plate or dish, are found along with the salt shaker. Lime juice is squeezed into mineral water, in soups, on broiled meats, on tacos, or on any other dish whose flavor might be enhanced. It is a habit as common as shaking a few extra grains of salt on food. Lime juice is also used to marinate fish and shellfish before cooking or to prepare a raw fish dish called *ceviche.* Limes (*Citrus limetta*), called *limones* in Mexico, also accompany tequila or beer. Lemonade (*agua de limón*) is made with lemon juice, as is a popular drink with tequila, the margarita. The bitter lime called *lima agria* is used only in the cuisines of Yucatán. It is an important ingredient in a soup called *sopa de lima*, which is a chicken-broth-based soup with fried tortilla strips and shredded chicken. The royal or sweet lemon, called *limón real*, can be found on the Pacific coast and has a slightly sweet flavor. It is used for making a beverage known as *agua fresca*, which can be made with any fresh fruit. Yellow lemons are seldom used in Mexico, since cooks prefer the more acid flavor of the Mexican lime.

Oranges are mainly used for squeezing fresh orange juice. Bottled or frozen orange juices are considered inferior products and are mainly used when the price of oranges becomes too high. Freshly squeezed juice is still a common item on restaurant menus as well as street stands, where it is squeezed at the very moment it is ordered. In tropical climates, oranges mature before the skin changes color; thus, most oranges arrive on the market as green oranges, even though they may be ripe, sweet, and juicy.

Sliced oranges served with ground chile and salt are popular foods served in street stands. *Naranjas agrias* (bitter or Seville oranges) are used in Yucatecan cooking. It is a flavoring for *cochinita pibil*, a pork dish wrapped in banana leaves and cooked underground in a barbecue pit. Bitter oranges are also used in fresh chile sauces in the Yucatán instead of limes.

The acid flavor of citrus fruit is much appreciated as an accompaniment to alcoholic beverages, such as *pico de gallo*, a mixture of pieces of oranges, *jícamas*, cucumbers, pineapple, and mangoes, flavored with lemon juice and chile powder. *Sangrita*, a typical accompaniment for tequila, is prepared with orange and lemon juice, syrup, and a sauce made of tomatoes, chile peppers, onion, and salt.

Citrus fruits, especially small tangerines (also called *mandarinas* or *clementinas*), are popular items to stuff the piñata during Christmas parties (*posadas*), held during the nine days before Christmas, that symbolize Joseph and Mary's search for lodging. These colorful decorated pots can be filled with a variety of candies, citrus fruits, peanuts, and small toys.

Fruits

Many other fruits were brought to Mexico in the sixteenth century from other parts of the world. Apples, pears, cherries, mangoes, grapes, strawberries, plums, peaches, bananas, melons, and watermelons all arrived in the sixteenth century. Most of them found an ecological niche somewhere in the country, where they could adapt to the local climate and altitude and prosper. Many have become so much a part of the local diet that it is hard to convince people that they are not native plants. The mango (*Mangifera indica*) is an example of this. Mangoes originated in the Indo-Burmese region and were introduced into Mexico by merchants from the Manila Galleon, which traded for 250 years between the ports of Acapulco and Manila, in the Philippines. Mangoes now grow abundantly in Mexico and have become one of the most sought-after fruits. People look forward to its appearance on the market at the end of May, before the rainy season begins. The mango season lasts throughout the wet season, until October.

When it is eaten as a fresh fruit, the flat mango seed is usually impaled on a three-pronged mango fork and unceremoniously eaten by

Fresh fruit juice vendor. © TRIP/S. Grant.

biting around the large seed. This method of eating a mango usually leaves one covered with sticky mango juice. A more delicate way of eating it is to peel the fruit, cut the pulp into halves, and eat it from the plate with a fork. It is a popular fruit, found on street-food stands, peeled and carved into elaborate shapes and sprinkled with lime and red chile-pepper powder.

There are several varieties of mangoes available in Mexico. The Manila mango has soft, delicate flesh and a wonderful aroma. It is considered the finest mango on the market. The Ataulfo mango looks like the Manila variety but is more fibrous, sometimes leaving the eater with a mouthful of stringy fibers. A large red-to-red-green variety is called *mango petacón*, which literally means "mango with large buttocks." This variety has firm flesh and is available on the market nearly all year round. Favorite desserts using mangoes include mango mousse or mango flambé made with tequila and flamed at the table.

Flambéed Mangoes

- 6 ripe mangoes, peeled and pitted
- 3 tablespoons dark brown sugar
- 3 tablespoons butter, cut into pieces
- zest of 1 lime and 1 orange
- 1 tablespoon fresh lime juice
- 1 tablespoon fresh orange juice
- 1/4 cup white tequila

Preheat oven to 400°. Butter shallow baking dish. Cut mango halves into slices and arrange, slightly overlapping, in prepared dish. Sprinkle with brown sugar and dot with butter. Scatter lime and orange zest on top. Drizzle lime and orange juice on mango slices. Bake until mango slices begin to brown, about 20 minutes. Remove from oven. Just before serving, reheat on top of stove, sprinkle tequila over mangoes, and ignite with a long match. Shake the pan for a few minutes until flames die out, then serve on individual plates. Serve with vanilla ice cream and mango sauce.

Meat

Wherever the Spaniards went, they took their animals with them. Animal foods were an important source of protein for the diet in New Spain and surpassed the plant foods in nutritional value. Cattle did not adapt well to the high plains area of central Mexico, but instead prospered in northern and western Mexico, where they found favorable pastures and unlimited space to graze and reproduce. Meat became cheaper on the Mexican market than in Spain, and animals were so abundant they were slaughtered for their hides to make leather goods.

In Mexico, beef is known as *carne de res*. It is considered the highest-status meat and the most expensive one as well, making it out of reach for many Mexicans. It is consumed in many ways: roasted on the grill, when it is called *carne asada*; as an ingredient in stews; or as dried beef, called *cecina, tasajo,* or *machaca. Cecina* is prepared in adobe, covered with a paste of chile peppers and seasonings that give it a special flavor. *Tasajo* is made with beef strips, partially dried and salted, allowing it to last for several days without spoiling. *Machaca* is a popular dish in northern Mexico and is usually presented finely shredded and used as an addition to scrambled eggs, along with tomatoes, onion, and chile peppers.

Many Mexican Indians proved to be lactose intolerant when milk was introduced into Mexico, and they could not incorporate milk into their diets; however, milk in the form of cheese did not affect them. Different parts of the country specialize in regional cheeses, which are now available on the national market. One of the most popular cheeses, called *manchego*, resembles a hard Spanish cheese with the same name. Fresh cream is an accompaniment to many typical Mexican dishes, such as tacos, refried beans, and many desserts. A braggart, or a person who speaks too highly of himself, is often described with the expression "He puts too much cream on his tacos."

Sheep and goats adapted well to their new surroundings, but were considered a menace by the local population because they invaded and destroyed the crops of the Indians. Mutton is popular for making barbecue by roasting it in a barbecue pit, while roast kid is a popular dish in the state of Nuevo León.

Pigs were one of the most popular animals to arrive in the New World and have caused significant changes in Mexican cooking. They were easily accepted by the Indian population because of their small size and the facility with which they could be raised. They contributed not only abundant meat to the new diet, but lard (*manteca de cerdo*) as well. Pre-Hispanic sources of cooking fat were scarce before the conquest, mainly coming from insects, squash seeds, and other sources. Lard proved to be an important contribution to Mexican cooking, because so many dishes now rely on the technique of frying.

Pork is a much-solicited and appreciated meat product in Mexico. A chopped, roasted pork dish, called *carnitas*, is prepared by browning the pork pieces in a large copper basin, using the fat of the pork for frying. This gives a crunchy texture to the pork, which provides a nice contrast in texture between the filling and the soft tortilla. *Tacos de carnitas de puerco* are typical fare in most taco restaurants and stands throughout the city.

Pork for Tacos (*Carnitas*)

- 2 pounds boneless pork with some fat, cut into 2-inch chunks
- 1/2 cup lard
- 8 cups water
- 1/4 onion
- 2 cloves garlic
- 1 tablespoon salt

Heat a heavy pot on top of stove for 20 minutes, until very hot. Add lard and brown pork pieces over low heat. Add water, onion, garlic, and salt. Cook, covered, over medium heat for 1-1/2 hours, until pork is tender. Transfer meat to a colander to drain off grease. Serve with corn tortillas and *salsa de tomate verde*.

Other popular uses for pork in the diet are *puerco con calabacitas* (pork with zucchini) and *puerco adobado* (made with a sour seasoning paste of ground chile peppers, herbs, and vinegar). Mexican cuisine makes ample use of pork as an ingredient, as well as lard to fry many finger foods and re-fried beans and as an additional ingredient to the *masa* of tamales to make them more fluffy. Fried pork skin called *chicharrón* is a favorite accompaniment for tequila or beer when it is served dry with lemon juice or chile pepper sauce. Pork meat is prepared in sausages, ham, hot dogs, and many cold cuts, some of them with chile pepper added.

Chickens were accepted by the Indian population almost immediately when they arrived from Europe because they were small and easy to keep, and because the Indians already knew how to care for turkeys and found the raising of chickens a similar task. Eggs soon became an extra source of income for the women of Indian households, who sold them weekly in the marketplace. Chicken meat is inexpensive in Mexico and is probably the most popular meat on the market. Chicken broth with rice or vegetables is a standby in many Mexican households and is also considered an effective remedy after a night out on the town.

Chicken in Chipotle Sauce (*Pollo al Chipotle*)

- 1 chicken, cut into pieces
- salt and pepper

- 3 cloves garlic
- 4 whole black peppers
- 2 whole cloves
- 1/2 teaspoon ground cumin
- 1/4 onion
- 1/2 cup water
- 2 tablespoons oil
- 2 onions, sliced
- 5 small tomatoes, sliced
- 3 whole canned chipotle peppers

Season the chicken with salt and pepper. Blend the garlic, black pepper, cloves, cumin, and onion with 1/4 cup water in blender jar. Sauté the sliced onions until they are transparent. Add purée mixture and let cook 10 minutes. Add the sliced tomatoes, and when the mixture begins to boil, reduce the flame, cover the pot, and let cook 5 minutes. Blend the chipotles with 1/4 cup water and add to pot. Add the chicken, cover, and let cook over a slow flame for 30 minutes. Serve with white rice.

In the contemporary diet, meat is an important item, for those who can afford it. Mexicans living in the northern part of the country are particularly heavy meat eaters and experience the negative side effects of a diet heavy in protein and fat, such as high cholesterol, high blood pressure, and a degree of obesity.

Rice

The cultivation of rice began centuries ago in Asia. It was introduced into Spain by the Moors in the eighth century and arrived in Mexico soon after the conquest. Because many of the conquistadores were from southern Spain, it was an essential ingredient in their diets. In present-day Mexico, rice is mainly cultivated in the states of Veracruz, Morelos, and Sinaloa.

It is a popular carbohydrate in the Mexican diet. It is consumed on a daily basis and can be compared to the use of the potato in American cooking. It is often served as a "dry soup" when it is served by itself and may be accompanied by fried plantains or other garnishes. It is also used as an ingredient in liquid soups or as an accompaniment to the main dish. There are several ways to prepare rice. All cooking styles require the rice to be soaked in warm water for half an hour to remove any excess starch and allow the rice to cook more evenly. It is then drained, allowed to dry, and fried in oil until lightly colored. Water, chicken stock, or puréed tomatoes are added, depending upon the type of rice prepared. White rice may have a few drops of lime juice added to it along with the stock to give it a whiter color. *Arroz a la mexicana* is a red rice, prepared with puréed red tomatoes and chopped vegetables, such as carrots and peas, added at the end of cooking. Green rice is made with fresh cilantro, parsley, and roasted poblano-type peppers that have been puréed and added with the liquid to the cooking rice. Strips of poblano chile peppers may be added to provide an interesting texture. Black rice is made with black bean broth from the bean pot, known as *frijoles de olla*. Rice is also used to prepare the typically Spanish dish paella (seafood cooked with rice).

Mexican Red Rice (*Arroz Rojo a la Mexicana*)

- 3/4 cup vegetable oil
- 1 cup white rice, rinsed and drained
- 2 tomatoes, chopped
- 1 small onion, chopped
- 1 clove garlic, peeled
- 1/3 cup carrots
- 1/3 cup peas
- 2-1/2 cups chicken stock
- 1 teaspoon salt
- 1 sprig parsley

Heat oil in medium saucepan until hot. Add the rice, stirring constantly, until slightly opaque. Strain oil from rice. Combine tomatoes, onion, and garlic in a blender until smooth. Pour mixture over rice and cook over medium heat, stirring for about 5 minutes. Add the water, carrots, peas, and salt and place parsley on top. Lower the heat, cover, and simmer for about 25 minutes or until rice is tender.

White rice is used in making rice pudding, *arroz con leche*, which is a favorite Mexican dessert. It is flavored with stick cinnamon and may have a tablespoon of brandy added on special occasions. The refreshing drink called *horchata* is made by soaking and then grinding raw rice, cinnamon, and a few almonds mixed with water and a bit of sugar, which is then strained and served over ice.

Spices

Mexican cooking is well known for its spicy flavor, which mainly comes from the chile pepper; nonetheless, many other spices are also used for flavoring food. Black pepper, cinnamon, cumin seeds, sesame seeds, aniseed, oregano, cloves, and nutmeg are only a few of the spices on the market regularly used in cooking. Mexicans are especially fond of cinnamon, used in desserts, coffee (*café de olla*), hot chocolate, and cinnamon tea, as well as in breads and cookies. Mexico is the principal consumer of cinnamon in the world. Local spices include annatto (*achiote*) seeds, used almost exclusively in the Yucatán peninsula in paste or powdered form. These are the base of many seasoning pastes famous in Yucatecan cooking. Green or white pumpkin seeds (*pepitas de calabaza*) are popular for cooking or for eating as snacks. *Pipián* paste can be bought ready-made, and with the addition of green chiles, herbs, lettuce, and tomatillos, a fast and tasty sauce can be prepared in a few minutes. Mole sauces originated in pre-Hispanic Mexico, when all sauces were called *mollis*. The moles prepared in Mexico are made with a combination of ingredients from both the New and Old Worlds. Many ingredients for *mole poblano*, such as turkey, chiles, chocolate, tomatoes, and peanuts are native to Mexico, while lard, onions, garlic, aniseed, black pepper, cloves, cinnamon, almonds, pecans, coriander, sesame, and cumin seeds were brought from Europe.

Chile peppers, garlic, onions, and tomatoes make up a seasoning often referred to as *a la mexicana*. The red, green, and white colors are said to be reminiscent of the Mexican flag. This flavor combination is chopped, diced, or ground and served raw or cooked and incorporated into many soups, meat dishes, and vegetables, as well as scrambled eggs.

The recent globalization of the world economy has had an important effect upon Mexican food traditions. New products available on the market have provided middle- and upper-class Mexicans with a more varied diet. These changes have had little effect upon the everyday diet of the mass of the population, who still cling to their basic diet of corn, beans, and chile peppers. They are, however, affected by the fast-food snacks that have invaded the food markets, providing food high in calories but with little nutritive value.

Sugar

Some Old World plants acquired new meanings and uses once they reached America. One of the products that found new uses in America was sugar, or sucrose, produced from sugarcane (*Saccharum officinarum*).

The sugar industry was established early in Mexico on land belonging to Hernán Cortés in the state of Morelos.

Sugar soon became a popular ingredient for making Mexican sweets and candy in the convents and nunneries. Sugar was also employed in the manufacture of a type of rum called *chinguirito*. It contained a high percentage of alcohol and was prohibited by the colonial authorities because it contributed to alcoholism, a severe problem in colonial Mexico.

The most important use of sugar today is in the manufacture of soft drinks, although these are generally manufactured with a fructose base. Mexico is, nonetheless, the highest consumer of sugar in the world. Mexican desserts are very sweet, but they are not consumed on a daily basis. Many people prefer fresh fruit as a dessert. *Cajeta,* also called burnt milk (*leche quemada*), is milk with sugar cooked in a copper pot for more than an hour until it is thick and condensed. This is a very sweet dessert and can only be consumed in small quantities. A favorite means of preparation is as *crepas de cajeta*, where the bland taste and texture of the crepes absorbs the taste of the sugar.

The local candy industry is well developed in Mexico, often as an artisan product. Several regions of the country are known for the particular type of candy they produce. For example, Saltillo, Coahuila, produces fine almond-paste sweets; Puebla is renowned for its yam-based fruit pastes, called *camotes*. Tequila jellies called *borrachitos* are favorites in Guadalajara, while Guanajuato uses its local strawberry production to make crystallized strawberries. Crystallized fruit in general is popular in Mexico and made with a great variety of fruits. Chile peppers are a common flavoring found in many types of candy. Specialized markets that sell only candy have become popular in recent years.

Wheat

The introduction of wheat into Mexico gave rise to the important Mexican bread industry. Wheat adapted well to Highland Mexico due to its similarity to the Mediterranean climate. By the middle of the sixteenth century, New Spain was producing enough surplus wheat to provide Caribbean markets with wheat, hardtack bread, and flour. Mexico was able to do this even during times of wheat scarcity because of abundant supplies of corn, which could be used as a substitute for wheat in times of wheat shortage.

Wheat is mainly used today as flour in bread making and for an abundance of cold cereals on the market, a direct influence from the United

States. From the beginning, bread making was a commercial enterprise, unlike tortillas, which were prepared as household labor. Bread stores, or *panaderías*, were established soon after the conquest. During the 300 years of Spanish rule, the ownership of *panaderías* was restricted to Spaniards or Creoles. In the beginning, Mexican bread stores produced and sold Spanish-style bread, but in time, Mexican bakers became innovative and developed many new local bread types, particularly sweet breads, called *pan dulce*. Mexican bread bakers produce over 500 varieties of sweet breads. Bread has always been a large-scale commercial enterprise, closely identified with urban consumption. Large bread stores still produce and stock a wide variety of breads. In recent decades, supermarkets have become important producers and sellers of fresh bread as well as packaged bread and pastries.

Dry, wheat-based cereals have flooded the supermarket stands since the North American Free Trade Agreement with the United States and Canada was signed in 1994. The variety of pastas on the market has also increased.

NOTES

1. John C. Super, *Food, Conquest, and Colonization in Sixteenth-Century Spanish America* (Albuquerque: University of New Mexico Press, 1988), 88.

2. Ellen Messer, "Maize," in *The Cambridge World History of Food*, vol. 1, ed. Kenneth F. Kiple and Kriemhold Coneè Ornelas (Cambridge: Cambridge University Press, 2000), 103.

3. C. Earle Smith, Jr., "Plant Remains," in *The Prehistory of the Tehuacán Valley*, vol. 1, *Environment and Subsistence*, ed. Douglas S. Byers (Austin: University of Texas Press, 1967): 225–26.

4. Jeffrey Pilcher, *¡Que Vivan los Tamales! Food and the Making of Mexican Identity* (Albuquerque: University of New Mexico Press, 1998), 77–78.

5. Josefina Morales de León, "Frijoles de colores y sabores," *Cuadernos de Nutrición* 15, no. 2 (1992): 38–41.

6. Kent V. Flannery, ed., *Güilá Naquitz: Archaic Foraging and Early Agriculture in Oaxaca, México* (New York: Academic Press, 1986).

3

Cooking

Throughout Mexican history, the role of preparing food has been considered women's work. In most hunting and gathering societies there is a sexual division of labor, where men are in charge of hunting game and women assume the role of gathering wild plants and foods, water, and firewood. This was the general rule in ancient Mexico and is confirmed by present-day ethnographic evidence on hunting and gathering societies.

In rural Mexico, women have always been in charge of preparing the daily food. They were also responsible for planting kitchen gardens, gathering wild plants and foods, and finding cooking fuel. Food storage also came under the domain of their activities. Women could assume responsibilities that did not interfere with child bearing, the early education of their children, and other chores that could be carried out near the household. Women horticulturists may have even played a role in domesticating plant species and adapting new plants imported from other areas. Innovative women probably contributed to the formation of new varieties by developing new cultivars with positive traits and suppressing undesirable features.

The botanical knowledge they obtained through the experience of gathering, collecting, harvesting, storing, and processing plant resources no doubt gave them status and prestige in their communities. Knowing where to find the right plant for a specific purpose, medicinal or culinary, would also have been valuable knowledge to acquire.

Cooking was a part of the life and education of Mesoamerican women. When a baby girl was born, her umbilical cord was buried under the *metate*. If she was a commoner, she was taught to cook, grind corn, and make tortillas by her mother when she was 13 years old. She was then considered a bread maker and was given permission to eat two tortillas a day. These were probably very large tortillas. Women ground the corn, made the sauces, shaped the tortillas and tamales, and did all the hard work cooking entailed.

The kitchen was one of the principal obligations of noblewomen, who were not allowed to work in the fields or sell in the marketplace. They were encouraged to learn how to make good food and beverages for the men in their lives, because in that way they would be honored and loved and their lives would be enriched. Perhaps we could make an analogy to modern Mexican society-women, who are encouraged to learn to prepare a meal in order to teach their servants how it should be done, even though they do not participate in the actual food preparation.

Mayan women were in charge of everyday cooking; however, men occasionally had a role to play in this endeavor. They took charge of outdoor cooking, especially when it involved barbecuing meat on a framework of sticks over an open fire. Maya hunters prepared meat in this way immediately after the hunt to preserve it from spoiling on the long, hot journey home. When they arrived, the meat was divided between the ruling Maya lord, the hunters' neighbors, and other members of the family. On the next hunt, the hunter might not be so lucky, and he could fall back upon his kin and neighbors to share their kill with him and his family.

Men were also involved in preparing the underground ovens called *pibs*. The Mayans were accomplished in this technique and used it for cooking wild boar; massive tamales; large fowl; and vegetables, which were placed in a vessel and cooked at the same time as the meat. The underground *pib* is still built in the same way as it was centuries ago. The procedure entails digging a large hole in the ground, lining it with stones, and placing a layer of wood on the top, which is lit afire and left to burn down. When the temperature rises to the proper degree, the wood and ashes are removed and maguey leaves are inserted into the pit to cover the stones. Food is then placed directly on the maguey leaves, covered with more maguey leaves, and cooked for the required length of time. Pork, turkeys, and lamb are favorite ingredients for this type of barbecue, practiced throughout the country. The process of digging and preparing the pit oven still falls to the men of the household.

The following recipe was originally written to be cooked underground in a pit barbecue. Today, it is usually baked in the oven.

Chicken Cooked in a Pib (*Pollo Pibil*)
- 4 chicken breasts, with skin removed
- 1/4 package ready-made *achiote* paste
- 1/4 cup orange juice
- 1/4 cup lemon juice
- 1 onion, sliced
- 3 jalapeño peppers, chopped
- 1 tablespoon vegetable oil
- aluminum foil
- 1 tablespoon dried epazote
- 4 tablespoons margarine

Dissolve the *achiote* paste in the orange and lemon juices. Prick chicken breasts with a fork and pour the *achiote* mixture over the chicken. Marinate for several hours. Sauté onions and chiles in oil until soft. Line a roasting pan with aluminum foil. Place chicken breasts on the foil and cover with the remaining marinade. Top with onions and chile peppers. Place a bit of epazote and margarine on top each piece of chicken. Fold foil over the chicken to make a small package, cover the pan, and bake in oven at 350° oven for 1 hour. Serve with rice.

Throughout history, men have participated as cooks for feasts, banquets, and funerary rites. The pre-Hispanic book known as the *Tudela Codex* describes burials of noblemen and women, who were wrapped in feathers and fine cloaks and buried with two, three, or four live Indians, depending upon their social status. The slaves were both male and female and accompanied the dead in order to prepare their food on the long journey to the afterworld.[1]

EARLY KITCHENS

Pre-Hispanic kitchens were simple and sparsely furnished. They were considered a place to cook, eat, and sleep and contained only the very basic and necessary elements. This was the central and often the only room in the house. Here the hearth, made with three stones, was located on the floor in the center of the room. The three stones were considered sacred, and to step on them was considered an insult to Xiuhtecutli, god of fire. Pine logs, leaves, cornstalks, long grass, and maguey leaves were used as fuel. Family members ate squatting around the fire. Here they cooked the food and the family gathered to eat it, with men being served first. Men and women ate separately. Men sat on palm-woven stools while women knelt on the floor near the fire with their legs tucked under them. A woven palm mat called a *petate* was used as a table; otherwise, people served themselves directly from the pot, ladling the food directly onto a tortilla. They fished tamales out of the steamer with their bare hands. Kitchens were closed rooms without windows, whose walls did not permit the circulation of air and smoke from the hearth, which continually filled the room and blackened the walls.

People ate two or three times a day. In the morning, before leaving for the fields, men drank a cup of *atole*, or corn gruel. The noon meal consisted of tortillas, salsa, and sometimes *pozol*. If there was food left over, they ate again before retiring to sleep. The first dish eaten was tortillas or tamales, served with a sauce. This was followed by fruit, of which the noble class was particularly fond.

Pre-Hispanic people were known for their hospitality to visitors and shared what food they had with unexpected guests (unless they were coming to conquer them). At first, the Spaniards marveled at the turkeys, tortillas, and fresh fruits given them; however, when the Indians discerned their true intentions, they became less generous.

FOOD PREPARATION

The most common form of food preparation in pre-Hispanic Mexico was cooking the food directly over an open fire. Later Mesoamericans developed a method of transmitting heat through another utensil, such as a griddle or pot. In this way, they could toast seeds, nuts, and vegetables or boil food in a pot of water. Using a more primitive method, hot stones dropped into water contained in skins, tightly woven baskets, or clay pots heated the water enough to cook the food. Boiling food allowed them to take advantage of certain vegetables that could not be eaten raw. Some raw vegetables contain poisonous substances that are removed through cooking; others are too tough to chew in the raw stage. Cooking made these ingredients edible and easier to digest and improves the flavor of food. Food was also cooked by boiling directly in water or by steaming. For steaming, in the case of tamales, they used an *olla*, a jug with a shallow water base and a light framework of sticks in the interior of the pot, to keep the tamales from touching the water. Food was also cooked buried in the hot ashes of the hearth. There were few sources of grease or lard, and frying was not a common cooking technique in pre-Hispanic Mexico.

NIXTAMALIZACIÓN

One of the great food-preparation discoveries of pre-Hispanic Mexico was the development of the process for preparing corn, called *nixtamalización*. In this procedure, corn kernels are soaked in a solution of crushed limestone, wood ashes, and water to help soften and loosen the outer hull of the grain, which makes the corn easier to grind. The alkaline processing changes the chemical makeup of corn by increasing the calcium and correcting the proportion of certain amino acids. The procedure improves the quality of protein in corn and makes both niacin and tryptophan more available to absorption by the human body. This prevents a niacin deficiency and the occurrence of pellagra, common in some corn-consuming areas, where the diet was based almost exclusively on corn.[2]

The next step in the process is for the corn kernels to be wet-ground, boiled, and ground again on a stone slab (*metate*) to form a fine cornmeal. This arduous and time-consuming process was considered women's work and had to be carried out every morning. The process could easily take up five or six hours of a woman's day. The dough could not be kept from one day to another, because it would begin to ferment. This procedure produces what is called *masa*, or corn dough, which is later shaped into

Mayan women have a small business making tortillas, Chetumal. © TRIP/ J. Greenberg.

tamales, tortillas, and other tortilla-based dishes. Women derived much of their self-esteem from their grinding skills and their ability to feed their family well. Chalupas are a tortilla-based, boat-shaped snack, topped with a variety of ingredients.

Chalupas

- 12 small tortillas or chalupas
- 2 cups refried beans
- 12 slices cheddar cheese
- 1 avocado, sliced
- vegetable oil for frying tortillas

Heat oil in frying pan. Fry tortillas a few at a time, until crisp around the edges. Drain on paper towels. Spread chalupas with refried beans. Top with a slice of cheese, then place under a hot broiler until the cheese melts. Garnish with avocado.

COOKING IMPLEMENTS

Many cooking utensils found in present-day Mexican kitchens are cultural remnants of pre-Hispanic implements. It is surprising that these utensils are still manufactured and used in the twenty-first century.

The three-legged grinding stone known as the *metate*, carved from a volcanic stone such as basalt or andesite and used for grinding grains, beans, chocolate, and other dry ingredients, was the most important implement in the kitchen. *Metates* are rectangular-shaped and slightly concave, to prevent the mixture from overflowing the edges. The front of the grinding stone is higher than the rear, which gives a slight inclination to the *metate*. The grinding itself is performed by a cylindrical stone known in Spanish as a *mano*, which is thicker in the center and tapers toward both ends. The back-and-forth movement of this uneven cylinder allows an efficient grinding of grains. Grinding stones are found in most Mexican kitchens; however, for everyday cooking, the food processor or food blender is now commonly used.

Another useful utensil known in Mexico since ancient times is the stone mortar and pestle called a *molcajete*, which comes from the Náhuatl term *molcaxitl*, made up of *molli* (salsa) and *caxitl* (bowl). The term can be translated as "sauce bowl."[3] It is generally shaped as a small, round bowl, with curved and diverging walls with deep incisions on the bottom for grinding. The mortar is made of a porous volcanic stone to facilitate the

Metate, used for grinding corn. Courtesy of Jorge Contreras
Chacel/Banco Mexicano de Imágenes.

grinding or crushing of seeds and vegetables, with the help of a small,
round, chopped-off cylinder, known in Spanish as a *tejolote*. After about
1500 B.C., clay *molcajetes* began to be shaped; however, the stone pestles
were conserved for the actual grinding process. Blenders or food proces-
sors have generally replaced this ancient implement in modern kitchens,
but most households keep one in storage and use it to make salsas for special occasions.

Clay pots have a long tradition in food preparation in Mexico, dating
back to almost 2000 B.C. in sites like Tehuacán; Puebla; and Puerto Marqués, Guerrero. They have been used for storing grains and liquids as well
as for cooking and serving foods. A variety of sizes and shapes have been
used throughout Mexican history: jugs, pitchers, pots, jars, basins, dishes,
plates, and griddles have been unearthed in archaeological sites throughout the country. Women were no doubt the potters who made pots for
their own domestic use, but men participated in the process when they
were manufactured on a commercial scale. There was a special section for
clay pots in the great market in Tlatelolco when the Spaniards arrived in

Tenochtitlán in 1519. Specially shaped vessels were used for drinking pulque or chocolate. Mayan ceramics found as funerary objects were beautifully painted with everyday life scenes or ceremonies that tell a story as the vessel is rotated. Clay pots are still being manufactured, many made by hand or thrown on a pottery wheel. Glazed pots are used for cooking beans, as people like the sweet flavor they impart. The glaze is high in lead and not recommended by the Mexican Health Ministry; nevertheless, the tradition is hard to break, and clay pots remain a popular option for cooking. It is important to know that acids such as vinegar or fruit juices release the lead in the glaze and should not be served in glazed pottery.

Clay griddles, or *comales*, are especially popular for cooking tortillas and for toasting seeds, nuts, and vegetables. This is a flat utensil, much like a flapjack griddle, roughly finished on the exterior to allow the heat to penetrate evenly with a polished interior surface. It became very popular during the Aztec phase of Mexican history, but there is little evidence of its use prior to 500 A.D. Archaeologists calculate that prior to that, people heated their tortillas on the side of a pot or on stone slabs. It was not known by the Maya until the Spanish conquest, leaving the question open of how the Mayans cooked their tortillas. The usual explanation is that this was done on flat stone slabs that were heated and used as a *comal*. Metal griddles have become popular as a substitute for clay plates, since they are unbreakable.

Small clay braziers, called *anafres*, shaped like a pot with three arms extending toward the center for the hot dish to rest upon, were common for heating foods. The 30 dishes prepared for Montezuma's daily fare were kept hot on small clay braziers. *Anafres*, now made of tin, are still being used in Mexico today and can be purchased in any large market.

COOKING IN NEW SPAIN

Spain contributed more than new plants and foods to the Mexican diet. The Spaniards also brought metal cooking utensils, new techniques of food preparation, new farming methods, and metal agricultural implements, as well as water-powered mills for grinding sugar and flour. All of these factors contributed to the new concept of eating in New Spain.

The Spaniards introduced the concept of the kitchen as a separate room, dedicated exclusively to the preparation and consumption of food. The *fogón* (Spanish-style stove shaped with stucco) was waist-high for easy cooking and was set into long kitchen walls. It came to replace the Aztec hearth and represented a significant technological improvement, as

Colonial kitchen in Pueblo, showing the type of stove intro-
duced by the Spaniards in the sixteenth century. By Eduoard
Pingret, *Cocina poblana* (eighteenth century). Courtesy of
CONACULTA-INAH-MEX. Reproduction authorized by the
Instituto Nacional de Antropología e Historia.

women could cook standing up and no longer had to kneel down before
the fire to cook.

Multiple burners on the new stoves helped modulate the cooking temperature, and the openings on the front of the stove were convenient for

storing charcoal and firewood, which soon replaced leaves, cornstalks, and maguey leaves. One of the important Spanish contributions was the formation of windows and a hole in the ceiling that permitted the smoke to escape from the kitchen.

It is not easy to describe a typical colonial kitchen, because there were so many different social and cultural levels in New Spain, each with its own culinary customs and special methods of food preparation. The stereotype that has come down through history is that of a large, spacious, sunny room, well equipped with the necessary equipment for preparing a large meal. Kitchens of this type were probably only found in convents, monasteries, and hospitals, where meals had to be prepared for a large number of people and where there were sufficient resources to spend on food preparation. An analysis of ordinary kitchens indicates that in reality home kitchens, even in the most elaborate homes, were dark, poorly equipped, and located near the servants quarters, because they were the ones in charge of food preparation.

It was in the mestizo kitchens that one could appreciate the mixture of New and Old World kitchen utensils. The kettles, cauldrons, saucepans, and casseroles made of iron and copper brought by the Spaniards in an effort to recreate the Spanish diet in America shared space in the cupboards with stone and clay implements, only rarely taking their place. An English traveler in the nineteenth century was surprised to see how few metal utensils were in use in Mexican kitchens.[4] The Indian and mestiza cooks, who were in charge of preparing the food, were more accustomed to the warmth of clay utensils than the cold, insensitive metal implements, and they were reticent to give up their clay pots for cooking.

Skillets were a novelty in New Spain, because they were unnecessary in Aztec kitchens where there was no custom of frying foods and little grease for doing so. The copper mortar and pestle, introduced by the Spaniards, never replaced the *metate* and *molcajete*, even though they served the same purpose. Nor did the tin or pewter cups brought from Spain replace the polished clay jugs, remnants of ancient Mexico. Cooking implements were hung on the walls around the kitchen in the same way they were in Spain. Instead of replacing the stone and clay implements of pre-Hispanic kitchens, the new cooking utensils merely shared kitchen space with the traditional utensils. Fresh meat was hung on hooks from a long, forked pole on an iron grate, which also served for hanging garlands of garlic or dried chile peppers when the household budget was not sufficient enough to buy meat. A variety of spits, chains, graters, hooks, trivets, and skewers were novelties in Mexican kitchens.

Molcajete, used for making sauces. Courtesy of Janet Long.

Some grand houses had special jars for storing olive oil, earthenware jugs for vinegar, and little pottery barrels that contained pickled olives, capers, and chile peppers.

A few kitchens contained large, heavy tables for kneading bread and ovens to bake it. Ovens were part of the new technology used for baking breads and cookies and roasting meats, but were generally limited to those places where food was prepared for a large number of people.

Adobe wood-burning ovens were located in a corner of the cloister, beside a patio, adjoining the room where the bread dough was kneaded and near a water well and the granary, where the wheat was stored. All the necessary elements were nearby, but it was located at a distance from the dormitories and closets to avoid the danger of a fire. Work in the bread-making room, as well as the kitchen, was considered chores of the lowest level; nevertheless, in some convents these tasks were shared by all members of the convent.[5] White bread, sweet bread, cookies, tarts, and turnovers were only some of the delicacies that came out of the convent ovens. The convents of New Spain were elaborate structures built with large rooms and several annexes such as storerooms; bread-making rooms; special rooms for preparing chocolate; bottling rooms to bottle wine and vinegar; a space for washing dishes; and small rooms off the refectories, somewhat like European *ofices*, where the last details were given to the food before it was taken into the refectories.

COOKS IN NEW SPAIN

Who were the cooks responsible for preparing food during the colonial period in Mexico? As long as the conquistadores were organized in military groups, there were specialized cooks among them who prepared the food. The local population often gave the Spaniards prepared foods or lent them women to grind corn for tortillas. Hernán Cortés received a gift of 15 to 20 Indian maidens in Tabasco to grind corn for their tortillas. This proved to be a stroke of good luck for Cortés, because one of the young girls was Malintzin, who was called La Malinche by the Indians and Marina by the Spaniards. Cortés depended heavily upon her knowledge of both Náhuatl and Maya, and she became invaluable to him as a translator. She was called Cortés's voice, as she quickly became fluent in Spanish and paved the way for the Spaniards' entrance into Mexico. She later became Cortés's lover and bore him an illegitimate son named Martín.[6] Cortés also fathered a legitimate son with the same name. Because Hernán Cortés already had a wife in Cuba, he married Marina to Juan Jaramillo, a fellow conquistador.

After the conquest was accomplished, each conquistador established himself in his own house or was awarded a land and service grant called an *encomienda*, with the right to the services and tribute of the Indians on his land. Food preparation then fell into the hands of local Indian women, especially during the early years. The tributary laws did not distinguish between cooks and servants, so it is impossible to judge who was employed as a cook and who was a cleaning woman.

There were few Spanish women among the early immigrants to Mexico. Several hundred arrived in 1535 and 1536 when New Spain reached the status of a viceroyalty government, or *virreinato*. The lack of Spanish women gave local women an opportunity to take charge in the kitchens and introduce local foods into the diets of the conquistadores. Even after the arrival of Spanish women, it is unlikely that they participated in the preparation of food, taking into consideration the condition and categories of the kitchens and the pretensions that many Spanish women had when they arrived in New Spain. Kitchens were not considered a proper place for ladies, and they left them in charge of Indian women, slaves, blacks, mulattoes, and mestizas. In later years, some families brought their cooks from Spain. The tenth viceroy, Don Juan Manuel de Mendoza y

Luna, disembarked from the ship in Veracruz in 1603 with 33 servants among his traveling companions.

COLONIAL DINING ROOMS

Dining rooms were not a part of sixteenth-century houses in Mexico. Following the custom of medieval Spain, people were accustomed to eating in the kitchen or pantry. When people of a certain status offered a dinner or a banquet, they merely placed a provisional table in the room, made with sawhorses or trestles and wooden planks, and covered it with tablecloths or strips of linen to serve as a temporary dining room. Afterward, the table was disassembled and the room returned to its former function.

In the years following the conquest, silver was so cheap and plentiful that dishes were forged of this metal, especially because there was no porcelain and little pottery available. Dishes, plates, soup bowls, salt shakers, serving bowls, fruit plates, pitchers, spoons, candelabra, and cutlery were made of solid silver. In Don Luis de Castillo's kitchen, even the minor kitchen utensils were crafted in silver.[7] According to his biographers, Hernán Cortés was no gourmet, but his table was set like that of a European prince. His dishes were made of silver and gold, and he possessed fine tablecloths and napkins. Setting a refined table contributed to his social prestige in the new colony.[8]

Dining rooms became more common in the seventeenth century, and by the eighteenth century they were found in many distinguished homes in Mexico City. The eighteenth century was a time of great prosperity in New Spain due to the development of the mining industry, commerce, and the great haciendas. All of this was reflected in the dining room. European and Asian-style dining rooms became popular, especially heavy Chippendale furniture with high-backed chairs covered in velvet or brocade brought from Europe, or the less formal leather, which copied the style of furniture popular in Cordoba, Spain. Fine inlaid marquetry chests and tables from Puebla encrusted with shell, ivory, and bone have become the antique dealer's delight in the past few decades. Religious art or family portraits were popular for decorating dining-room walls. The blue and white china from the East India Company became a matter of social prestige, and many pieces bore the family coat of arms, ordered specially from the manufacturer. They were considered proper wedding gifts for a new couple.

Glazed white *mayólica* pottery was manufactured in the city of Puebla, reproduced from the pottery made in Talavera de la Reina in Spain. Large pieces such as washbasins, jars, bowls, plates, and serving dishes were pro-duced for convent and home use. This colorful pottery, now called *talav-era*, is still being manufactured in Mexico with the same colonial designs made popular in New Spain.

INDEPENDENT MEXICO

Nineteenth-century kitchens were rustic and simple. They contained one or two tables for preparing food; a long, narrow table to eat upon; a cupboard to store the dishes; a stove; some water jugs; and garlands of clay mugs that decorated the kitchen walls. Some visitors insisted that the only cutlery used or needed were tortillas.

It was not until this time that many Mexican houses had a separate din-ing room, although most upper-class homes in Mexico City acquired this space in the eighteenth century. Before a space was designated for dining, the food was normally prepared and eaten in the kitchen. Mexicans found it more comfortable to eat in the kitchen, where tortillas could be eaten hot off the griddle. Dining rooms were reserved for festive meals, special events, and visitors. On these occasions, they were decorated with flower vases and still-life paintings (*bodegones*) on the walls. Breakfronts were useful for displaying prized collections of silver and Chinese porcelain.

Because the food served was complicated to prepare, housewives spent many hours in the kitchen. Even in the homes of the wealthy, the lady of the house was expected to spend a good part of her time supervising the preparation of the food. Food was purchased and prepared on a day-to-day basis for lack of refrigeration.

The itinerant merchant became important during the second half of the nineteenth century. Almost any product could be delivered to the house by these merchants, who canvassed the neighborhoods, wheeling their stores or machines ahead of them. Meat sellers brought whole sides of beef and sliced off the cut the housewife asked for before her front gate. The bread seller carried a variety of breads on the upper side of a huge hat, which he carefully balanced on his head, and the ice-cream seller sold his products from a metal cart with a small bell that he rang constantly as he traveled the streets of Mexico City.

People became accustomed to eating outside the home. So much food activity took place in the street kitchens, *fondas*, and cafés that American visitor Brantz Mayer questioned whether Mexican homes even had kitchens.[9] A worker left his home in the morning with a few pesos in his pocket that he used to pay an Indian woman for tortillas and a street vendor for a bit of stew (*guisado*) or salsa, which constituted his morning meal.

During the late nineteenth century, innovative Mexican engineers became intrigued with the invention of corn-grinding mills and hand-operated tortilla presses to facilitate the making of tortillas. These inventions required decades of research and development before yielding a marketable product. Industrially processed tortillas went through a three-step process: (1) mechanical corn mills, (2) the tortilla press, and (3) the invention of *nixtamal* flour. It was not until the twentieth century that the inventions were perfected and placed on the market for public consumption. After producing an efficient corn mill and a user-friendly tortilla press, the next step was the invention of dehydrated tortilla flour that could be mixed with water to produce tortillas. This was not accomplished successfully until 1949.

Industrial tortilla presses were developed where the *masa harina* or *nixtamal* flour could simply be poured into a spout on the machine, and with the addition of water, acceptable tortillas could be produced without using human hands. Conveyor belts were adjusted that flipped the tortillas as they dropped from one belt to another, to imitate the turns given by a cook using the traditional *comal*.[10]

These inventions liberated the Mexican woman from many hours of grinding corn and patting out tortillas, which left them with time to pursue commercial interests or become merchants in the marketplace. The inventions were initially rejected by Mexican men, who believed that without the discipline of the *metate*, their wives would become lazy and promiscuous and may become involved in all sorts of mischief. Tortillas, which up to this time had been considered women's work, were now placed squarely in the realm of men, when it became culturally acceptable for them to manage tortilla shops (*tortillerías*) and be in charge of their packaging and distribution. Men could also become involved in the manufacturing of tortillas by using mechanical tortilla makers, as these no longer entailed delicately patting them out between the hands.

THE TWENTIETH CENTURY

By the early twentieth century, the principal cities of the country were connected by railroads and seaports. Electricity contributed to the expansion and modernization of communications, services, and industry in Mexico City. Some of the new industry was connected to food preparation.

One of the new uses to which electricity was applied was in the use of the electric stove. This appliance was eventually rejected by the public, who preferred cooking with gas. The electric stove never became a commonly used appliance in Mexico, partly because of the high cost of electricity and the belief that the heat of gas stoves could be regulated more easily.

New technology was imported or developed locally for the wheat-flour industry, the chocolate and sugar industries, the alcohol industry (which produced pulque, mezcal, and tequila from the maguey plant), the meat-packing industry, and as many others that experienced a significant improvement with the new technology.

In the 1920s electric refrigerators took the place of iceboxes, which also eliminated the ice deliveryman who came by daily with a fresh block of ice. Refrigerators, however, were available to only a small proportion of the Mexican population at this early date. It was not until after World War II that household technology was diffused from the United States on a large-scale basis. Pressure cookers were a useful contribution to the Mexican kitchen, as they allowed beans to be prepared in 30 minutes instead of the usual four or five hours of simmering on a back burner. Stoves with four burners, an oven, and a plate warmer became popular in Mexican kitchens at about the same time.

By the end of the 1940s other electrical implements that revolutionized cooking were becoming common in Mexican kitchens. Electric blenders, which facilitated grinding ingredients for soups and salsas without the use of the metate or the molcajete, were easily accepted. Food mixers, hand beaters, toasters, waffle makers, and juice extractors also contributed to making food preparation easier. Special cookbooks were published in the 1950s to teach women how to cook with their new appliances. The new implements did not completely take the place of traditional utensils. Most women still kept a metate and a molcajete in storage, for use on special occasions.

Foreign technology helped in the preparation, preservation, and mechanization of the food industry, but it was up to the Mexicans to develop their own solutions to problems of distribution and retailing of food products. The highways built during the 1920s and 1930s were taken advantage of by the soft-drink and beer industries to take their production to the interior of the country. No matter how bad the roads, the beer trucks and Coca Cola distributors always found a way to deliver their products. In this way, they helped incorporate rural consumers into national markets.

Cooking is still considered women's work in Mexico. A large percentage of women form part of the workforce, but men are reticent about participating in food preparation. Middle-class women are more receptive to convenience foods on the market because of a lack of time to prepare a traditional Mexican meal.

Upper-class and professional women generally can afford to pay kitchen help to prepare the food. Nonetheless, household help is becoming scarce and expensive. Many young women, who formerly made up part of the servant class, prefer to look for work as undocumented workers in the United States, where they can command a higher salary.

In a recent study of the food customs of Tláhuac, one of the most traditional and conservative areas of the city, many improvements were made in the lives of the inhabitants of the area during the twentieth century: electricity was introduced into the area; water pipes were laid out; drainage was put in; the streets were paved; and in the 1970s, the first gas stoves were purchased.[11] During this same decade, refrigerators and blenders were purchased, and corn mills for grinding nixtamal were finally accepted.

Tortilla presses were not accepted by the community until about 1955, even though they recognized that this would give them time to carry out other activities. The women in Tláhuac were reticent about purchasing machine-made tortillas and continued to pat them out by hand or use handheld tortilla presses until well into the 1980s. Because part of their education was centered around the importance of making tortillas by hand, they believed their very essence was connected with the making of tortillas. The act of making tortillas by hand confirmed their worth as "true" and good women. Besides making tortillas, they were expected to cook; embroider; wash; iron; clean the house; educate the children; take care of animals; and take the noon meal to their husbands, who were working in the fields.

The young women interviewed in the study stated that they were no longer brought up to learn to cook, because more emphasis was now placed upon education. They have a high-school education or commercial-school studies, which enables them to find work outside the home. They also stated that they did not spend more than two hours a day preparing food for the family, because they could find everything nearby and did not waste time shopping. They do not make tortillas; rather, they buy them in the supermarket or from women who sell them on street corners by the dozen. They make use of convenience food products such as cubes of chicken broth and mixes for preparing stews and soups. Products they do not like to buy are instantaneous or semiprepared beans, mole paste, and mixes for preparing cream soups, which they prefer to cook from scratch. Young Tláhuac cooks use gas stoves and ovens; heat their food in microwave ovens; and equip their kitchens with refrigerators, blenders, mixers, beaters, fryers, skillets, and Teflon-lined pots. They do not make traditional dishes, but eat them if they are made by their mothers, grandmothers, or mothers-in-law. It is clear that they still like traditional food, but do not want to take the time and effort to prepare it.

TLÁHUAC KITCHENS

Gas stoves combined with electric ovens or microwave ovens are common in most kitchens in Tláhuac today. Most kitchens include refrigerators, blenders, mixers, hand beaters, deep fryers, juice extractors, and Teflon-coated pots and skillets, as well as the latest status symbol: microwave ovens. Kitchen implements made of plastic, glass, or other materials form part of every kitchen. When large quantities of food have to be prepared, they use clay casseroles, pots, basins, or steamers and large aluminum pots. The younger generation of housewives do not like to use clay pots, vessels, and jars. Beans are still cooked in clay pots in spite of the long hours of cooking time because of the sweet flavor they impart. Microwave ovens are used for making popcorn and for reheating food. On Sundays, the noon meal is usually eaten outside the home to give the women a rest from cooking.

MIDDLE- AND UPPER-CLASS KITCHENS

Kitchens in middle- and upper-class homes in Mexico City are as well equipped as many American kitchens and include dishwashers, microwave ovens, blenders, hand beaters, garbage disposals, gas or electric ovens, toasters, electric coffee pots, and any other equipment they wish to buy. The North American Free Trade Agreement has opened up the Mexican borders to receive American appliances at reasonable prices.

In spite of the interest in food in the last decades, upper-class Mexican women are not known for their interest in the kitchen. They usually have household help for daily meals, and when they invite friends for dinner, they may use one of the very fine caterers that are now available in Mexico City.

It is interesting to observe the continuity in Mexican food traditions and preparation. Many pre-Hispanic dishes, as well as implements and methods of preparation, are still in use.[12] Mexicans value tradition, and this is reflected in their conservation of their basic diet and preparation techniques.

Up until a few decades ago, the Mexican kitchen was not given much attention or importance in the house, because it was mostly occupied by kitchen help. This is a change from pre-Hispanic Mexico, when the kitchen was the most important room in the house. Today, more women are cooking, due to a shortage of kitchen service, and are more aware of the need for comfort and efficiency in the kitchen, to make the cook's life more pleasant.

NOTES

1. José Tudela de la Orden, *Códice Tudela* (Madrid: Ediciones Cultura Hispánica del Instituto de Cooperación Iberoamericana, 1980), 283.

2. Ellen Messer, "Maize," in *The Cambridge World History of Food*, vol. 1, ed. Kenneth F. Kiple and Kriemhold Coneè Ornelas (Cambridge: Cambridge University Press, 2000), 103–4.

3. Janet Long-Solís, *Cápsicum y cultura: La historia del chilli* (Mexico City: Fondo de Cultura Económica, 1986), 17.

4. William H. Bullock, *Across Mexico in 1864–65* (London and Cambridge: Cambridge University Press, 1866), 201.

5. Rosalía Loreto López, "Prácticas alimenticias en los conventos de mujeres en la Puebla del siglo XVIII," in *Conquista y comida: Consecuencias del encuentro de dos mundos*, ed. Janet Long (Mexico City: Universidad Nacional Autónoma de México, 1996), 482–87.

6. Peggy K. Liss, *Mexico under Spain, 1521–1556* (Chicago: University of Chicago Press, 1975), 65.

7. Janet Long-Solís, *El sabor de la Nueva España* (Mexico City: Instituto Mora, 1995), 16.

8. Miguel Ángel Fernández and Victor Ruiz Naufal, *Mesa mexicana* (Mexico City: Fundación Cultural Bancomer, 1993), 109–10.

9. Brantz Mayer, *México, lo que fue y lo que es* (Mexico City: Fondo de Cultura Económica, 1953), 67.

10. Jeffrey Pilcher, *¡Que Vivan los Tamales! Food and the Making of Mexican Identity* (Albuquerque: University of New Mexico Press, 1998), 99–123.

11. Verónica Isabel Torres Cadena, "La alimentación en Tláhuac, Distrito Federal. Estudio de caso sobre cultura alimentaria en México" (master's thesis, Universidad Nacional Autónoma de México, 2003), 122–23.

12. Ancient magical-religious elements can still be observed in the preparation of tamales in Tláhuac. A knife, a few coins, and the grinding stone (*tejolote*) of the *metate* are sometimes placed at the bottom of the tamale steamer (*tamalera*).

The coins are used to test if the water in the steamer has evaporated, because the tinkling sound of a bubbling coin indicates that there is still water in the pot. On top of these objects, a bed of straw (*zacate*) is placed to accommodate the tamales in a vertical position. Care must be taken to not make the cook angry, because if this happens, the tamales may come out all stirred up (*batidos*) or uncooked. A remedy for this kitchen failure is to place veins of dried chile peppers on top of the tamales or, better yet, for the cook to learn to control her temper. María de la Luz del Valle, "Rituales alimentarios y ciclo de vida en Villa Milpa Alta, D. F." (master's thesis, Universidad Nacional Autónoma de México, 2003), 114.

4

Typical Meals

The definition of a "typical Mexican meal" depends upon cultural group, setting (rural or urban), age group, social and economic level, and geographic region. One can, however, speak in general terms about Mexican food traditions. In this chapter, typical meals will be described in accordance with these categories.

Corn is combined with beans, squash, chile peppers, tomatoes, and tomatillos to form the basic diet of the country. Secondary foods, which are eaten less frequently but are consumed throughout the country, are represented by native vegetables such as cactus paddles (*nopales*); avocados (*aguacates*); vegetable pears (chayotes); *jícamas*; and greens known as *quintoniles*, *verdolagas*, or *quelites*. Peripheral foods may include seasonal crops such as insects, mushrooms, chokecherries, the fruits of the prickly pear (*tunas*), and small cactus fruits known as *biznagas*. These foods are produced during the rainy season and are generally collected by the rural population.

Tortillas and hot chile sauces accompany meals throughout Mexico in all social levels. These two elements can be considered a common food denominator among social classes. The pungency of the sauces depends upon the type and quantity of chile used, based upon regional or personal preferences. Small plates of salt and cut limes are common table accessories. Meals are eaten two, three, or more times a day, depending upon the occupation and resources of the family and how one defines a meal. Some classify a cup of tea or coffee as a light meal. Fruits and sweets, considered snacks, are eaten at any time of the morning, afternoon, or evening. More substantial snacks, known as *tentempies*, which translates as "a little something to keep you on your feet," may consist of a corn-based snack (*antojito*) such as a quesadilla or *sope*. Beverages vary and include coffee, tea, hot chocolate, *atole*, soft drinks, beer, wine, and hard alcohol, depending upon the type of food served.

INDIAN GROUPS IN RURAL MEXICO

A recent investigation of the nutritional status of Mexicans entitled *Changes in the Nutritional Situation in Mexico 1990–2000* (*Cambios en la Situación Nutricional de México 1990–2000*), published by the Mexican Health Ministry, puts special emphasis upon the extreme nutritional risk for the rural Indian population.[1] This is most severe in the southern states of Guerrero, Oaxaca, and Chiapas, where there are large ethnic groups, many of whom live in very precarious conditions. The daily diet of some of the elderly members of these groups consists of tortillas, chile sauce, and little more. Many people can only aspire to eating a piece of meat during the yearly patron-saint fiestas. The nutritional risk of Indian groups is shown to have increased between 1990 and 2000, especially among children under the age of five, expectant mothers, and the elderly. Malnutrition is twice as common in rural areas as it is in urban areas. (See also chapter 8, "Diet and Health.")

DIETARY PATTERNS AMONG RURAL INDIAN GROUPS

Corn is the most important ingredient in the diet of rural Indian groups. It may be prepared in a variety of ways: as tortillas, tamales, gorditas, tostadas, roasting ears, *pinole*, *pozole*, fermented corn beverages, and many other ways. Corn products make up about 85 percent of the diet of the rural Yucatecan Maya.[2] In addition to the basic Mexican diet already described, wild fruits and greens are used as complementary items. Other variations in the diet are based upon regional customs, such as mustard greens and small game in the Tarahumara Indian diet in Chihuahua, and sweet potatoes, yucca, and *jícama* in the diet of the rural Yucatecan Maya. The Zapotecs in the Valley of Oaxaca have access to several tropical fruits and dried fish with which they complement their basic diets. The Tzotzil Indians in Zinacantan, Chiapas, cultivate cabbage and potatoes, which are part of their daily diet, when available. Indian diets may be supplemented by small game obtained by hunting, or seasonal fruits and greens, the products of collecting and gathering. Fruit, if consumed, is treated as a snack and eaten between meals.

Food and meal schedules in rural Mexico vary considerably according to local activities, resources, and customs. Breakfast may be eaten any time between 5 and 7 A.M., depending upon daily activities. Farmers usually rise very early, have a light breakfast of atole or tortillas and chile. They take their midday meal, which may consist of corn prepared as pozol, made of fresh or fermented corn and water, in the cornfield. After they return home in the afternoon, a meal that includes hot tortillas, beans, chile sauce, and coffee or atole is eaten between 4 and 6 P.M. These are the general guidelines for the Indian diet.

The definition of a meal, as described by the Mixtecs, is "food eaten at home, on a fixed schedule, served in a plate, hot, cooked, salty, spicy and accompanied by tortillas, which also serve as a spoon to transport the food from the plate to the mouth."[3]

In general terms, a typical Mixtec meal in the Mixteca Alta region of Oaxaca consists of a bean broth or soup served with tortillas and green chiles or with a hot, spicy sauce. When sufficient resources are available, bits of meat or eggs may be added to the broth. For special occasions, Mixtec cooks may prepare pozole, bean tamales, or a mole based on beans, mushrooms, or meat. Between-meal snacks may include tropical fruits, candy, sticks of sugar cane, candied squash, and sweet rolls. Chiles and salt are common items on the Mixtec table. When working in the fields or on a trip, the Mixtecs take a taco (shita in the Mixtec language) made with any of the above ingredients, without broth. Pulque, beer, and mezcal are favorite drinks consumed by the men of the community during fiestas.[4] Mezcal is the preferred drink for men when they are not celebrating a fiesta.

Among the Nahua Indians in Hueyapán, Morelos, food is closely identified with identity or "being Indian." In one investigation in the 1970s, informants explained that being Indian meant that one ate "ordinary food," nothing delicious. What they consider ordinary food includes tortillas, beans, chiles, tamales, squash, pulque, tejocotes, and mole. Unlike city people, who they said enjoyed good-tasting delicacies preserved in tin cans, the Indians complained that they ate only common things.[5]

There is a popular saying among the Tarahumara Indians of the state of Chihuahua: "Without corn, the Tarahumara could not exist." An analysis of their diet proves this saying to be true, as at least 50 percent of their diet is based upon corn.[6] The most common food of the Tarahumara Indians is pinole, which they call kobisi. This is parched, toasted corn flour, ground to a fine powder, then dissolved in water, with no other flavoring added. It makes a nutritious and refreshing drink. When the Tarahumara go on a trip, they carry the fine *pinole* powder with them in a little bag, which allows them to prepare their own sustenance wherever they may be. Tortilla *masa* or *atole* can be made from this same mixture.

Esquiáte is another dish made from toasted and ground corn with added water. The major difference between *pinole* and *esquiáte* is that while the corn is being ground for *esquiáte*, water is poured over the *metate* with one hand every few seconds. The result is a white, thin, soupy substance that is mixed with ground herbs or cornflowers. *Esquiáte* is very refreshing. It is kept in liquid form in a pot and dipped out at meals, to accompany beans, greens, or whatever else is served. During hot weather, most Taramuhara houses keep a jar of *esquiáte* ready to offer unexpected visitors.[7]

Pozole, called *oliki* by the Tarahumara, is made with tender corn, to which bits of beef or pork meat may be added. Tortillas and tamales are less important in the Tarahumara diet than they are among other Indian groups. Their favorite beverage, *tesgüino*, is also made of corn, in a fermented stage. It is of low alcoholic content and represents the most traditional and popular beverage for the Tarahumara. Some possess herds of goats or sheep, but meat contributes less than five percent of their food. Beans supply most of their protein. Small game such as mice, rats, squirrels, rabbits, lizards, and deer are hunted, and beans, greens, chile peppers, potatoes, onions, and broad beans are consumed when available. Wheat is not considered an important item in their diet. It does, however, serve as a substitute for corn, as it is harvested in the summer, during the annual famine period, when corn supplies are getting low and the corn is not yet ready to harvest. Their major sustenance is corn and corn products.[8]

The Huichol Indians, who live in isolated parts of western Jalisco and Nayarit, follow the traditional Indian diet. They eat corn in the form of tortillas, *atoles*, *pinole*, tamales, and roasted and boiled ears of fresh corn. They also eat amaranth, chiles, maguey, cactus products, and orchard fruits grown in the area. They supplement their diet with seasonal wild plants, fruits, nuts, greens, insects, and mushrooms. Like the Tarahumara, they manufacture the fermented corn beer called *tesgüino*; however, they add *sotol*, which they obtain from the agave plant, to make a more potent drink.

The urban Zapotecs of San Pablo Mitla, Oaxaca, generally eat two hot meals a day, defined as tortillas with a cooked sauce or beans, accompanied by soft drinks. Potatoes, rice, and wheat-flour pasta soups have become a substitute for beans when resources are not sufficient to purchase them. These items provide a less nutritious meal than beans, which are high in protein, especially when accompanied by corn. Few proteins of animal origin are consumed, although insects serve as extra sources of protein during the rainy season. If a family has the resources for meat only once a week, it is prepared for the Sunday meal. Primary foods in the Mitla Zapotec diet are corn and beans, secondary foods comprise starches and proteins, and spices and condiments make up the third category. Snacks of fruits and nuts complete the diet.[9]

Rural Yucatecan Maya Indians generally get up at dawn and have a cup of coffee, *atole*, or tortillas, made the day before. At noon, if the men are working their fields, they may prepare *pozol* by adding water to fresh or fermented cornmeal. When they arrive home after a day's work, their wives may serve them a vegetable stew with tortillas and beans and a hot sauce or chile peppers. The evening meal consists of beans and tortillas, with tea or coffee to drink. Fruit may be eaten between meals as a snack, but it does not form part of the meal structure. Citrus fruit is common in Yucatán, as are certain tropical fruits such as papayas, *anonas*, and *zapotes*.

THE INDIAN DIET IN MEXICO CITY

Indians who migrate to Mexico City to find work often become day laborers in the construction industry and are known in Spanish as *albañiles*. They immediately become part of the proletarian, urban sector in Mexico City. Most continue to survive on the traditional Indian diet, complemented by a heavy consumption of soft drinks, which provide much of the energy they need to perform their jobs.

Popular opinion has it that workers on a construction site pool their resources for purchasing food and are thus able to have a very good stew prepared for them, which they eat as a filling for tacos with chile-pepper sauce. This is called a *taquiza*. There is a common belief among the population that these stews are very good. This popular belief was discounted a few years ago when the National Consumer Institute (Instituto Nacional del Consumidor) carried out a study of the diet of 418 construction workers in Mexico City. The Consumer Institute found that little more than half of those interviewed ate a breakfast of high-energy food such as bread, tortillas, *atole*, or tamales, accompanied by coffee or tea. Four percent of those interviewed consumed only soft drinks and industrialized snacks, such as tortilla chips, during the entire workday. Those who ate bread, tortillas, wheat-pasta soups, and rice made up 35.2 percent. Only 49 percent ate a diet rich in proteins, such as beans, lentils, broad beans, chickpeas, beef, chicken or pork, tripe, eggs, and fish. A mere 2.4 percent of those surveyed had access to a dining room for employees, and 11 percent prepared their own foods while on the job; 40 percent brought food from home, while another 40 percent bought their food at street stands or supermarkets.[10] The study effectively destroyed the popular belief of the "good food" enjoyed by *albañiles*.

THE URBAN POOR

Cactus paddles (*nopales*) form part of the typical meal of the urban poor in Milpa Alta, a traditional suburb of Mexico City, located in the Xochimilco area. This is predominantly a rural area where local inhabitants produce potatoes, beans, chile peppers, broad beans, and especially *nopales* in household plots as well as in extended fields. The region is more suitable for the cultivation of cacti than for corn because the land is irregular and very uneven. Cactus plants have replaced corn as a subsistence plant, with the added benefit of *nopales* being in high demand in Mexico City markets. Milpalteñses have a repertoire of more than 300 recipes in their local food tradition for preparing this vegetable. They may be grilled and eaten as a filling for tacos; added to salads and soups; combined with vegetables, legumes, cheese, eggs, shrimp, fish, meat, or tamales; and even put in sweets and desserts.

Beans are served at every meal, either whole, in a liquid broth, or refried and topped with bits of pork cracklings. Potatoes are included in many stews, fried in oil, or boiled to make mashed potatoes or fritters. Local vegetables may be greens such as *verdolagas* or *quelites*, vegetable pears (chayotes), and zucchini, cooked with chile peppers and accompanied by tortillas and hot sauce. Mushrooms, fruits, and greens are gathered on the hillsides surrounding the town during the rainy season. A few pigs and chickens may be kept in household corrals and can be sold or eaten by their owners on special occasions. Additional sources of protein are obtained through hunting or by consuming seasonal insects.[11]

A typical midday meal of lower-income (although not poor, because this is often a relative category) groups may be represented by those who live in Tláhuac, in southern Mexico City. The meal begins with a liquid broth or a dry soup, followed by a stew and a plate of beans. The menu is always accompanied with tortillas and a hot sauce, which are requisites at every meal. Plain water or fruit-based beverages, *aguas frescas*, are served at weekday meals. Soft drinks are reserved for weekend meals. Desserts are not part of the food tradition, nor are soups always on the menu. The close proximity of Tláhuac to Lake Xochimilco ensures the availability of water insects, fish, turtle, *axolotl* (a local amphibian), and wild duck on the menu.

Until the 1950s, a very traditional diet prevailed in the seven Tláhuac towns. Most of the dishes were prepared with corn, chile, beans, and squash, plus amaranth, greens, and fish from the lakes.

GASTRONOMIC PATTERNS AMONG MIDDLE-CLASS MEXICANS

In spite of the many differences in the diet, a traditional order and sequence of meals can still be observed in middle-class Mexico. Many Mexicans start the day with a cup of coffee, herbal tea, or hot chocolate. These beverages may be accompanied by a sweet roll, but in most cases people just want something hot in their stomachs after a long night.

The beverage is followed later by a heavier meal called an *almuerzo*. This may be eaten around 10 A.M., depending upon the work schedule and whether it is taken at home or in a restaurant. A variety of dishes can be served at this meal. Juice and fresh fruit are common dishes to begin the meal. Eggs, meat, beans, stew, sauce, and tortillas are the general elements of breakfasts. Cereals, toast, and sweet rolls may also be served.

The most important meal of the day is served in mid-afternoon, sometime between 2 and 4 P.M. Outside Mexico City, families try to take the main meal of the day together; however, in large urban areas, it is generally no longer possible for the family to gather at home to eat, because of work schedules and heavy traffic at this time of day. The meal may begin with a snack or *antojito*, such as a quesadilla, or directly with a bowl of hot soup. The custom of serving both a liquid broth or creamy soup followed by a dry soup, such as rice or pasta, has become less popular in recent years due to the extra calories two soups represent. The main course may be meat, fish, or chicken served with a salad or vegetables. The most popular carbohydrate for accompanying most dishes is rice. Beans may be served with the main course or as a separate dish, following the principal dish. Desserts may include fresh fruit, ice cream, rice pudding, sherbet, or a custard called a flan. The dessert is also often eliminated because of the extra calories it contains. The most common after-dinner beverage is coffee.

Mexican Custard (Flan)

- 3 cups milk
- 3/4 cup sugar
- 2-inch cinnamon stick

- 1/2 teaspoon vanilla
- 3 egg yolks

Stir milk, sugar, and cinnamon together in a saucepan over medium heat. Bring to a slow boil, stirring until sugar is dissolved. Reduce heat to low and simmer gently until mixture is thick enough to cover the back of a spoon, about 20 minutes. Strain mixture and let cool slightly. Preheat oven to 325°. In a bowl, beat egg yolks until blended. Add vanilla. Add 1/3 cup hot milk, stirring constantly, then pour egg mixture into the rest of the milk mixture, stirring constantly. Divide mixture among 6 flameproof dishes on a rack in a baking pan and pour hot water into the pan to a depth of 1 inch. Bake until a toothpick inserted in the middle of the custard comes out clean, about 1 hour. Remove custard from water bath and arrange on a baking sheet. Place under the broiler until the tops are browned. Let cool and refrigerate for several hours, until well chilled.

After eating a substantial meal in mid-afternoon, most people do not feel like eating a heavy meal at night. A light meal (*merienda*) may be served around 8:30 or 9 P.M., when light snacks (*antojitos*), tamales, soups, sweet rolls, or leftovers from the noon meal may be eaten. Fresh fruit is a popular choice for a light evening meal. A more formal dinner (*cena*) may be shared with family and friends on special occasions.

Sunday is usually a day for getting together with the family for a relaxed midday meal. This may be at home when extended family members get together or in a favorite restaurant. Sunday is the most popular day for eating out.

This gastronomic scheme is by no means standard throughout the country. The majority of the population do not have sufficient resources to eat on such an elaborate scale.

Typical Meals

The menus for typical middle-class meals presented in this section will be divided into breakfasts (*almuerzos*), lunches (*comidas*), and suppers (*meriendas*). The menus have been chosen from five different regions of the country: Yucatán, northern Mexico, Oaxaca, Tlaxcala, and Mexico City.

Yucatán

A businessman or white-collar worker in Mérida, Yucatán, may begin his day with a cup of coffee or juice before rushing to the office. About 10 in the morning, he will have a snack (*tentempie*), which may consist of a *torta* with a filling of *cochinita pibil,* another meat filling, or some other *antojito.* This is an important time to share experiences with fellow employees, although some comment that it is not healthy because of the high-fat food eaten during this office recess.[12]

If it is Monday, his midday meal will probably be a dish of beans with pork (*frijol con puerco*), as this is the typical Monday menu in middle- and upper-class homes and restaurants in Mérida. The dish may be accompanied by a vegetable soup, rice, and tortillas or bread and fruit-based water or a soft drink. The evening meal, taken at home or at a restaurant, may consist of a Yucatecan *antojito* such as *panuchos* (small bean-stuffed tortillas, fried and topped with chicken, pork, or turkey and pickled red onions) served with Yucatecan hot sauce. A dark Yucatecan beer usually accompanies this dish.

More leisurely meals are enjoyed on Sundays, when breakfast may begin with citrus juice; fresh fruit; and Motul-style eggs (*huevos motuleños*), a dish made with fried eggs and served on a fried tortilla, covered with fried beans and topped with ham, peas, and fresh cheese. Coffee with milk would complete the breakfast. Sunday lunch often includes a light soup called *sopa de lima,* or lime soup. The typical Sunday lunch dish in Mérida is a stew called a *potaje* or *cocido,* made with beef or pork and vegetables. Barbecued pig (*cochinita pibil*) served with Yucatecan-style black beans is another popular Sunday meal. The evening meal would be a light snack after a heavy lunch, such as *antojitos,* served with a cold, dark Yucatecan beer.

Lime Soup (*Sopa de Lima*)
- 3 corn tortillas, cut in strips
- 2 chicken breasts
- 1 small onion, chopped
- 2 cloves garlic, chopped
- 5 whole black peppercorns
- 1 3-inch stick cinnamon
- 4 lime slices for garnish
- 8 whole allspice berries
- 1 tablespoon oregano
- 4 cups chicken broth
- 1 tomato, peeled and chopped
- 2 tablespoons lime juice

- 1 serrano chile pepper, chopped
- fresh cilantro

Fry tortilla strips in hot oil until crisp. Remove and drain. Place chicken, onion, garlic, peppercorns, cinnamon, allspice, oregano, and broth in a pot. Bring to a boil, reduce heat, and simmer, covered, for 40 minutes. Allow chicken to cool in the stock. Remove chicken from broth and shred the meat. Strain broth and add enough water to make 4 cups of liquid. Reheat broth with the tomato, lime juice, and chiles. Add chicken and simmer until hot. Place a few tortilla strips in a soup bowl, add the soup, garnish with lime slices and cilantro, and serve hot.

Northern Mexico

A cattle rancher in northern Mexico may begin his day with a hearty plateful of *machaca con huevos*, which is dried and shredded beef fried with tomatoes, onions, and green chile peppers cooked with scrambled eggs and served with cowboy-style pinto beans (*frijoles charros*), flour tortillas, and a mug of strong black coffee. If he is in Monterrey for lunch, he may be served a cheese soup (*caldo de queso*), pickled shrimp (*camarones en escabeche rojo*), and broiled kid (*cabrito al pastor*) with guacamole, onion, tomato, coriander, and chile peppers, served with pot beans (*frijoles de olla*) sprinkled with cheese and *pico de gallo* sauce. A good selection to accompany this meal would be a cold Bohemia beer manufactured in the city. The evening meal would no doubt include a broiled strip of beef (*carne a la tampiqueña*) served with red enchiladas, beans, and guacamole, to be washed down with yet another cold Monterrey beer. Northern Mexican men are noted beef eaters and beer drinkers.

Cheese Soup (*Caldo de Queso*)
- 2 tablespoons butter
- 1 onion, finely chopped
- 1 clove garlic, minced
- 2 large tomatoes, peeled and chopped
- 4 cups beef broth
- 2 canned mild green chiles, drained and chopped
- 1 cup milk or half-and-half
- salt and pepper, to taste
- 3/4 pound cheddar cheese, shredded
- 4 green onions, finely chopped

In a heavy pot, melt butter and sauté onion and garlic until opaque. Raise heat and add tomatoes. Cook, stirring, for about 5 minutes. Add beef broth and chopped chiles. Simmer a few minutes, lower heat, and add milk or half-and-half, salt, and pepper. Cook until heated. Divide shredded cheese into warm bowls and add soup. Garnish with green onions and serve.

Oaxaca

A fruit and vegetable market vendor, or *marchanta*, in the Central Market in Oaxaca may have time to interrupt her transactions long enough to go to a market food stand; sit at a long, rustic wooden table with other clients; and enjoy a hearty Oaxacan breakfast. This usually begins with fresh juice and is followed by roasted cheese in green sauce (*quesillo oaxaqueño*), black turtle beans seasoned with avocado leaves, large hot corn tortillas called *tlayudas*, and coffee with brown sugar and cinnamon or hot chocolate. Oaxaca produces a diversity of sweet rolls, which are also favorite breakfast items. At midday, she may go back to the same restaurant stand and order a cactus paddle and shrimp soup (*caldillo de nopales y camarón*) or an appetizer of tacos, filled with Oaxaca cheese in corn tortillas and a sauce. Pork in yellow mole sauce, simply called *amarillo*, served with black beans may be her choice for a main dish. The meal may end with ice cream, for which Oaxaca is famous, and black coffee. Her evening meal could well be Oaxacan tamales wrapped in banana leaves and served with *atole* or hot chocolate.

Jalisco

An agave-producing hacienda owner from the state of Jalisco would be able to have more leisure meals, as agave plants require only seasonal care. Guadalajara, the state's capital, is one of the culinary capitals of Mexico. A typical breakfast (*almuerzo*) menu may include juice, fresh fruit, Jalisco-style enchiladas (*enchiladas tapatías*) filled with shredded chicken breasts and a sauce made with ancho chiles, beans in their broth (*frijoles de olla*), and coffee. For the main meal, served in early afternoon, he might have an appetizer of tequila with a *sangrita* chaser, squash-blossom soup (*crema de flor de calabaza*), peppers stuffed with cheese (*chiles rellenos con queso*), mutton stew (*birria*), white rice, pinto beans, custard (*jericalla*), and coffee. The evening meal (*merienda*) may include Jalisco-style *pozole* served with individual bowls of hot sauce, finely chopped onions, thinly sliced radishes, finely shredded lettuce, and wedges of limes. Beer may be the drink of choice for an evening meal.

Tlaxcala

Tlaxcala, in central Mexico, has a deep-rooted Indian culture, which is evident in the daily diet. Insects, maguey worms, and century-plant dishes are popular in the local food tradition. Tlaxcalan food has much in common with Puebla-style food, but is more hearty fare. A middle-class breakfast may begin with fruit or fruit juice, followed by Mexican-style scrambled eggs (*huevos a la mexicana*) with chopped tomatoes, onions, coriander, and green chile peppers. Corn tortillas, refried beans, and a hot sauce are usual accompaniments for this breakfast. The main meal of the day may begin with Tlaxcala-style red rice served with a green sauce and accompanied with corn-fungus *huitlacoche* quesadillas or tacos. Corn and chile soup or steamed pork in maguey leaves (*mixiote de puerco*) may be served with pot beans seasoned with epazote, hot sauce, and tortillas, accompanied by a cold, freshly drawn mug of *pulque*. Dessert may be a cactus pudding (*dulce de nopales*) and coffee.

Mexico City

A college student in Mexico City, acutely aware of her figure, may drink nothing more than a glass of orange juice on her way out the door to her morning classes. At mid-morning, hunger forces her to forget her diet and join friends between classes to eat *chilaquiles*, *molletes*, quesadillas, or other high-calorie snacks. She may eat a nutritious and health-conscious meal at home with her mother and siblings, which could begin with a vegetable soup, broiled chicken or meat, and a fresh green salad. She could forgo dessert. In the afternoon, she might join friends for coffee and cookies, and at night order a fruit cocktail or salad to counteract the afternoon excesses.

Molletes

- 6 *bolillos* or hard rolls
- 2 cups refried beans
- 1/2 pound cheddar cheese, grated

Preheat oven to 400°. Butter a large cookie sheet. Cut rolls in half and scoop out the dough inside the rolls. Fill space with refried beans. Sprinkle with grated cheese and bake about 10 minutes or until cheese melts. Serve with Mexican hot sauce.

Fresh Mexican Hot Sauce

- 1 tomato, chopped
- 1/2 onion, chopped

- 5 sprigs coriander
- 3 serrano chiles
- 1/2 teaspoon salt
- 1/2 cup water

Mix all ingredients together and serve with *molletes*.

Children and Adolescents

When children and adolescents eat at home in a family atmosphere, their dietary habits usually conform to those of their parents. When they eat outside the home, they prefer fast foods like pizzas, hamburgers, hot dogs, potato chips, French fries, sandwiches, small cakes, doughnuts, cookies, and soft drinks. Adolescents represent the age group most affected by North American food imports. The high content of sugars and fats in these foods has contributed to an increase in the obesity of young people, especially in Mexico City and northern Mexico. This international diet coexists with that of Mexican-style *antojitos* such as tacos, quesadillas, *esquites*, enchiladas, *molletes*, *tortas*, tamales, *pozole*, and many others. On weekends, adolescents usually eat only twice a day because they get up later and only eat lunch and dinner.

The Upper-Class Mexican Diet

The upper-class Mexican diet does not vary substantially from the middle-class diet. This level of society is more aware of keeping a slim figure and probably consumes less sugar and fat than the middle class. They also have more resources to spend on gyms, spas, and exercise classes. Their higher income allows them to frequent expensive restaurants, and they tend to be more knowledgeable about international food trends due to their frequent travels to the United States and Europe. Generally, upper-class Mexican women have a kitchen staff and do not have to prepare the meals for their families.

NOTES

1. Instituto Nacional de Ciencias Médicas y Nutrición, *Cambios en la Situación Nutricional de México 1990–2000* (Mexico City: Salud Pública de México, no. 45, suplemento 4, 2003), 15–17.

2. Alfonso Villa Rojas, "The Maya of Yucatán," in *Handbook of Middle American Indians*, vol. 7, *Ethnology*, ed. Evon Z. Vogt (Austin: University of Texas Press, 1969), 244–75.

3. Esther Katz, "La influencia del contacto en la comida campesina mixteca," in *Conquista y comida: Consecuencias del encuentro de dos mundos*, ed. Janet Long (Mexico: Universidad Nacional Autónoma de México, 1996), 344–45.

4. Ibid.

5. Judith Friedlander, *Being Indian in Hueyapan* (New York: St. Martin's Press, 1975), 74–75.

6. The Tarahumara corn beer, called *tesgüino*, is closely identified with their identity and religion. To dance and drink *tesgüino* symbolizes a communication with God. A small offering is poured upon the ground before they drink, as God must always be the first one served. A refusal to drink *tesgüino* in public defines a person as a follower of the Protestant religion, as they are discouraged from drinking by church officials. Claudia Molinari, "Beber o no beber tesgüino, identidad y conversión en la Tarahumara," in *Identidad y cultura en la Sierra Tarahumara*, ed. Claudia Molinari and Eugenio Porras (Mexico City: Instituto Nacional de Antropología e Historia, 2001), 155–61.

7. Tarahumara etiquette orders that when a person has finished drinking *pozole* or *esquiáte*, he or she should scrape the bottom of the calabash with a curved finger and then suck on it. This is not done due to a lack of food; it is merely proper Tarahumara manners.

8. John G. Kennedy, *Tarahumara of the Sierra Madre* (Pacific Grove, Calif.: Asilomar Press, 1978), 53–58.

9. Ellen Messer, "Plantas alimenticias zapotecas: Transformación de dos culturas," in *Conquista y comida: Consecuencias del encuentro de dos mundos*, ed. Janet Long (Mexico City: Universidad Nacional Autónoma de México, 1996), 320–21.

10. Wenceslao Huerta, "¿Qué comen los albañiles de la ciudad de México?" *Cuadernos de Nutrición* 10, no. 5 (1987): 47.

11. María de la Luz del Valle, "Rituales alimentarios y ciclo de vida en Villa Milpa Alta, D. F." (master's thesis, Universidad Nacional Autónoma de México, 2003), 101–7.

12. Gabriela de la Riva, "¿Por qué come lo que come la población de Mérida?" *Cuadernos de Nutrición* 21, no. 5 (1998): 36–42.

5

Regional and Cultural Differences

A discussion of the Mexican food system has to take into consideration
the regional differences in diet. Mexico has many cuisines, some dishes so
different from others that one finds it hard to believe that they all stem
from the same cultural tradition. There are many reasons for these dis-
tinctions. Some are historical, others are cultural, and still others depend
upon the diet of the ethnic groups that live or lived in the area. Other reasons can be attributed to the natural resources, geography, climate, and
even the type of chile peppers developed and cultivated in the area. The
country occupies an area of 2,000 miles from north to south, with diverse
plant and animal life, which must also be considered.

The Mexican diet has a common substratum throughout the country,
based upon corn, beans, and chile peppers. At the same time, there are
many ways of preparing corn, different varieties and methods of preparing
beans, and a great diversity of chile peppers and sauces that are popular in
each region. Mexico produces a plenitude of fresh fruits and vegetables,
whose preparation is also regional.

A country's cuisine is influenced by its invaders, its conquerors, and its
commercial contacts. Mexican cuisine has been most affected by the
Spaniards and Americans and, to a lesser degree, by the presence of
French, English, Chinese, and Japanese immigrants in the nineteenth
century. In Santa Rosalia, Baja California, French-style bread is still
baked using the same nineteenth-century utensils brought by the French.
The influence of Chinese and Japanese food remains evident in the Baja

California diet. Modern transportation and refrigeration have removed many of the natural barriers that helped developed regional cuisines. Many ingredients are found in greater abundance on local markets, but can often be found in the large wholesale market in Mexico City, called La Central de Abasto. The demographic movement of the Mexican population, starting after the Mexican Revolution and accentuated during the 1950s, also helped to circulate food products and introduce regional food traditions in Mexico City. Practically any kind of regional Mexican food can now be found and eaten in Mexico City restaurants.

The most dominant influence in recent decades has been that of the United States, due to their close proximity and the open border for importing food products.

For the purpose of this chapter, the country has been divided into six regional areas based, on the whole, on gastronomic rather than political boundaries: northern Mexico, the Pacific coast, western Mexico, central Mexico, the isthmus of Tehuantepec, and the Maya area.

NORTHERN MEXICO

Northern Mexico comprises the six frontier states that border the United States. This region extends some 1,800 miles from Baja California on the Pacific coast to Tamaulipas on the Gulf of Mexico, and also includes the states of Sonora, Chihuahua, Coahuila, and Nuevo León. This section of the country has diverse geographical characteristics, including two mountain ranges: the Sierra Madre Occidental, which runs along the west coast, and the Sierra Madre Oriental, which pushes up along the east. High, arid deserts in the states of Chihuahua and Sonora; deep canyons; rivers; waterfalls; and humid, fog-moistened valleys, which are home to Mexico's finest vineyards, form part of the landscape. The area includes natural wonders like Copper Canyon, which includes six ravines, one of them over 6,000 feet deep. Copper Canyon is four times larger in area and more profound than Arizona's Grand Canyon. The Tarahumara Indians live in and around the canyons, enjoying the solitude and isolation that enables them to continue their own way of life and follow their own traditions in food and dress. This allows them to avoid being incorporated into modern culture, where they would be considered part of the proletarian class. In many respects, they live much as they did nearly 500 years ago when the Spaniards arrived in the area.

Spanish explorers preceded the Catholic priests, both of whom forged northward from central Mexico to extend the boundaries of the Spanish

empire and spread Christianity. At the same time, the explorers were able
to gain control of lands and riches for themselves. Wherever the
Spaniards went, they took their animals with them. In this case, it was
cattle that thrived and prospered on the virgin grasslands that heretofore
had been unexploited. Soon, many escaped from the domestic herd, and
in a matter of years, wild herds of cattle were roaming the northern plains
at will. There was such an abundance of cattle that they were slaughtered
for their hides and the meat was left to rot or be eaten by wild animals.
Mexico's finest beef still comes from northern Mexico.

There are similarities in diet throughout the region. A typical meal in
any of the northern states would include beef, red beans, wheat-flour tortillas, and coffee. Beef is the most popular meat in the region, most often
as a broiled T-bone; sirloin steak; or a local cut called an *arrachera*, which
is a thick strip of meat cut from the flank of the animal. Beef is also prepared in a variety of stews, such as *cocido* (prepared with chickpeas, corn,
green beans, squash, carrots, potatoes, and cabbage) and *menudo* (made
with tripe, cow's feet, corn, spearmint, coriander seeds, chopped onion,
and lemon).

Machaca, or dried and shredded beef seasoned with onions, tomatoes,
and green chiles, is used for tacos, in stews, and scrambled eggs. Other beef-
based specialties in the diet are ground meatballs; *picadillo*, which is ground
beef cooked with tomato sauce; and tacos and enchiladas with a beef filling. Other northern specialties include *sopaipillas*, made with wheat-flour
tortillas cut in quarters and fried to accompany savory dishes, as well as
burritos and *chivichangas* filled with *machaca*, beans, ham, or cheese. Pork
dishes include *pozole* and *mochomos*, made with finely shredded pork or
beef and fried, and *chilorio*, a chile-seasoned pork, served in tacos. Sauces
are not as spicy as those served in central and southern Mexico.

Food specialties from Chihuahua include the local cheese, produced by
the Mennonites, who arrived from Holland in the nineteenth century to
be free to practice their own religion and way of life. They settled on bar-
ren, agricultural land and have made it flourish and produce through hard
work and modern technology. They also keep dairy cattle and soon began
producing a local cheese called Chihuahua, which they sell on the national and international markets. Several dishes are made with local Chihuahua cheese, such as chile with melted cheese; cheese soup; beans with
cheese; and quesadillas with a variety of stuffings, such as cheese, shredded
beef, or eggs and sausages.

The Spaniards introduced wheat into the area in the sixteenth century
and developed a large, wheat-flour tortilla. This type of tortilla is made

with flour, lard, salt, and water and is shaped by extending a ball of dough between two sheets of waxed paper with a rolling pin, instead of being shaped by hand or with a tortilla press, as corn tortillas must be. The wheat-flour tortilla accompanies most meals in northern Mexico.

Beans are so popular in the area that they are said to be eaten three times a day. Red or pinto beans are prepared in a variety of ways. Drunken beans (*frijoles borrachos*), are made with pinto beans spiked with local beer. Hobbled beans (*frijoles maneados*) are cooked, puréed, and served with a sauce made with ancho chiles and stringy Chihuahua cheese—thus the name of "hobbled" or "tied-up" beans (with the stringy cheese). Cowboy beans (*frijoles charros*) can be quite spicy as they are prepared with chile peppers, herbs, and bits of meat.

Monterrey, Nuevo León, is not only Mexico's most important industrial center, it is also the home of spit-roasted young kid, or *cabrito al pastor*. Goats fare well in the arid north because of their ability to thrive on very short vegetation and the rocky terrain. To make *cabrito*, young goats are soaked in a large stock pot with vinegar, salt, and water for about two hours, while a fire is built on the ground with mesquite wood, which is then allowed to burn down to white coals. The kids are then removed from the water, threaded on the spits, and allowed to roast slowly for two to three hours, until the meat is tender and juicy, while basting with salted water. It is then served with guacamole, chopped onion, tomatoes, coriander leaves, and chile peppers. Cowboy beans sprinkled with grated cheese usually accompany the dish as along with large wheat-flour tortillas and sauce. The meat may also be shredded and used as a filling for tacos.

Northern desserts include a bread pudding called *capirotada*, rice pudding (*arroz con leche*), fritters or *buñuelos* with molasses syrup, caramelized milk, and *chimangos*. *Chimangos* are fritters made with wheat flour molded into a rhomboid shape, fried, and accompanied with syrup. There are many sweets distinctive to northern Mexico as well as fruit pastes, called *ates*, made with a variety of fresh fruits. Coahuila, in particular, produces a great variety of sweets, candies, *cajetas*, and other milk-based candies.

Several beverages and alcoholic drinks are popular, such as *bacanora*, tequila, and *mezcal*, all made from the sap of the maguey plant. *Tesgüino*, a fermented drink prepared with corn, brown sugar, and water is popular among the Tarahumara Indians. Beer is a favorite drink, and wine may be served on special occasions. Festive food may include any of the dishes described here as well as tamales with diverse fillings. Food from northern Mexico is hearty, filling, unpretentious fare.

BAJA CALIFORNIA, SONORA, AND TAMAULIPAS

Baja California, Sonora, and Tamaulipas will be given separate treat-ment, as they have many miles of coastline, a rich marine life, and some-what different food traditions, although typical dishes from northern Mexico, already mentioned, also form part of their diets. The Sea of Cortés, in Baja California, contains more than 250 species of fish, such as grouper, yellowtail, pompano, marlin, and bonito, and an abundance of shellfish as well. Fish are used locally in soups, salads, seafood cocktails (*ceviches*), and in fish balls known as *albondigas de pescado*. Fish fillets may also be served breaded and fried or Japanese-style, *en tempura*. Wheat-flour tortillas, beans, and coffee complete the daily menu. Baja California is also home to Mexico's finest wine-producing area, the Valley of Guadalupe, considered by many to be Mexico's Napa Valley.

A famous dish from the area is Caesar salad, the brainstorm of Italian immigrants Alex and Caesar Cardini, who had a small restaurant in Ti-juana in the early 1930s. The salad, made with crisp romaine lettuce and a dressing of garlic, anchovies, Worcestershire sauce, and Parmesan cheese, is served with croutons and a coddled egg. Today, it can be found on menus of restaurants around the world.

The port cities of Guayamas and Ciudad Obregón, Sonora, are well known for their shrimp and seafood dishes, such as grilled shrimp *al mojo de ajo*, tacos of *machaca de pescado*, and a variety of seafood soups and broths.

Seafood is an important part of the Tamaulipas cuisine, due to the state's location on the Gulf of Mexico. Among their most popular dishes are a shrimp soup called *huatapé de camarón*; several pickled fish dishes; stuffed crab; and a crab soup the state shares with its southern neighbor, Veracruz, called *chilpachole de jaiba*.

Tamaulipas's most famous dish is grilled beef *a la tampiquena*. This dish was invented by José Luis Loredo in Tampico in the early twentieth cen-tury. It consists of a thin strip of grilled beef served with enchiladas, beans, and guacamole. It is a hearty plateful and is still a popular item on local restaurant menus.

THE PACIFIC COAST

The Mexican coastline extends for more than 6,000 miles around the country. This measurement would include the Pacific and Gulf of Califor-nia coasts, as well as the Gulf of Mexico and Caribbean coastlines, which surround the Yucatán peninsula.

The Pacific-coast area extends from the state of Sinaloa in the north to
the popular tourist state of Guerrero in the south and includes the states
of coastal Jalisco, Michoacán, Colima, and Nayarit. Seafood is one of the
specialties of these six oceanfront states and is consumed by the thousands
of tourists from cold northern climates who flock to the beaches to enjoy
Mexico's ever-present sunshine. Remote fishing villages and small restaurants set up on the beaches provide visitors with an endless variety of
local-style seafood. Shrimp, red snapper, snook, sea scallops, crab, oysters,
marlin, and sailfish are only a few of the seafood varieties prepared in *ceviches*, soups, salads, stuffed crepes, or as toppings for tostadas and as fillings for tamales. Seafood may be broiled, baked, pickled, smoked, or fried;
served with hot sauce to stimulate jaded appetites; and accompanied by a
basket of hot corn or wheat tortillas, depending upon the local tradition.
Food in Nayarit is accompanied with corn tortillas rather than the wheat-
flour ones popular in northern Mexico.

The specialties of the Pacific-coast area are not confined to seafood
dishes; every one of the states has as many dishes made with a variety of
meats and vegetables. Michoacán and Jalisco, especially, have a long cultural tradition of meat and corn dishes. Because they border the ocean,
some seafood specialties they are known for will be included in this section.

Sinaloa is famous for several fish dishes, such as smoked marlin, prepared with bay leaves and served as a fish dish or used in seafood salads.
The fish may be prepared with mesquite wood or smoked slowly in special
ovens. Shrimp is also abundant in the state and is served in cocktails;
smoked; as *machaca*; breaded and fried; in sauces; and stuffed with vegetables, if they are large enough. Sinaloa is also the home of *pescado zaran-
deado*, which might be translated as "shaken-up fish," prepared with soy
sauce; tomato sauce; and a blend of herbs, salt, and pepper. It is then
grilled over a low flame and served with rice and wheat tortillas. On the
island of Mexcaltitlán, the local specialty is called by the Náhuatl name
of *tlaxtihuilli* and consists of a very spicy shrimp broth served at the fiestas
of Saints Peter and Paul.

Sinaloa is an important farming state, with large extensions of irrigated
land. Farmers here are the principal producers of tomatoes, rice, watermelon, and eggplant. They also produce large quantities of chile peppers,
melon, sugar cane, wheat, sorghum, and soy. Much of this produce is ex-
ported to the United States, especially the tomatoes and chile peppers.

Colima is one of Mexico's smallest states, but has several gastronomical
feathers in its cap, such as a cold coconut soup prepared with fresh coconut, coconut milk, sugar, heavy cream, and milk. This soup is very re-

Woman carrying tostadas for sale on her head, Zi-
huatanejo. © TRIP/S. Grant.

freshing on a hot summer day at the beach. The state also produces a variety of fish and shrimp dishes. Colima is the home of a dish called
tatemado made with meat; cooked in a *chile pasilla* sauce and tomatoes; and
flavored with bay leaves, ginger, pepper, and cumin. Iguanas are considered a delicacy in this region and other coastal areas and are prepared in a
multitude of ways.

The favorite chile pepper used in Guerrero-style cooking is a bright red
chile called *chile costeño*. One can see mountains of these chiles drying in
the sun like burning fires. Grilled red snapper, often prepared as *pescado a
la talla*, is a specialty of Barra Vieja, located on the outskirts of Acapulco,
and is prepared before one's own eyes on the beach. The fish is sliced open
in a butterfly cut, the intestines removed, and the fish seasoned with lime

juice, salt, and pepper. It is then grilled on an outdoor grill over a charcoal fire for 30 or 40 minutes while basting with an ancho- and *pasilla*-chile sauce. At serving time, melted butter and a good squirt of lime juice give it the finishing touch.

Chile Pasilla Sauce

- 4 *pasilla* chiles
- 1 clove garlic, peeled
- 1/2 teaspoon salt
- 3/4 cup cold water
- 1 tablespoon onion, minced

Toast chiles on a griddle and blend with the rest of the ingredients. Put sauce in sauce bowl and garnish with minced onion.

There are many sophisticated and complex recipes for making fish and shellfish dishes, but undoubtedly the very best is prepared with a just-caught fish skewered upon a stick; broiled over a low fire of dried coconut shells; and eaten, accompanied by a spicy chile sauce and a cold beer, in the shade of an umbrella on a sunny Acapulco beach.

WESTERN MEXICO

States grouped into this area, based on a gastronomic affinity, are Guanajuato, Querétaro, Aguascalientes, San Luis Potosí, Zacatecas, eastern Jalisco, and eastern Michoacán. The states border each other in the central western part of the country. Guanajuato, Michoacán, San Luis Potosí, and Querétaro form a region called El Bajío, known as the "bread basket" of New Spain during colonial times because wheat adapted well to the area and was the source of much of the wheat flour produced during that time. El Bajío was the birthplace of Mexico's struggle for independence from Spain in the nineteenth century. This is a very traditional and conservative part of the country, which is reflected in the diet.

Jalisco is probably best known as the home of mariachi music and tequila, made from the *Agave tequilana*. Tequila is traditionally served in a small shot glass and accompanied with cut limes; salt; and a chaser called *sangrita*, which is a mixture of orange juice, ground onion, *chile piquín* or *chile de árbol*, salt, and sugar. A sauce called *pico de gallo* (rooster's beak) is also a common accompaniment for tequila. The sauce is made with *jícama* and orange slices topped with ground *chile piquín*. Western Mexican food is hot and spicy, due to the *chile de árbol* pepper sauce that usually accompanies the meal.

Popular dishes in the region are thick, meat-based soups made with beef, pork, mutton, or kid and prepared with a variety of vegetables. These may be in the form of *birria*, *pozole*, *menudo*, or *cocido*. Jalisco-style *birria* is Guadalajara's most popular dish. It is a mutton or kid soup or stew made with large pieces of lamb or goat meat and covered with a thick mixture of spices, ground chile peppers, and other seasonings, then steamed in a large pot for several hours with a bit of liquid until it is thoroughly cooked. It may be served with chopped onions and dried oregano, or the meat shredded and made into a taco. It is served in small food stands along the roads outside the city and in local restaurants. *Pozole jaliscience* is also a typical Guadalajara dish, made in a red chile sauce and, when the garnishes are added, thick enough to be considered a whole meal. *Menudos* and *cocidos* are popular throughout the region, as are enchiladas, tostadas, *sopes*, and gorditas. *Sopes* are said to have originated in Guadalajara.

Michoacán has a rich culinary tradition and many specialties; perhaps the best known is called plaza chicken or *pollo de plaza, estilo Morelia*. It is actually an enchilada stuffed with chopped chicken breasts; garnished with ancho-chile tomato sauce, grated feta cheese, carrots, potatoes, and jalapeño chiles; and served on a bed of romaine lettuce. Restaurants surrounding the San Agustín Plaza, in Morelia, put this dish on sale every afternoon at 6 P.M. Another Michoacán contribution to Mexican cuisine is a delicate white fish from Lake Patzcuaro called *pescado blanco rebozado*. The fish are coated in a beaten egg-white batter, fried, and served with lime juice. Michoacán is also famous for its tamales. *Corundas* tamales with pork bits are shaped in triangles and wrapped in fresh corn leaves instead of dried corn husks. Unfilled tamales called *uchepos* are made with fresh corn and served with thick cream and sauce.

Regional soups in the area include *caldo michi*, made with catfish or carp from Lake Chapala in Jalisco, and melon soup from Apatzingán, Michoacán, where a large harvest of melons is produced every year. *Sopa tarasca* is a popular bean soup served in Morelia. It received its name from the local Tarascan or Purépecha Indians, who are the predominant Indian culture in that state.

Zacatecas, Guanajuato, and San Luis Potosí were important silver-mining areas during Mexico's colonial period, which is reflected in their contemporary gastronomic specialties, called "miner's-style" dishes. Guanajuato and San Luis Potosí both have miner's-style enchiladas and tostadas as part of their culinary tradition. San Luis Potosí enchiladas are filled with a feta-type cheese and served with guacamole sauce, cheese, and onion, while the Guanajuato miner's enchiladas or tostadas are made with fried chicken breasts, potatoes, carrots, and beans and fried in hot oil. The tostadas are spread with hot bean paste with chopped chicken, lettuce, avocado, and cream and topped with a slice of chile pepper. These are served hot from small braziers in the market square.

Guanajuato and San Luis Potosí are famous for a Spanish-type dish called *fiambre* made of cold meats such as cooked tongue, pig's feet, and chicken; served with herbed vinaigrette sauce; and garnished with carrots and potatoes. A rich stew called a *puchero* is popular throughout western Mexico. It is originally of Spanish origin and recipes vary from state to state. In some states it goes by the name of *cocido*.

The culinary specialties of Aguascalientes include *birria*, *pozole*, and *menudo*. The local version of *menudo* is said to be rejuvenating and a good remedy for a night on the town. This state is also the most important center of guava production and dried chile peppers. *Guajillo*, *puya*, *pasilla*, chipotle, *cascabel*, and *bola* peppers are dehydrated in large ovens or spread out on mats to dry in the sun.

The desert areas of the region take advantage of the fruits of the desert, such as *cabuches*, which are the blossoms of the *biznaga* cactus. These are cooked and prepared in a salad with a vinaigrette sauce. Another desert fruit is heart of palm from the tender trunk of the Brazilian palm tree. Cactus paddles (*nopales*) are prepared in soups and salads throughout the area.

The region is famous for its many sweet desserts and candies, such as curds or *chongos Zamoranos*, invented in Zamora, Michoacán. The city of Celaya, Guanajuato, is an important producer of a caramelized goat's milk known as *cajeta*. Thin crepes bathed in *cajeta* make a marvelous dessert after a light meal. Jalisco claims a rich custard called *jericalla*, popular throughout western Mexico, as its own invention. The small town of Jericó, Colombia, also claims this distinction. Querétaro makes a yam-based sweet called *dulce de Querétaro*. *Buñuelos* and *arroz con leche* are popular desserts in Zacatecas and throughout Mexico in general.

Fruit-based beverages, called *aguas frescas*, made by combining pineapple, prickly pears, melon, and many other fruits are popular accompaniments for any of these dishes from western Mexico, as is a cold beer or a shot of tequila.

CENTRAL MEXICO

Central Mexico is often referred to as Highland Mexico, in reference to the high elevation of most of this area. It includes the states of Mexico,

Morelos, Puebla, Tlaxcala, and Hidalgo, as well as the Federal District, where Mexico City is located. Important cities in the region are Mexico City, Puebla, Tlaxcala, Toluca, and Cuernavaca; all of these are well-known gastronomic centers with specialties of their own.

The area has always been rich in gastronomic resources due to its central location and the fact that it has been the center of power since pre-Hispanic times. Food products from all parts of the country traditionally converge in the area. This was the region most affected by the influx of imported food products from Europe after the conquest, because more Spaniards settled in the area. Meat and meat products, such as milk, cheese, and eggs; wheat; sugar; rice; citrus fruits; wine; some vegetables such as onions and garlic; and condiments such as parsley, coriander, oregano, and cloves were combined with local products to produce the Mexican diet as we know it today. Highland Mexico was soon considered the nutritional center of the country and has remained so throughout history.

The animals most quickly adopted by the Indian population were the pig and the chicken, because they are small animals and relatively easy to care for. Pigs, especially, adapted well to the Valley of Toluca, in the state of Mexico. Throughout the years, the valley has become famous for its fine pork products, such as Toluca sausages. Red and green chorizos are prepared as seasoned links of fresh sausage and are popular items in the diet. Green sausages are colored with fresh herbs and chiles, while the red sausage contains ancho chiles, pork fat, sweet paprika, and a variety of spices. Eggs with chorizo is a popular item on the breakfast menu in Toluca, and is usually garnished with fresh cheese and served with a green sauce and tortillas. The sausage called *longaniza* is one that has not been sectioned off; rather, it is cut from one continuous piece. Toluqueños also produce a blood sausage, called *moronga*. Pig's head cheese, called *queso de puerco*, is made by simmering a pig's head with flavorings; cutting it into small pieces; and placing it in a small basket, like a pâté. Other well-known pork dishes from the state of Mexico are fried pork bits called *carnitas*, garnished with cilantro and finely chopped white onions. Freshly made tortillas are served on the side, so diners can make their own tacos with their sauce of choice. Chopped zucchini with pork, *calabazitas con puerco*, is a popular everyday dish, as is a pork stew called *cocido de puerco*. Barbecued mutton or goat meat is prepared for festive occasions. Twice-fried pork cracklings are served with guacamole or a chile sauce and a few drops of lime juice.

Wild mushrooms can be collected in the Toluca area during the rainy season, from May through September. Unusual red mushrooms called *santigüeros* are popular for local consumption, as are yellow mushrooms called *canarios*. Blue mushrooms are favorites for serving with pork. Better-known mushrooms from the area find good reception in Mexico City markets. The San Juan market is known for its wide selection of mushrooms during the summer. Morels, cèpes, chanterelles, *escobetillas* (little brushes), and very small ones called *clavitos* (little nails) are popular for preparing soups, stews, and tacos. Mushrooms are most often sautéed with onions, garlic, serrano chile peppers, and epazote (*Chenopodium ambrosioides*). This herb brings out the full flavor of mushrooms and is a common accompaniment for them. Mushrooms are also used as a filling for tacos, quesadillas, and other finger foods. Collecting mushrooms can be a good source of income for many women, who rise early to collect them before sunrise and sell them in carefully constructed piles on Mexico City sidewalks, near the markets.

Another specialty from the area is blue tortillas made with blue corn, which are said to be more nutritious than white or yellow ones. *Tlacoyos* are made with large, thick, oblong-shaped tortillas, filled with refried beans and potatoes, and fried with onions or Oaxaca cheese. In the region of the Valley of Toluca, especially in Tenancingo, fruit-based alcoholic liquors are important products. To make them, the fruit is placed in refined alcohol for a period of time, then reduced into sugar syrup. Chokecherries, guavas, limes, *nanches,* apples, oranges, pears, crab apples, and blackberries are used in the preparation of the liquors. Toluca is also famous for its local candies made with fruit, such as *ates,* candied fruits, and jellies.

Morelos

Due to its temperate climate, the state of Morelos produces a large variety of tropical fruits, such as mangoes, figs, bananas, avocados, and guavas. It is also an important producer of sugar, rice, and tomatoes. Specialties of the region include the semidried beef called *cecina* from Yecapixtla, Morelos, which is sold in long strips, ready for broiling. Green mole made with squash seeds and served with chicken, pork, or beef is a favorite on local restaurant menus, as is beef in a green chile pepper sauce and Cuernavaca's own style of meatballs.

The inheritance left by the Indian diet is reflected in the consumption of many insects and insect eggs in several towns in the state, such as Cuautla, Amilcingo, and Jumiltepec. *Jumiles* are sold live in the markets stands in Cuautla and are used as a condiment with certain dishes. The usual method of preparation is by toasting them on a griddle, then grinding them with chile pepper and adding them to rice soup. They are also eaten live in tacos, without cooking, and served with a highly seasoned chile sauce. *Acociles, chapulines* (grasshoppers), and ants' eggs, called *escamoles,* are prepared in a similar fashion. Insects have been a nutritious complement to the diet since pre-Hispanic times, as they provide good sources of protein.

Puebla

The city of Puebla was one of the first cities to be founded by the Spanish conquistadores after the conquest of Mexico. The city soon became a crossroads for immigrants, armies, and merchants who traveled between the port of Veracruz and Mexico City. It was established in a fertile area of the country, where wheat and other agricultural products adapted well to the local conditions. Puebla is often called the gastronomic capital of the region and the birthplace of Mexican cooking. After the introduction of Christianity, Puebla soon became an important religious center, with many convents and monasteries within and around the city limits. These religious centers became famous for the fine cuisine developed in convent kitchens, where some of Mexico's most famous recipes were invented. *Mole poblano, chiles en nogada, rompope,* and a wide variety of sweets have made Puebla a renowned gastronomical center that is still considered the best of Mexican cuisine.

When a plant, food product, or even culinary dish attains an important place in the culture of a country, people often invent stories or myths around its origin or its introduction into the country. These stories are often associated with an historical or mythical figure, to give them additional credibility. In Mexico, *mole poblano* is a good example of this tradition. A series of legends have grown up surrounding its origin that have been repeated so often that they are almost accepted as truth. According to one version, the dish was invented in the Santa Rosa Convent by a Dominican nun named Sor Andrea de la Asunción when she was preparing a banquet to honor Viceroy Tomás Antonio de la Cerda y Aragón on one of his visits to Puebla in 1680. Known for her culinary inventiveness, the nun came up with an intricate blend of spices, chocolate, and turkey. The legend goes into great detail about how a gust of wind blew the right amount of spices into the cooking pots and allowed her to produce this delectable dish. This is a clever and charming story, but it is only that—a fanciful story, not based upon facts. *Mole poblano* had its origin in pre-

Tile kitchen in the Santa Rosa de Lima Convent, Puebla. From *La cocina mexicana a travès de los siglos*, Vol. IV, *La Nueva España*. Courtesy of Secretaría de Cultura/Puebla.

Hispanic Mexico, when it was called *molli* and was made with turkey and served on festive occasions. The arrival of the Europeans brought many new spices and ingredients that have been incorporated into the dish, modifying its flavor. Today, half of its ingredients are of European origin, while the other half are native to Mexico. It is a good example of the culinary syncretism that the two food traditions underwent in colonial Mexico. What is more, the dish is still undergoing a transformation, as sophisticated Mexico City and Puebla restaurants now serve moles made with blackberries, tamarind, plums, and many other flavors.

Another signature dish from Puebla is called *chiles en nogada*. Some authors consider this dish a national culinary icon, because the finished dish has the three colors of the Mexican flag, namely green, red, and white. This is one of Mexico's best-known festive dishes and consists of poblano peppers stuffed with ground or chopped meats, tomatoes, candied citrus fruits, chopped nuts, and a long list of additional ingredients. It is topped with a creamy sauce of fresh walnuts and cream and decorated with sprigs of green parsley and a sprinkling of red pomegranate seeds. This makes a colorful and showy dish that is traditionally prepared in August or September, when poblano peppers are at their seasonal peak and walnuts and pomegranates can be found on the market. It is associated with Mexico's Independence Day festivities on September 15 and 16.

The legend spun about the origin of *chiles en nogada* also attributes it to another nun from a convent in Puebla, who was asked to prepare the banquet in honor of Mexico's emperor, Agustín Iturbide, who was passing through the city of Puebla during the 1820s. This is also an amusing tale, with no factual basis. Walnut sauces were not a local invention; rather, they were used to embellish cooked vegetables during the Italian Renaissance. Many dishes from the period passed into the Spanish cooking tradition after appearing in Diego Granados's well-known cookbook published in 1599. The sauce probably arrived in Mexico through the Viceregal Palace kitchen as a dish of Spanish tradition. *Chiles en nogada* is considered one of Mexico's examples of haute cuisine. Today there are so many versions of this dish that it would be impossible to know which was the original or under what circumstances it was created.

Another dish often associated with Puebla cooking is chalupas, which are similar to *sopes* but are usually flat and topped with a red or green sauce and shredded chicken. *Tinga* is a popular dish in Puebla, made with shredded pork, chicken, or beef; pulque; chipotle chile peppers; and tomatillos. *Tinga* can also be served as a filling for French-roll sandwiches called *tortas*, or for topping tostadas and garnished with shredded lettuce and avocado slices.

The delicate fricassee called *pipián*, made with ground pumpkin seeds and fresh green or dried red chiles, has been made in Mexico since pre-Hispanic times. The convent nuns of Puebla improved the dish by adding European herbs and spices and used it as a sauce to serve with chicken or pork. It has become a common dish throughout Mexico under the name of *mole verde*. Other varieties of mole from the region are *mole de olla*, which is a more liquid type of mole, more like a soup than a sauce. It is said to have its roots in the Spanish one-dish meal called *puchero* and contains beef as well as a variety of vegetables, such as corn, zucchini, green beans, tomatoes, onions, and vegetable pears. It is a filling and comforting dish. Still another mole is known as *mole de cadera* and is made with goat meat and bones prepared in the autumn, after the goats are driven northward from southern Puebla and slaughtered in the city of Tehuacán, Puebla.

Tlaxcala

The state of Tlaxcala is located to the north of Puebla, and they share many similarities in their food traditions. The name, *Tlaxcala*, can be translated literally from the Náhuatl language as "the land of corn." They were one of the few Nahua tribes unconquered by the hated Aztecs, who engaged in "flower wars" with them to obtain sacrificial victims. Anyone struck by a flower was obliged to surrender to the enemy. After initially resisting the Spaniards, the Tlaxcaltecans soon formed an alliance with them against the Aztecs and were essential to the Spanish in their conquest of Mexico. Many Tlaxcaltecans were also instrumental in settling northern Mexico as they were sent as settlers to the area, and consequently took many Tlaxcalan food traditions to the area of Saltillo.

Tlaxcala is known for its moles and the cultivation of the century plant, which has several uses in food preparation. Chile-seasoned mutton, chicken, or fish called *barbacoa en mixiote* is wrapped in the transparent skin of the leaves of the maguey plant and then steam-roasted in stone-lined barbecue pits covered with maguey leaves. Another important product made from the sap of the century plant is pulque. This was one of the region's most lucrative products during the colonial period. Haciendas dedicated to the cultivation of maguey were important up until the second half of the twentieth century. Beer has taken the place of this popular drink; however, it is still drunk in the countryside, where it is also used as an ingredient in Mexican cooking. Another product of the maguey plant is the worms that the plant produces during the rainy season. *Gusanos de maguey* may be fried and served with a spicy sauce in taco shells. Black ant eggs called *escamoles* are also highly prized and highly priced delicacies for filling tacos.

Hidalgo

Hidalgo's principal claim to culinary fame comes from the huge tamale called *zacahuil*, as made in the Huasteca hidalguense. The Huastec area, which includes a strip of land from Hidalgo and Puebla, is humid and temperate and has fertile soil. Indigenous groups of Nahuas, Tepehuans, Totonacs, Huastecs, and Otomis are the dominant cultural groups in the area. They lived in isolation for many years, which enabled them to preserve their own culinary traditions, and they were less affected by Spanish cuisine. The *zacahuil* tamale is at least three feet long and can envelope a complete suckling pig, a turkey, or a chicken, after which it is well seasoned with dried chile peppers, garlic, and onions; wrapped in a soft dough of white corn; and wrapped in banana leaves and left to cook for several hours in an underground oven. Sometimes a variety of meats are used for making this famous dish, which may include vegetables as well.

Cactus plants are much appreciated in parts of this arid region. Cactus paddles known as *nopalitos* are a standard dish throughout the country. They are eaten as an ingredient in stews, salads, or soups, in a variety of recipes. Ant eggs, maguey worms, and other exotic insects are part of the traditional cuisine in Hidalgo.

Mexico City

Mexico City is undoubtedly the gastronomic capital of the country. In recent years it has become a very cosmopolitan city, where fine restaurants representing food traditions from all corners of the world can be found.

Today, Mexican food has become fashionable not only internationally but in Mexico City as well. This can be measured by the great number of good restaurants specializing in Mexican food that have opened their doors in recent years. This interest in fine Mexican food is relatively recent in restaurant circles and can be traced to some 25 years ago. Before this time, French, Italian, or Chinese food was preferred in restaurants or for entertaining in upper-class homes in Mexico City. This began to change in 1981, when several distinguished women chefs and women with a special interest in Mexican food got together to form the Mexican Culinary Circle, known as the Circulo Mexicano de Arte Culinario. The main objective of the group was the promotion and preservation of traditional Mexican food, including the regional dishes of Mexico. They set about developing and modifying many dishes from family recipes to make them more compatible with contemporary palates, sharing recipes of traditional dishes, and developing new interpretations of old recipes. This sparked an interest in local food.

Well-known dishes traditional to Mexico City cuisine include a hearty soup called *caldo Tlalpeño*. Tlalpan, now a suburb of Mexico City, was once a town outside the city, with beautiful colonial haciendas.

Tlalpeño-Style Soup (*Caldo Tlalpño*)
- 1-1/2 quarts chicken broth
- 1 whole chicken breast, without skin
- 1 tablespoon cooking oil
- 1/2 onion, chopped
- 1 large carrot, peeled and diced
- 1 zucchini, sliced

- 1 avocado, peeled and sliced
- 2 cloves garlic, chopped
- 1 *chile chipotle en adobo*, chopped
- 1 fresh sprig of epazote
- 1/2 teaspoon salt
- 1/2 teaspoon black pepper
- 1 can chickpeas, drained and rinsed

Cook chicken in broth until well cooked. Remove chicken and let cool, then shred the meat and set it aside. Do not discard the chicken broth. Heat the oil in a large soup pot over medium heat. Add onion and carrot and sauté about five minutes. Add garlic and sauté for a few more minutes. Pour in the broth and add the zucchini, chile, epazote, salt, and pepper. Bring to a simmer and let cook 20 minutes, uncovered. Add chickpeas and simmer another 10 minutes. Add shredded chicken and heat well. Serve the soup decorated with avocado slices and lime wedges. Serves 6 people.

Tortilla soup is another favorite dish that originated in the capital. It is perhaps Mexico's most famous soup, and it combines the traditional flavors of the country, such as chile peppers, tomatoes, avocados, tortillas, and epazote for flavoring. Black-bean soup flavored with epazote is comfort food for many Mexicans and often appears on the menus of Mexico City *fondas* and restaurants. The Aztec casserole (*budín Azteca*), made with layers of tortillas, vegetables, chicken, sauce, and cheese, is an earthy dish and can be quite heavy when eaten in the evening.

Another earthy dish popular on the everyday menu is called *ropa vieja*, which translates as the unlikely name of "old clothes." It is a simple dish of shredded beef with vegetables and can be used as a taco filling or as a salad, when it is prepared with a vinaigrette dressing. Corn-fungus crepes with poblano sauce are said to have been invented in Mexico City and constitute a good example of Mexico's haute cuisine. This is a festive dish mainly reserved for special occasions. Many regional dishes are equally at home on Mexico City menus.

Most aspects of life are affected by fashion, which is known to be very short-lived. It can be said that Mexican food is now in fashion both locally and internationally. It is in Mexico City where new trends in cooking are developed and introduced from other countries and diffused to restaurants in other parts of Mexico. The interest in Mexican food is apparent in many ways. Several Mexico City universities have recently began offering courses in the history of Mexican food. New cooking schools attract many students who plan to make a formal career as a chef in the food industry. An organization called La Cofradía de la Mayora Mexicana is dedicated to the training and assistance of the most important woman chef in a Mexican restaurant, called *la mayora*. Women who fill this position are the called the souls of Mexican restaurant kitchens. Every year, the Cofradía gives special recognition to an outstanding woman chef.

THE ISTHMUS OF TEHUANTEPEC

The states of Oaxaca, Tabasco, and southern Veracruz make up the region known as the Isthmus of Tehuantepec. This is a narrow strip of land, only 125 miles across, from the Gulf of Mexico to the Pacific coast. It includes areas of great fertility due to almost constant moisture in some states, as well as dry and desolate areas in parts of others.

Oaxaca is one of the most Indian states of Mexico; some 31 different ethnic groups live in the state. Zapotecs and Mixtecs inhabit the Valley of Oaxaca, and their food customs have influenced the local cuisine. Oaxaca is the "land of the seven moles." Black mole, *mole negro oaxaqueño*, is probably the most famous dish; nonetheless, other moles are equally popular. Yellow mole, simply called *amarillo*, is really more like a stew, because it contains pork meat, a diversity of vegetables, and small *masa* dumplings. It was originally made with the yellow chile, *chilcoztli*, which gave it a deep yellow color. Because the *chilcoztli* chile pepper is hard to find outside Oaxaca, ancho and *guajillo* chiles can be substituted, which gives the dish a more reddish tone. Pork, chicken, or beef can be used in preparing this mole. Red mole does not include chocolate, a typical ingredient of most moles. Little red mole, called *coloradito*, contains boiled potatoes, to be added at the last moment. There is also a green mole, which goes by the name of *mole verde*, made with fresh chiles and green tomatoes. *Chichilo* is a dark mole made with *chilhuacle* peppers, which give it its characteristic dark-brown color. The seventh mole also goes by the name of *mancha manteles*, or "tablecloth stainer." This is essentially a red mole with chicken, pork, and fruit.

The mainstay of the Isthmus diet is black turtle beans flavored with avocado leaves. Oaxaca is also known for its large tortillas, called *tlayudas*. These are thick tortillas left on the griddle until crisp, so they will last for several days without spoiling. They are usually prepared by spreading the residue of rendered pork lard on the tortilla, after which a *pasilla* chile sauce is added and the tortilla is topped with fresh Oaxaca cheese, onion rings, and chopped parsley. This dish is filling enough to be considered the main course at lunch.

Oaxaca produces a diversity of cheeses in many shapes and sizes. The most famous goes by the name of Oaxaca cheese. It is soft, white, and stringy and is sold in the market rolled into balls, in braided strips, or shaped into very small balls that can be added individually to a soup or stew at the last minute. A common way of cooking with this cheese is to place it on the griddle until it begins to melt and then add it to a green sauce made of tomatillos and green chile peppers. Prepared in this way, it is called *quesillo asado en salsa verde.*

Tamales are another mainstay in the Oaxacan diet; they have many shapes, forms, and fillings. They are eaten as a festive food and as an everyday dish for breakfast or supper. Tamales made with *mole negro* and pork or turkey wrapped in softened banana leaves are the most well known. Others are made with yellow or red mole, pork *chicharrón* (fried pork cracklings), or beans with avocado leaves or a licorice-flavored herb called *hoja santa.* Sweet tamales containing raisins and tinted a delicate pink are also popular, especially with children.

Oaxaca's drink of choice is *mezcal,* a distilled alcoholic drink similar to tequila and also made from the agave plant. It is a favorite drink for accompanying before-meal snacks such as fried peanuts with garlic and *chile piquín;* pieces of stringy Oaxaca cheese; green mangoes or plums steeped in *chile pasilla* vinegar; tostadas made with marinated vegetables in a sauce of chile, garlic, oregano, and other spices; tiny tacos filled with *chicharrón;* and many other popular snacks.

Like most regions of Mexico, Oaxaca produces an astonishing number of sweets, said to be an inheritance left by the nuns of the colonial convents. This is also the home of the dessert called *antes,* which is made only in Oaxaca. These have a base of cake bread soaked in a syrup with a variety of paste fillings, which may be made of fruits or nuts.

Oaxacan food is distinct in its use of chile peppers. Some of the peppers, such as *chilcoztli* or *chilhuacle,* are difficult to find outside Oaxaca. Oaxaca produces a light green chile called *chile de agua* that is similar to the California Anaheim chile pepper. Pepper nomenclature can be confusing: for example, the jalapeño chile goes by the name of *chile pasilla* in Oaxaca, which has no resemblance to the *chile pasilla* of central Mexico. The fiery red *chile costeño* is also used to enhance the flavor of local dishes.

TABASCO

Tabascan cuisine is said to be varied and very good; however, it is not well known outside the state itself. The warm, humid climate makes it an ideal place for producing rice, bananas, coffee, cacao, and tropical fruits such as mangoes and mameyes. Bananas are one of the most important revenue-producing products of the state.

Fish are an important part of the Tabascan diet. One of the state's most famous fish dishes is made with a fish called *pejelagarto*, which looks like a small crocodile because of the shape of its mouth and the tough scales on its skin. The fish is usually roasted and served with green sauce, served in a stew, or grilled on a spit and served as a snack with lime juice and pickled chile peppers. The state also has an important beef industry. Both fish and beef are important elements in the local diet.

Herbs commonly used in Tabascan cooking are *achiote*, made into a paste from the hard, red seeds of the annatto tree. This provides a deep yellow-orange color to foods and a distinct flavor. Local herbs or leaves, such as *chaya*, *chipilín*, and *momo*, are used to wrap fish and flavor casseroles. If these herbs are not available, watercress or chopped spinach leaves can be substituted.

Desserts include egg bread served with a chocolate sauce and cake breads called *marquesotes*. These can be served with a sprinkling of powdered sugar or as a more elaborate dessert served with a wine or fruit syrup. These go by the name of *paneletas* in Tabasco. Another popular dessert made with a local ingredient is bananas flambé with rum, called *plátanos flameados con ron*. This can also be made with plantains, ignited with rum, and served with vanilla ice cream.

Like most Mexican regional food, the Tabascan diet is a combination of indigenous and Spanish-style food. The most important Indian group in the area is the Chontal ethnic group, whose members live in the center of the state and are mostly farmers. Their contribution to the diet is a large variety of tamales, such as *chipilín* tamales wrapped in banana leaves; tamales filled with pork and *achiote* paste; black beans with *hoja santa* (a large, licorice-flavored leaf); and, finally, those made with *shish*, the residue of rendered pork fat. Food of Spanish influence is consumed by the mestizo population, such as a stew called *estofado*, made with a variety of meats and condiments.

VERACRUZ

The food from Veracruz is strongly influenced by Caribbean, African, and Spanish cuisines. The port of Veracruz was the most important entrance into Mexico for over 400 years; many European and Caribbean food products passed through this port of call en route to central Mexico.

Spanish conquistadores; African slaves; English, Dutch, and French pirates; and American marines were active in the port during different periods of history.

Seafood can be eaten at any time of day at one of the seafood stands located on the beach, near the port. Fresh shrimp waiting to be peeled, shredded crab prepared as *salpicón de jaiba*, and crab legs are popular appetizers served before lunch at restaurants in Alvarado and Boca del Río, fishing towns south of the city of Veracruz, which are popular for Sunday outings. People not only go to enjoy the fresh seafood but also to listen to the vivacious musicians called *huapangeros*, who provide fast music and are also very clever at inventing on-the-spot verses to entertain their clients. These leisure Sunday lunches are often begun with a light alcoholic drink called a *torito*. This is a thick, slightly sweet drink made with ground peanuts. A type of local paella called *arroz a la tumbada* is a typical dish, made with rice and seafood. Another popular dish is a whole fish wrapped in the large leaves of an anise-flavored herb, which is called *hierba santa*. Octopus in a black sauce is usually served with white rice and fried bananas. The most famous fish dish in Veracruz is called *pescado a la veracruzana*, a delicious dish that successfully combines Mexican and Spanish ingredients.

Veracruz-Style Fish (*Pescado a la Veracruzana*)
- 6 fillets of sea bass
- lemon juice
- olive oil
- 2 lbs. tomatoes, peeled and chopped
- 1/2 cup chopped onion
- 1 green bell pepper, cut into strips
- 1 teaspoon salt
- 1/2 teaspoon black pepper
- 4 cloves of garlic, chopped
- 2 bay leaves
- 1 teaspoon dried oregano
- 1/4 cup capers
- 1/2 cup chopped green olives
- canned jalapeño chiles for garnish

Wash the fish and marinate it in salt, pepper, and lemon juice. Roll in flour and sauté in hot oil until it is lightly browned. Remove it from the skillet. In another skillet, heat 1 tablespoon oil and sauté onion and garlic for a few minutes. Add the tomatoes and let the mixture boil. Add the bell pepper strips and cook, stirring, for a few minutes more. Correct the seasoning, add bay leaves and oregano, and let it simmer over low heat for 10 minutes. Just before serving, add the capers, olives, and fish fillets and place over low heat until just heated through. Garnish each fillet with a jalapeño chile on top of each serving. The dish can be served with fried plantains and dishes of black beans and rice, called *moros y cristianos*.

Veracruzanos admit to being addicted to coffee. This is the favorite drink in restaurants and coffee shops as well. In port coffee shops, a light tapping of a metal spoon on a coffee glass is all that is needed to signal a waiter that a refill is requested by a customer.

THE MAYA AREA

The Maya culture was one of the great civilizations of Mesoamerica. At the time of the European conquest, Maya-speakers occupied an area in southern Mexico, the Yucatán peninsula, Belize, Guatemala, and parts of Honduras and El Salvador. The basis of the Maya diet was corn, beans, squash, and chile peppers. Corn was the most important food in the Maya diet. The sacred book of the Maya, the *Popul Vuh,* relates that the gods created people out of corn dough and that only then were true human beings created.

In Chiapas, Mexico's southernmost state, the influence of the Maya culture can still be noted in the great diversity of tamales that form part of the Chiapanecan diet. Some tamales are elongated and stuffed with chicken and a wonderful combination of cinnamon and saffron; others are round like a ball and stuffed with pork and chile sauce; still others are stuffed with chicken, olives, and chopped hard-boiled eggs and steamed in pliable banana leaves. Another specialty in Chiapas is tamales stuffed with fresh flower petals, called *tamales de puchulu.* Dried shrimp, beans, and pumpkin seeds are the filling for the *tamal juacane,* which is then wrapped in large leaves of *hoja santa,* a licorice-tasting herb.

A bread soup popular in Highland Chiapas is known simply as *sopa de pan.* It is assembled with layers of French-style bread, cooked onions, tomatoes, plantains, zucchini squash, green beans, and boiled potatoes, with a topping of almonds and raisins. Chicken broth is poured over the dish and it is baked for 30 minutes. It is called a soup but is generally served as a main course, because it is very filling.

Chiapas chiles are generally very hot. Because the indigenous diet is based on tortillas and beans, they need the flavor and pungency of peppers to give added interest to their diet. The small, hot chile called *chile de siete caldos* is said to be hot enough to season seven pots of stew. The tiny, wild *chile piquín* goes by the name of *max* or *mashito*. It is also very, very hot.

The Yucatán Peninsula

The food of the Yucatán peninsula, which includes the Mexican states of Yucatán, Campeche, and Quintana Roo have a similar cooking tradition because the three states make use of the same ingredients. The most common seasoning in the area is made from *achiote* paste, from the seeds of the *Bixa orellana* plant. Small rectangular blocks of this paste are sold in all the local markets. The paste is diluted with bitter orange juice made from Seville oranges and used to marinate chicken, fish, or pork, then prepared as a barbecue called *pibil*. The meat is marinated for some time, then wrapped in banana leaves and slowly roasted in a stone-lined pit prepared as an underground oven called a *pib*. This type of barbecue has been compared with the Hawaiian luau. Yucatán's most famous dish is *cochinita pibil*, or barbecued pig served with pickled red onions.

Yucatán cooking is also famous for its *masa*-based snacks, or *antojitos*. *Panuchos* are small tortillas filled with black beans, and topped with shredded fowl, and sauce. In Campeche, *panuchos* are made with shark meat (*cazón*). *Papadzules* are small tacos covered with a sauce of ground pumpkin seeds, then a tomato sauce, and finally chopped hard-boiled eggs and a few drops of pumpkinseed oil.

The most well-known soup in the Yucatán diet is a lime and chicken soup called *sopa de lima*. The soup is served with fried tortilla strips, avocado slices, and additional limes to give more flavor to the soup.

Chile peppers from the Yucatán peninsula include the yellow or orange bonnet-shaped habanero chile. It is the hottest of all Mexican peppers and is usually prepared in a sauce to accompany the dish rather than forming part of the ingredients of the dish itself. There is no Maya-language nomenclature for this pepper. It is a latecomer to the Yucatecan diet and was probably not part of the food tradition before the nineteenth century, when it arrived from the Caribbean. An elongated pale yellow pepper carries the Maya name of *x-cat-ik*, so we can assume that it was part of the

Maya diet in ancient times. Another usual pepper used in Yucatecan cooking is called *chile dulce*, which looks somewhat like a badly formed bell pepper. It is a sweet pepper and used for Spanish- or Lebanese-style dishes, which are important influences on Yucatecan cuisine.

Yucatán also has unique tamales that are served on festive occasions. A tamale called *el tamal de la novia* is a typical wedding dish. A leaf reminiscent of Swiss chard called *chaya* is often chopped in tamales or used to wrap them and gives them a special flavor.

6

Eating Out

Good food and good cooking have become fashionable in Mexico in recent years. The number of eating places, from simple *taquerías* that offer unpretentious fare to elaborate, upscale restaurants where clients gather both to eat fine food and to see and be seen, have increased tenfold since the early 1980s. Urban Mexico has become a delight for gourmets. In the 1970s, restaurants served mostly nondescript international food to fill the demands of the tourist industry; although fine restaurants existed, they were few in number. Today, eating places are filled with the local population, who have become demanding customers, knowledgeable about food and possessing refined palates.

The number of food stalls, *taquerías*, *torterías*, *fondas*, *loncherías*, cafés, and elegant restaurants catering to different social and economic levels is truly prodigious. People living in urban areas are increasingly eating outside the home, because the increase of women in the labor force gives them less time and energy to spend in the kitchen. Daily food preparation is less complex than it used to be, but even so, it is easier and sometimes even less expensive to eat out. In terms of nutrition, it is preferable to prepare home-cooked meals, but because this is not always feasible, people have learned to make use of other options to fill their nutritional needs. Street foods play an important role in providing food for a large percentage of the Mexican population.

STREET FOOD

Mexico has a long tradition in selling street food. This has been described as food and drinks sold on public streets, ready for consumption, prepared and offered by nonpermanent sellers in the city streets.[1] The proliferation of food stands is not only a reflection of busy schedules or the lack of time for leisurely eating—although these two factors are important in explaining the abundance of street-food establishments—but is also the continuation of a long-established tradition in eating habits. Long before the arrival of the Spaniards in sixteenth century, Aztec vendors set up food stalls in the markets to serve the general public, who came to purchase the many stews, fish, insects, sauces, and tortillas prepared daily for sale there.[2] This custom continued throughout the colonial and independent periods of Mexican history and continues on an even larger scale today.

There are many reasons for the increase in street-food establishments; among them is the deterioration of the economic situation in rural Mexico, resulting in a lack of available jobs in those areas, which contributes to the migration of able-bodied workers to the cities. The expansion of Mexico City forces workers and students to travel long distances from their homes to their places of work or universities, making it almost impossible for them to return home for their midday meal. Street food is also a reflection of unemployment and underemployment of people who are not qualified for more complex jobs.

The majority of the Mexican working class cannot afford to eat in a restaurant or even a *fonda*, and there are many options in street stands available for those who need to find a quick, inexpensive meal. Street food is the most convenient choice for many, in terms of both location and price. Some people take a hard-roll sandwich (*torta*) from home, while others choose to order a more substantial meal from a street vendor.

Temporary food stands can be found on city corners; outside bus or subway stations; near markets; in public parks; near factories, office buildings, or hospitals; or wherever there are plenty of people looking for a good, quick lunch. Some vendors serve food from the trunks of their cars or from inside vans. When they have finished selling all the food, they merely drive away with their empty pots and pans and return the following morning with a fresh supply of prepared food. Other vendors are truly itinerant and carry a basket of tacos or *tortas* to sell on a staked-out street corner.

Some stands are semipermanent, in which case they may have access to electricity and running water. A portable gas tank may be connected to the grill and used to cook or heat the food, or they may use a round metal griddle placed over a charcoal brazier, which gives good, even heat for long periods of time. Most street stands do not have these conveniences and offer few amenities such as a washbowl or paper towels to wash and dry the hands. Plastic plates, forks, and spoons are generally provided, as well as paper napkins. If the food being served is tacos, they may be served on large squares of butcher paper that absorb the dripping sauce and hot oil and can be tossed into the garbage pail after eating. Tacos are eaten by holding them between the thumb and fingers, so no cutlery is needed. Some stands offer a complete meal consisting of soup served in a plastic or Styrofoam cup, a meat stew, Mexican red rice, beans, and tortillas, served on a small, rectangular Styrofoam tray. A soft drink, to be drunk straight out of the bottle, and extra hot sauce complete the meal. This type of food is nutritious, filling, inexpensive, and probably cheaper than what a housewife could prepare at home. It is also within the Mexican food tradition, which many customers look for when choosing a place to eat.

There are many types of food offered by street stands; the most common ones provide one or more foods from the following groups of foods:

1. Peeled and sliced fruit, which may be eaten with the fingers, is offered by fresh-fruit stands. Peeled and carved mangoes impaled on a wooden stick are popular choices, as are slices of apples, oranges, pineapple, watermelon, or pears. *Jícamas*, carrots, and cucumbers are also favorite selections. Ground chile pepper, lemon wedges, and salt are usually offered to accentuate the fruit's flavor. Fruit stands offer nutritious food that is a good source of vitamins, minerals, and fiber.

2. Shaved ice (*raspados*) made from syrups of natural fruits are popular; however, care must be taken to make sure the ice is made with clean water. Ice-cream bars and popsicles sold from small refrigerated carts are a safer purchase and have almost taken over the market.

3. Hot snacks such as quesadillas and *sopes* are good choices since they are made on the spot, served hot, and have less chance of being contaminated. They are traditional high-energy foods, made of a wide variety of choices. Quesadillas may be filled with cheese, potatoes with sausage, squash flowers, *huitlacoche*, chicken in a tomato sauce, or shredded beef.

4. Tacos, especially those called "perspiring tacos" (*tacos sudados*) are a popular traditional food, served from a basket; however, if they are kept at room temperature for too long, they may spoil and become a source of intestinal infections.

5. Stews are traditional dishes made with meat and served with tortillas for making tacos. The meat mixture should be kept hot to prevent spoilage.

6. Tamales and *atole* are considered excellent choices, as tamales can be kept warm in a metal tamale steamer, while *atole* maintains its warm temperature if kept in a thermal jug.

7. Fresh corn on the cob (*elotes*) is a favorite street food and can be found in the
   evenings on many street corners, especially near movie theaters. Tender ears
   of corn are pulled out of a pot of hot water and served covered with grated
   cheese, chile powder, mayonnaise, or simply with a generous sprinkling of
   salt.

These fried-food stands were traditionally set up in urban squares, in
parks, or near churches in the evenings. They can now be found throughout the city at all hours of the day. Occasional hot-dog stands appear on
the scene, but they appear to have less of a public than traditional Mexican snacks or light foods.

Setting up a street-food stand is a rather simple process. Little capital or
experience in the management of food is required. Temporary stands do
not bother getting a license or permit to sell food, so technically they are
illegal businesses. A more serious problem may be finding a good location
on a busy street corner that has not been already taken by a previous vendor. Boundaries must be respected by newcomers to the area. More
women than men are involved in serving street foods. Often it is a single
mother who involves her entire family in the business. Family members
may participate in the purchasing, preparation, and selling of the food.
Wholesale markets are used to purchase basic products in large quantities
at lower prices. The average age of vendors fluctuates between 20 and 50
years old.[3] The level of education of people in this profession is low; many
are illiterate and would have difficulty finding employment in other areas.
A street-stand owner makes approximately double the minimum wage
and thus has a higher income than a factory worker, and works between 5
and 12 hours a day.[4] The average client of a street-food stand is a worker
who has a similar profile as the food sellers, with a low level of education
and little regard for cleanliness in the handling of food.

On the positive side, food stands offer quick, nutritious, and sometimes
very good food at minimal prices and at convenient locations. On the
negative side, the food served may be contaminated by dust, lead, or car
fumes from passing traffic. Uncovered pots of food are an attraction for
flies and other insects. Cleanliness is not usually the priority of the food
vendors, especially if they do not have water available. In those stands
where there is only one attendant, he or she may handle the money when
charging a customer and serve the food as well, without washing his or her
hands.

People who patronize street-food stands were once disparagingly called
los agachados, or "those who eat squatting on the ground," because there
were no stools or chairs for them to sit on. This is now a common way of

eating for millions of people, and there is no longer a social stigma attached to eating at a street stand.

Street food is a necessity in the everyday life of modern cities. City authorities realize the important role played by street-food stands in providing quick and nutritious meals for the public and, even though many stands operate without a license or permit, they choose not to close them down. They do not pay city taxes, and they contribute to the lack of cleanliness of the city streets and may even be a source of bacterial infections. Occasionally the media will warn the public of the danger of eating at food stands or provide recommendations on what to look for in choosing an appropriate stand.[5] There are too many in the city, and they are too mobile for the Health Department to be able to exercise much control over them.

Permanently established food vendors, called *cocinas económicas*, operate from fixed installations and offer a full menu of soups, rices, pastas, stews, beans, and even desserts for a modest price. They must, however, follow city regulations and health requirements and pay taxes, which puts them at a disadvantage with regard to street-food stands. They are popular with working housewives, who must divide their time between the workplace and home.

FONDAS

Another option for eating away from home can be found in small eateries called *fondas*. These are usually small restaurants with simple, unpretentious decoration that cater to office workers and set up their establishments near office buildings or wherever there are large groups of employees as potential customers. Many offer fixed menus, which are posted at the entrance, showing the food for the day. They usually offer chicken broth or another liquid soup, which may be a cream-of-vegetable soup. The second course will be a choice of Mexican rice or some sort of pasta with tomato sauce, paradoxically called a "dry soup," or *sopa seca*. The main dish may be tacos, enchiladas, stuffed vegetables, or even a meat dish in a sauce. The latter choice would raise the price of the meal. Most *fondas* offer dessert, which is likely to be a custard known as flan, rice pudding, gelatin, or sliced bananas topped with cream and served with coffee. Any drinks, including bottled water, carry an additional charge. The fixed menus have set prices and can be quite economical if one considers the amount of food received. *Fonda* owners consider street-food stands unfair competition as they do not have to pay rent, city taxes, or for the public services they use, and can offer food at much lower prices. Food served in *fondas* is under stricter controls on the part of health authorities and is generally more hygienic than food sold on the street.

Dry Vermicelli Soup (*Sopa Seca de Fideos al Chipotle*)

- 3 or 4 canned *chipotle chiles en adobo*
- 4 garlic cloves, unpeeled
- 5 large tomatoes
- 1/2 cup vegetable oil
- one 10-ounce package vermicelli noodles, in nest shapes
- 1 cup beef broth
- 1 teaspoon dried oregano, preferably Mexican
- 1 teaspoon salt
- 2 medium zucchini, cut into 1/4-inch cubes
- 1/2 cup thick cream
- 2/3 cup finely grated Mexican *añejo* cheese or Parmesan
- chopped coriander, for garnish

Roast the unpeeled garlic on the griddle for about 15 minutes. Cool, then peel. Roast half of the tomatoes on the griddle until black and charred. Cool, then peel.

In a food processor or blender, process the tomatoes, canned chiles, and garlic to a purée. Heat 1 tablespoon oil in a Mexican clay pot over medium-high heat. Add the purée and stir for 5 minutes until it thickens. Set it aside. Brown the vermicelli a few nests at a time in hot oil in skillet. Add vermicelli and fry until quite browned. Remove with slotted spoon, draining as much oil as possible back into the skillet. Drain on paper towels. Continue until all vermicelli nests have been browned.

Add the broth, oregano, and pepper to the tomato sauce. Chop the remaining pound of tomatoes. Add them to the sauce and simmer briskly for about 5 minutes. Taste and season with salt. Add the vermicelli nests, pulling them apart when they are soft enough. Add the zucchini and simmer until noodles are tender but firm, about 2 minutes.

Add cream, raise heat, and boil quickly for a few minutes. Stir in half the grated cheese, serve in warm soup bowls, and add remaining cheese on top with coriander for a garnish.

Many *fondas* specialize in regional foods, such as Oaxaca, Yucatán, Puebla, or Veracruz dishes. These are informal restaurants; some of them make use of patios or gardens to serve the public and are in reality too large to be called *fondas*. There are many medium-sized restaurants that specialize in very good Mexican food and have been in business for decades. In a classification of restaurants, they would fall somewhere in between *fondas* and restaurants.

Eateries that specialize in vegetarian menus usually fall into the category of *fondas*. Small sidewalk cafés may specialize in serving snacks, sandwiches, or pastries and soft drinks, as well as more substantial meals. Some cafés called *churrerías* specialize in Spanish-style deep-fried pastries called churros, which children and teenagers, who don't have to worry about the extra calories, like to frequent.

Ice-cream shops often include sidewalk tables and chairs for the comfort of their customers, and it is common to see entire families out for Sunday ice cream. Mexico has a long tradition of making ice creams and sherbets from tropical fruits, some of them very exotic and refreshing. Many neighborhoods have a favorite ice cream shop that local residents patronize, and long lines form around these popular outlets.

Coffee houses have become popular in recent years. Starbucks has recently made incursions in upscale neighborhoods, and they become popular meeting places for the younger crowd, who consider it very hip to meet and order a chai latte at Starbucks. Sandwiches, salads, ice cream, cookies, and other pastries are popular items on the menu.

Fondas that Specialize in Specific Meals

Breakfasts have become popular meals in Mexico, both for the businessman or lawyer who uses this time and occasion to close a deal in an informal atmosphere and for Mexican women who do not work and can spend the entire morning over coffee and gossip at the latest "in" café or restaurant.

Some *fondas* cater to the breakfast crowd and open their establishments as early as 5 or 5:30 in the morning and close at noon. The early morning hours are said to be for the benefit of those who have spent a night on the town and would like to eat some solid food before confronting family members at home. Hot, spicy food is said to make the body perspire and eliminate the effects of too much alcohol. More than likely, it is to benefit those who start an early workday and have no one to make their food at home at such an early hour. Many are neighborhood *fondas* that cater to the people in the local area.

An example of this type of eatery could be a *fonda* on the south side of Mexico City that has operated for nearly 50 years. It is located in a rustic

warehouse-type building with the only amenities offered being trouba-
dours who entertain the public with traditional guitar music and song.
Ten long, Formica-topped tables are used for seating clientele, who sit on
long benches and share the tables with fellow companions in a most unpretentious atmosphere. Plastic containers on the tables hold the necessary cutlery. Small bowls of hot sauce and plates of dried and fried *chiles de
árbol* decorate the tables along with small plates of chopped onion, lemon
wedges, and dried oregano leaves. There are no tablecloths or placemats.
The menu is different every day of the week. There is space for about 100
customers at a time. Service is informal, fast, and efficient. The long line
outside the building discourages one from lingering over coffee, nor is this
encouraged by the staff, who clearly want a quick turnover to serve as
many customers as possible. Huge *mole ollas* decorate the walls and are
used in the preparation of the food in the open kitchen. These, as well as
cooking vats, are placed over large braziers called *anafres* burning thick
blocks of charcoal. A typical breakfast menu may include tripe, pork
cracklings in green sauce, beans and scrambled eggs (presented in the
shape of a long tamale), pork in green chile sauce, long sausages called
longanizas and eggs, beef in *chile pasilla* sauce, tortillas, and a variety of
other dishes. Orange juice, soft drinks, or boiled coffee in a pot called *café
de olla*, sweetened with brown sugar, accompany the meal. Freshly fried
Spanish-style pastries called churros may finish the meal, or you may prefer to purchase delicate puff-paste breads called *campechanas*, sold from a
canasta at the exit of the restaurant. The food is delicious; inexpensive;
clean; and served in a friendly, informal atmosphere. This particular *fonda*
serves thousands of breakfasts each week and no doubt represents a good
business for the family owners.

Beef with Green Chile (*Carne con Chile Verde*)

- 2-1/4 pounds stewing beef, cut into 1/2-inch cubes
- 3 cloves garlic, peeled and finely chopped
- 2 teaspoons salt
- 2 cups water
- 3 tablespoons vegetable oil
- 1 onion, finely chopped
- 1-1/2 tablespoons flour
- 12 Anaheim chiles, charred and peeled, cut into squares
- 2 small tomatoes, broiled and chopped

Place meat cubes in a heavy pan, in two layers. Add the salt, garlic, and 1/2 cup water, then cover the pan and cook over a very low flame until the meat is almost tender, the liquid evaporated, and the fat rendering out, about 1 hour. Add more water, if necessary, to prevent the meat from sticking. Shake the pan and turn the meat over from time to time. Add enough oil to the fat in the pan to make 3 tablespoons. Turn the heat to medium, then add the onion and brown the meat lightly. Sprinkle the flour into the pan and let it brown lightly, stirring constantly. Add the chiles, tomatoes, and 1-1/2 cups water, then cover the pan and cook over low heat for 20 minutes. Adjust the seasoning and serve hot.

In provincial Mexico, small *fondas* called *cenadurías* open at 5 P.M. and stay open until midnight. These small restaurants cater to the evening crowd, who want a light supper. *Antojitos* are the favorites on the menu, although more substantial meals can also be ordered.

MARKET FOOD

Mexican markets are known to sell almost all of life's necessities, especially a plethora of fruits and vegetables, as well as prepared foods. The Coyoacán market, on the southern side of Mexico City, is famous for the quality of market food it serves. The soft voices of the food sellers perme-

Eating at market, Queretaro. © TRIP/J. Highet.

ate the entire market as they call out to each passerby, "¿Qué le damos, marchanta, qué va a llevar?" ("What can we sell you, lady, what are you going to buy?")

Somewhere in between the stalls of carefully constructed pyramids of fruits and vegetables and those that sell medicinal herbs that profess to cure nervous tension, headaches, and impotence; products to remove an enemy's curse; and rose-petal candles—which are a sure thing for recovering a lost love—there are food stands that open early for breakfast but really get into full swing around 10:30, when the *almuerzo* crowd arrives. The market is famous for its many stands, offering crisp tostadas layered with refried beans, shredded chicken, lettuce, avocado, onion, and tomato and topped off with sour cream, fresh cheese, and hot sauce. The protein, vitamins, and carbohydrates all in one dish make a balanced meal. Each stand offers as many as 20 different kinds of tostadas, ranging from pickled pigs feet (*pata*) to delicate seafood toppings.

Chicken Tostadas (*Tostadas de Pollo*)

- 12 corn tortillas
- 1-1/2 cups refried beans
- 3 cups shredded lettuce
- 1 whole chicken breast, cooked and shredded
- 1 onion, chopped
- 2 tomatoes, sliced
- 1 avocado, peeled and cut into strips
- 1 cup sour cream
- 3/4 cup crumbled feta cheese
- salsa

Heat 1/2 inch oil in skillet and fry tortillas until they are crisp and golden. Drain on paper towels. Heat refried beans and spread each tostada with beans and top with lettuce, chicken, 2 slices of onions, 2 slices of tomato, and a strip of avocado. Place a tablespoon of cream on top and sprinkle with cheese. Serve sauce separately.

Taquerías

Tacos are Mexico's favorite fast food. They can be eaten at any time of day and are sold in all types of eateries, both large and small. They can be nutritious when filled with stews, chopped meat or chicken, fish, or even shrimp and a good ladle of hot sauce. Some are called "nothing tacos"

Device used for making shepherd's tacos (*tacos al pastor*). From *La cocina mexicana a travès de los siglos*, Vol. VII, *El pan de cada día*. Courtesy of Gabriel Figueroa/Editorial Clío.

(*tacos de la nada*), as they are merely rolled up tortillas with a few grains of salt. Taco fillings go from the simple to the complex; the latter may include a dark mole sauce with pieces of turkey meat, barbecued lamb, or deep-fried pork (called *carnitas*). "Perspiring tacos" (*tacos sudados*) are commonly found during early morning hours at transportation stations and near schools, served from a basket by an enterprising woman in need of money to buy food for her family. This type of taco is said to have originated in the mining towns of Pachuca, Hidalgo, and Guanajuato and is called a "miner's taco" or *taco de itacate*, which means "taco on the go."

Small *taquerías* keep a close tab on the tacos customers order, one at a time, depending on how filling the tacos are and how hungry the customer is. At the end of the meal, the tally is agreed upon by both the client and vendor, probably based upon the number of tortillas eaten.

Deep-fried tacos are called "flutes," or *flautas*, because they resemble long, smooth flutes; they are fried until they acquire a deep golden tone and are crunchy. These are dipped in hot sauces with each bite, as they can't be opened up to add the sauce.

Another popular type of taco is called a shepherd's taco (*taco al pastor*), also known as "*taco oriental*," as it was inspired by the Turkish kebab. Thin layers of pork are marinated and layered together on a vertical spit that revolves in front of a fire that cooks the surface of the meat as it spins slowly around. Taco makers are adept at slicing off the meat in thin diagonal slices with a long, sharp knife and placing the pork quickly in a hot tortilla along with chopped onion that has been broiled below the spit. Chopped fresh cilantro, a bit of hot sauce, and a few pineapple chunks from the whole fruit roasting on top of the spit completes the taco, which the taco maker manipulates as deftly as any kebab maker in an Istanbul market.

In the past few decades, tacos, like tequila, have become upscale foods and can be purchased in large restaurants that cater to the young crowd, who are known taco consumers. Some, such as a famous one in the Colonia Roma in Mexico City, are favorite meeting places for the young crowd

Preparation of a barbecue pit. Photo by José Ignacio González Manterola.

around two o'clock in the morning, after a late movie or a visit to a nightclub. One very large restaurant that specializes in tacos and barbecued meat serves thousands of customers a week, especially on weekends. The restaurant offers multiple dining rooms for special occasions, while a band of mariachis, musicians who play loud, popular music, perform with great gusto throughout the meal. A typical menu consists of soup, plates of fried pork called *carnitas*, barbecued lamb, a salad of cactus paddles, and cowboy-style beans called *frijoles charros*. Baskets of fresh tortillas are constantly brought to the table so clients can make their own tacos and add the hot sauce of their choice. Small woven baskets of Mexican-style candies are served after the meal. A festive environment; good, hearty food; and good spirits make up the dominant atmosphere of this popular, informal restaurant.

Torterías

Tortas are the Mexican equivalent of sandwiches. They are prepared on an oval-shaped, hard Spanish-style roll called a *telera*, which is sliced horizontally and then stuffed with a variety of fillings. The bottom half of the roll may be spread with refried beans and a layer of lettuce followed by the main filling, which may be chicken, turkey, ham, cheese, or beef; this is then topped with pickled carrots and chile sauce. One well-known *tortería* always hides a very spicy chipotle chile in the center of the *torta*, which takes unsuspecting eaters by surprise when they bite into it. There are fewer types of *tortas* than there are tacos, but many areas of the country have their specialties. *Tortas ahogadas*, or "drowned tortas," are the favorites in Guadalajara and receive their name from the fact that they are literally submerged in a very hot chile sauce. One has to be a real *torta* and chile-pepper fan to enjoy a *torta ahogada*.

Another variety of *torta* is called a *guajolota*. This is also made from a *telera* roll, sliced horizontally and filled with a tamale. They are extremely dry and not easy to eat without some sort of beverage to help you get them down. *Guajolotas* are often considered funeral foods, as it is common for them to be served at a wake.

COMPANY DINING ROOMS

Another possibility for those eating away from home is the company dining room, which serves only employees of the company. These meals are generally subsidized by the company and are offered to employees at a modest price in order to solve the problem of where to eat and to enable employees to have access to clean, healthy food at an affordable price. This way, employees do not take too much time for eating lunch and generally do not even leave the company premises. The most frequent complaints of the employees is that they are not at liberty to choose a menu.[6]

AMERICAN RESTAURANT FRANCHISES

Transnational companies such as McDonald's, VIPS, Kentucky Fried Chicken, Burger King, Subway, Domino's Pizza, Tele Pizzas, and Pizza Hut have a foothold on the Mexican medium-priced fast-food restaurant industry. These serve the same high-fat foods popular in the United States. Many foods are given a Mexican touch, such as chile sauces on hamburgers and hot dogs and chile peppers and hot sausages on pizzas. Prices are not necessarily low, but the food is appealing to the young crowd, who consider it status food. These establishments can be found throughout the city, at all economic and social levels.

RESTAURANTS

Mexico City has become a cosmopolitan city in recent decades, where restaurants that specialize in food from all parts of the world can be found. Asian, African, Mediterranean, Caribbean, South American, European, North American, Middle Eastern, and Mexican restaurants abound throughout the city. Foreign-eating traditions are represented by small, simple fondas or loncherías as well as their counterparts in elegant establishments with fine service and first-rate foods. For example, Mexico City has innumerable sushi bars, which are inexpensive and serve very good food, but Japan is also represented by fine restaurants that charge according to their status. French-style bistros have become popular in recent years. The fusion of Mexican-style food with foreign food traditions is used to present novelty dishes that are currently popular, because chefs have to be constantly looking for something to attract new clientele. The "lite" food trend can also be noted on many menus, with recommendations of certain dishes that have fewer calories. Restaurants that specialize in meat or seafood dishes divide the culinary tastes of the public.

Many restaurants belong to consortiums, with several restaurants sharing publicity and other expenses, which may be owned by the same group of investors. The public is noticeably fickle and may flock to a newly opened restaurant because it has gotten a good review in the press and

A floating restaurant on Lake Xochimilco. © TRIP/
F. Nichols.

then abandon it just as quickly when a new review of a different restaurant is published. The competition is fierce for upscale restaurant customers.

Some small foreign restaurants, such as authentic Japanese, Korean, or
Indian eateries, cater to people from those countries living in Mexico,
who appreciate genuine food from their countries. They do not try to attract a Mexican clientele, whose palates may not be attuned to their authentic food. Chinese, Mediterranean, South American, and Caribbean
restaurants in general prepare food that is appealing to middle- and upper-
class Mexicans. Fine French, Italian, Spanish, and Chinese restaurants
have established clientele. Some traditional restaurants, such as San-
borns, have been in business for almost 100 years and are reliable places to
eat simple Mexican food. Some restaurants are housed in ancient ha-

cienda buildings that are now inside the city and offer a beautiful background and a colonial atmosphere, along with standard-to-good food. They generally serve a menu of international food with a few local specialties, because they are favorites on the tourist circuit.

In recent years, Mexico City has seen the emergence of a few top-notch restaurants that specialize in serving fine Mexican food. These are no doubt the finest Mexican restaurants in the world. The food served in these restaurants is truly haute cuisine by any standard. The menus list such unusual foods as blue and white tortilla soup in duck broth, lobster enchiladas in a green mole sauce, foie gras lightly sautéed in a chocolate sauce with guava paste and habanero chile peppers, chicken breast in a pistachio-nut *pipián* sauce, barbecued lamb steamed in a banana leaf, vermicelli in a black mole sauce, and a very delicate dessert of mamey pudding decorated with an edible gold leaf and carnation-petal jelly. They are found in upscale neighborhoods and have fine decor, and the prices on the menu reflect the quality of both the food and the decor. It is interesting to note that women are often the chef-owners of these fine restaurants. When asked how they explain the recent upsurge in the interest in fine Mexican food, two proprietors explained that it is essentially a search for the roots of Mexican food and a desire to recuperate their own food traditions.[7] This may be a nationalistic response to so much foreign influence in the local food industry, or it may be that the time and circumstances are right for fine Mexican food to come into its own, on its own merits.

NOTES

1. Elba Durán and Martha Kaufer Horowitz, "La venta de alimentos en la vía pública," *Cuadernos de Nutrición* 21, no. 3 (1998): 21–28.

2. Bernardino de Sahagún, *La historia general de las cosas de la Nueva España* (Mexico City: Edtl. Porrúa, 1961), 305–6.

3. Durán and Kaufer Horowitz, "La venta de alimentos," 24.

4. Ibid., 21–28.

5. Elba Durán and Martha Kaufer Horowitz, "Hacia la reordenación sanitaria de la venta de alimentos en la vía pública," *Cuadernos de Nutrición* 21, no. 3 (1998): 30–34.

6. Monserrat Sabio Busquets, "Servicios de alimentación," *Cuadernos de Nutrición* 17, no. 5 (1994): 7–12.

7. Patricia Quintana, conversation with author, 24 April 2004; Marta Ortíz Chapa, conversation with author, Mexico City, 8 May 2004.

7

Special Occasions

Mexicans love a good fiesta (celebration) and readily admit to being a fun-loving people when they say, "*Somos muy fiesteros*" (We are a very festive people). They have many opportunities to celebrate throughout the year, as the Mexican calendar is full of official, unofficial, and religious holidays. In 1988, the Department of Popular Cultures published a calendar of fiestas, *Calendario de Fiestas Populares*, that listed 5,083 ceremonies that have maintained their festive-religious character.[1] All in all, the researchers found some 10,000 fiestas still being held throughout the country. If rite-of-passage fiestas such as baptisms, First Communions, 15-year-old coming-out parties, weddings, and funerals as well as birthdays, saint days, graduation parties, and many other occasions are added, one can get a good panorama of Mexican social life. The fiesta cycle can be considered one of Mexico's most distinctive cultural traits.

Noted Mexican poet Octavio Paz described the Mexican attitude toward fiestas when he wrote,

Fiestas are our sole luxury. They are a substitute for, and perhaps have the advantage over theatre and vacations. [They take the place of the] Anglo-Saxon weekends, cocktail parties, bourgeois receptions and the Mediterranean café.... What is important is to go out, open up a way, get drunk on noise, people, colors. Mexico is in fiesta. And this fiesta, shot through with lightning and delirium, is the brilliant opposite of our silence and apathy, our reticence and gloom.[2]

Some festive occasions have become customary throughout the country and are considered national fiestas. National fiestas may coincide with religious or civic fiestas.

Rite-of-passage celebrations are most likely carried out on a personal or family level. These include the baptism ceremony, confirmation in the Catholic Church, First Communion events, 15-year-old coming-out parties for young girls, weddings, and funerals. Birthdays, saint days, and fiestas to celebrate graduation from different educational levels may also be included in this type of celebration.

Some religious fiestas must be considered localized events. They may involve the entire community or be carried out on a private and personal level. The introduction of the Catholic religion in Mexico brought about many changes in the Mesoamerican/Mexican diet. Church restrictions regarding diet, such as the prohibition of eating meat on Fridays and diet restrictions during Lent, had an important effect upon Mexican eating traditions.

Harvest festivals are generally held in early autumn, when most agricultural produce is harvested or the harvest is about to begin. Rural people may be giving thanks for a particularly good harvest or ask for protection of the crops until they can be gathered. Harvest fiestas are very common in southern Mexico.

To these activities, one must add a list of civic fiestas such as the Day of the Constitution, celebrated on February 5; the Battle of Puebla, held on May 5; Independence Day festivities, held on September 15 and 16; and the Day of the Revolution, on November 20. These are official holidays in Mexico when banks, schools, and government offices are closed and people can participate in government-sponsored festivities if they wish to do so.

FIESTA FOOD

Food and drink are important elements in the fiesta cycle. Specific dishes may be associated with certain celebrations and are traditionally served at those functions. Typical fiesta dishes include tamales in all shapes, sizes, and flavors; a variety of mole dishes served with turkey, chicken, or pork; a codfish stew called *bacalao*; poblano-type chile peppers stuffed with a chopped meat and dried-fruit stuffing and topped with a nut sauce, called *chiles en nogada*; barbecued kid, lamb, and beef; a pork and hominy dish called *pozole*; and many, many others.

No particular foods are reserved for special occasions; the same food can be eaten on nonfestive occasions. However, when the dishes are prepared for a fiesta, cooks may use better-quality ingredients and take greater care in the preparation, and more people may be involved in the process.

When food is prepared for a community fiesta, the responsibility is shared by several members of the community.

Festive food may depend upon the customs of the particular region of the country preparing the celebration. It also depends upon the economic resources of the participants and the social level of those involved.

NATIONAL FIESTAS

Fiestas celebrated on a national level begin the year with the New Year's Day lunch or dinner, when friends and family get together to celebrate the beginning of the new year. This particular celebration is often shared by friends rather than family. There is no fixed menu for this day; however, food and drink may be similar to that prepared for December festivities and may include roast suckling pig (*lechón al horno*) or roast turkey stuffed with a ground or chopped meat (*picadillo*) and fruit dressing. Another favorite is a codfish stew called *bacalao* (prepared with small boiled potatoes, pickled chile peppers, olives, and tomatoes) or a fricassee of breaded shrimp patties in mole sauce cooked with an herblike vegetable resembling rosemary (*romero*), which explains its name in Spanish: *revoltijo de romeritos*.

Mexican-Style *Bacalao* (*Bacalao a la Mexicana*)

- 1 lb. dried codfish
- 3 lbs. puréed tomatoes
- 1 head roasted garlic
- 1 large onion, sliced
- 1 bunch finely chopped parsley
- 1 can (8 oz.) pickled *chiles güeros*
- 1 can (8 oz.) red pimento, cut in strips
- 1 lb. small potatoes, cooked and peeled
- 1/2 cup olives, stuffed with pimento
- 1/4 cup raisins
- 1/4 cup almonds, peeled and chopped
- 2 cups olive oil

Cut the codfish in pieces and soak overnight in water, changing it 3 or 4 times. The next day, boil the fish in clean water until it is cooked but does not fall apart. Remove it from the water and shred it, not too finely. Put oil in a saucepan and fry the sliced onion lightly. Add the puréed tomato, parsley, and head of garlic. Let it cook until the liquid is reduced. Add the fish, boiled potatoes, raisins, and almonds. Let boil gently for 10 minutes. The pimentos, the *chiles güeros*, and the olives are added just before serving.

For dessert, a tray of candies, such as Spanish *turrones* and *mazapanes*; Mexican sweets and candied fruits; or *buñuelos* (deep-fried flour tortillas served with a molasses syrup) may be offered.

THE FIESTA OF CANDLEMAS

A few days later, on January 6, Mexican families gather to share three-kings' cake, known as *la rosca de Reyes*. This day marks the arrival of the three wise men, or *los reyes Magos*, who arrived at the stable in Bethlehem where Jesus was born, bearing gifts for him. Catholics commemorate the event by giving gifts to their own children. On the night of January 5, small children fill their shoes with straw and place them at the foot of the Christmas tree or at the entrance to the house. The straw symbolizes the manger in which Jesus lay. The Mexican custom of giving Three Kings' Day gifts to their children is more widespread than the tradition of giving them gifts on Christmas Eve. Many more toys are purchased to be given on January 5 than on December 24. Some lucky children receive gifts on both occasions.

The three-kings' cake is a ring-shaped sweet bread that originated in medieval France and arrived in Mexico via Spain. Over the centuries, it has become Mexicanized by local bakers and is now decorated with crystallized fruits such as pineapple, figs, citrons, and oranges. Small plastic dolls representing Jesus are baked in the dough; the number of dolls depends upon the size of the cake. Very large *roscas*, purchased for a large family or for an office party, may contain many dolls.

The slicing and serving of the cake has become a ritual in Mexico. Each person present is served a slice of the cake, and the one whose slice contains the doll is obliged to offer a tamale party, called a *tamalada*, on February 2, the Day of Candlemas (Día de la Candelaria), and must invite all those present at the table. Three-kings' cakes are traditionally accompanied by hot chocolate, coffee, or a variety of fruit- or chocolate-flavored *atoles*. This custom is deeply entrenched in Mexico, when bread shops and supermarkets bake and sell thousands of *roscas de Reyes* the first week of January.

Three-Kings' Cake (*Rosca de Reyes*)

- 1/2 cup warm water
- 2 packages active dry yeast
- 1/2 cup unsalted butter
- 1/2 cups sugar
- 4 eggs, separated
- 1 tablespoon grated orange zest
- 1 tablespoon grated lemon zest
- 1/2 teaspoon orange flavoring
- 1 teaspoon salt
- 5 cups flour
- 1 cup chopped crystallized fruits
- 1/2 cup chopped pecans
- 2 or more plastic dolls

Decoration

- 2 eggs
- 1 tablespoon cream
- crystallized figs, oranges, and a citron, all cut into strips
- 1/3 cup sugar

Pour warm water into a large bowl, sprinkle on the yeast, and let stand for 5 minutes. Stir in the melted and cooled butter, sugar, eggs, orange and lemon zests, orange flavoring, and salt. Add 3 cups of flour and beat for 3 minutes with a wooden spoon. Add the rest of the flour, a little at a time, and beat until the dough begins to pull away from the sides of the bowl. Turn dough out onto a floured surface and knead, adding more flour if necessary, until it forms a smooth, elastic ball. Oil a large bowl and turn the bread ball in it until it is covered with oil. Cover with a damp kitchen towel and leave it in a warm place for about 1-1/2 hours, or until it is doubled in size. Grease 2 baking sheets with oil. Divide dough in two parts and turn out onto a lightly floured surface. Sprinkle each piece with candied fruits and nuts and knead the dough until they are incorporated into the dough. Press one or more small plastic dolls in each piece of dough. Roll each piece of dough into a log about 25 inches long and 2-1/2 inches in diameter. Form each log into a ring, pinching the ends together. Place one ring on each baking sheet. Place an oiled metal bowl in the center to help the ring keep its shape. Cover lightly with a kitchen towel and let it rise for 1 hour. Preheat oven to 375°.

Topping: Beat eggs and cream together. Brush the rings with the egg mixture. Decorate with strips of crystallized fruits alternated with wide bands of sugar.

Bake about 25 minutes or until the top is lightly brown. Transfer the rings to racks to cool.

Another aspect of this fiesta is the blessing of plants and seeds by the priest in the church of San Francisco in Xochimilco on February 2. Farmers who cultivate vegetables and flowers on the *chinampas* in the area consider this ritual a means of insuring that the plants will produce a good harvest.

Yet another tradition associated with the Day of Candlemas is the tradition of honoring Jesus on this day, to commemorate the Virgin Mary's presentation of the child before the Church 40 days after his birth. Life-size figures of the baby Jesus called *niñopas* are dressed in new clothes and taken to the cathedral by their godparents, who have taken care of them for the past year, to be blessed during the mass. At this time, the dolls will be delivered to new godparents, who will care for them in their home for one year. Mariachis fill the atrium of the church with popular music, and food stands are set up to sell snacks (*antojitos*) such as tamales with *atole*, *pambazos*, quesadillas, and tacos. A lunch is also offered by the retiring godparents for the new couple, who have committed to caring for baby Jesus during the following year. The menu of the luncheon is at the discretion of the hostess. This is a prestigious position and gives the couple considerable status in the community. In 2004, the waiting list of couples who have requested the opportunity to care for the baby Jesus extended to 2,035.[3] This can be an expensive proposition, as the godparents have to provide the *niñopa* with fresh flowers every day and the appropriate new clothes throughout the year.

Preparations for the ceremony begin some four months before, when the sponsor (*mayordomo*) collects a fee from every household in the neighborhood to help pay for the mass, music, flowers, and decoration of the church. The fiesta lasts from February 2 to February 8. On the second and eighth day, thousands of people arrive to view the baby Jesus. Every neighborhood presents its own *niñopa* to be blessed on the Día de la Candelaria.

THE CARNIVAL

Carnivals are celebrated five days before Ash Wednesday. The cities of Veracruz, Mazatlan, Campeche, Manzanillo, and Tampico have become famous for putting on a good carnival and are popular among tourists for celebrating before Lent begins. Music, dance, and food mark the celebration of carnivals. Parades with flower-decorated floats are organized, and a "king and queen of the carnival" are chosen. The queen is chosen for her beauty, but the king is appointed for his "ugliness." The public dons masks and costumes and dances, eats, and drinks during the three days of the carnival.

The food served reflects the fact that the popular carnival locations are coastal cities. Thus, seafood dishes, such as fresh fish marinated in lime juice (*ceviche*), or quesadillas, tacos, and tamales filled with fish, are popular as carnival fare. Carnivals are also celebrated in Mexico City, where fast foods such as potato chips, *chicarrones* (fried pork rinds), oranges sprinkled with powdered chile or hot sauce, cotton candy, cookies, yogurts, juice, soft drinks, and beer are sold in a fairlike atmosphere. Typical Mexican snacks such as tacos, quesadillas, and *huaraches* (a tortilla-based snack in the shape of a sandal sole, served with pork or beef) are popular during the carnival.

Fresh Fish Cocktail (*Ceviche*)
- 1 lb. white fish, cut into 1 × 2-inch pieces
- 1-1/2 cups white-wine vinegar or lime juice
- 2 tomatoes
- 4 canned pickled serrano chiles
- 1/4 cup olive oil
- 1/2 teaspoon oregano
- 1/2 teaspoon salt
- freshly ground pepper

Garnish
- 1 small avocado
- 1 small onion
- 1 tablespoon finely chopped coriander

Place fish in a glass dish and cover with vinegar or lime juice. Let fish marinate in the refrigerator for several hours, stirring from time to time. Peel, remove seeds, and chop tomatoes; chop chile peppers and add them to the fish. Add olive oil, oregano, salt, and pepper. Let season for 1-1/2 hours in the refrigerator. Garnish each cocktail with slices of avocado and onion rings and sprinkle with coriander at the time of serving.

LENT AND HOLY WEEK

The 40 days of Lent are considered a time for religious contemplation and reflection in Mexico. Many people restrict their diet as a form of penitence at this time of year and eat mostly fish-based dishes with vegetables. Meat is not eaten on Fridays during Lent, although Catholics may eat meat on Fridays in Mexico at other times of the year. People show a preference for soups, such as a shrimp broth called *caldo de camarón*; pastas stuffed with spinach or sardines; tuna dishes; shrimp patties; Veracruz-style fish called *huachinango a la veracruzana*; and turnovers prepared with fish, such as codfish stew or tuna. Vegetable fritters such as potato patties (*tortas de papa*) and cheese-stuffed chile peppers are popular as substitutes for meat. A favorite dessert prepared at this time of year is a bread pudding called *capirotada* made with fried wheat-flour rolls and served with a syrup of brown sugar, raisins, cinnamon, and shredded cheese. A similar dessert called *torrejas*, made with egg-dipped bread, fried, and served with a cinnamon-flavored syrup and shredded lime peel, is also popular.

LA FIESTA DE LA SANTA CRUZ

The fiesta of the Holy Cross (Santa Cruz) is celebrated in Mexico on May 3. It is best known in Mexico City as the Fiesta of Construction Workers, or El día del albañil, for on this day a cross is set up on construction sites, and the architect, engineer, or owner of the house or building under construction are obliged to give a feast for all the construction workers employed on the site. This is usually called a *taquiza*, or taco meal, because the workers make tacos of the stews (*guisados*), which are served with an abundance of tortillas and sauces. There is no set menu for these celebrations, but the food must be easy to eat, as it is consumed on the construction site without plates and a minimum of cutlery.

In Zitlala, Guerrero, the fiesta of the Holy Cross is held from May 3 to 7 and is celebrated as an act of purification, as well as a ceremony to solicit spring rains. Young men and boys don jaguar masks and costumes and beat each other with whips and ropes to show their valor and to convince the gods of their sincerity in soliciting the needed rains. This ceremony can become very violent when the beating gets out of hand and the local police have to step in and establish order.

INDEPENDENCE DAY FESTIVITIES

Mexico gained its independence from Spain in 1821, after 300 years of Hispanic domination. On September 15 and 16, Mexicans celebrate their independence in a very festive manner. Throughout the month of September, small Mexican flags flutter in the air, from the antennas of taxicabs, private cars, and municipal busses. Some homes, office buildings, and businesses show their patriotism by displaying the Mexican flag on a pole in front of the buildings. Flags are sold by itinerant street merchants or at newspaper stands. The celebration on the night of September 15 commemorates the cry for independence given at 11 P.M. by the provincial parish priest Father Miguel Hidalgo in 1810. Independence Day is observed on September 16.

The entire month of September is considered a time of celebration. As the 15 of the month nears, people go to La Merced market or other markets to try and purchase firecrackers and rockets, notwithstanding the fact that the city government has declared their purchase illegal. The Mexican president repeats the original cry for independence on September 15. At 11 P.M., he steps out on the balcony of the second floor of the National Palace and recites the names of the principal insurgents who fought in the battle for independence, then ends with a resounding "Viva Mexico!" which he repeats three times, to which the masses, gathered in the Zocalo, or main plaza, in front of the Palacio Nacional, in turn answer, "Viva Mexico!" This is an emotional ceremony and is repeated in all the municipal palaces throughout the country, in villages, towns, and cities, with the mayor taking the president's place in the ceremony. It is also carried out in U.S. cities with large Mexican populations.

Food is an important part of the ritual, as small booths, food stands, and women with portable braziers and canastas set up their temporary restaurants to cater to the demands of the thousands of Mexicans who flock to the main square to celebrate the cry for liberty, or El Grito, as it is known in Mexico. People also celebrate the ceremony at home, in housing projects, and in restaurants and fondas (small eateries). It is an occasion when everyone tries to make sure he or she has an invitation to a fiesta or dinner party to attend, so that he or she will not lose face with friends and family.

Some of the popular dishes typical of this fiesta are green enchiladas (stuffed tortillas covered with a green sauce); enchiladas with black mole; and several tortilla-based snacks called garnachas, gorditas de frijol, picaditas, or sopes. The last two are similar and may be filled with refried beans, fresh feta cheese, chopped onions, and hot tomato sauce and topped with cheese. Fried tortillas filled with barbecued goat meat, tacos, and masa fritters stuffed with chorizo sausage and potatoes, called molotes, are other popular foods for this special occasion.

Public fiestas are held in the evenings on streets and squares where a pork and hominy soup called pozole is served with chopped lettuce,

radishes, powdered chile pepper, lime juice, and oregano. Another favorite is a hard-roll sandwich made with a Spanish-style bread roll and
filled with diced potatoes fried with chorizo and chopped lettuce and flavored with chipotle chiles. This snack is known as a *pambazo*, a word that
comes from the term *pan bajo*, or "bread eaten by the poor."

A more sophisticated dish served in private homes and restaurants associated with Independence Day festivities is the well-known *chiles en nogada*, made with poblano chile peppers; stuffed with a variety of ground or
chopped meats and a dried fruit mixture; covered with a smooth, ivory-
toned nut sauce; and topped with a few parsley leaves and bright red
pomegranate seeds. This dish is an explosion of color in green, red, and
white, which is said to symbolize the colors of the Mexican flag.

Traditional Mexican desserts associated with independence festivities
include the large deep-fried wheat tortillas called *buñuelos*, served with
molasses syrup. These are popular as fiesta food throughout the year.

THE DAYS OF THE DEAD

The Day of the Dead (Día de los Muertos) celebration is Mexico's most
distinctive fiesta and one of the most important rituals in the Mexican fiesta cycle.[4] It can best be described as a festival to welcome the return of
the souls of the dead on November 1 and 2 and provide them with the
pleasures they enjoyed while living. The fiesta incorporates elements of
pre-Hispanic religious beliefs and practices, which differentiates it from
other more orthodox Catholic feasts on All Saints' and All Souls' Day.[5] In
Mexico it is celebrated like in no other Catholic country in the world.

The Day of the Dead is essentially a private or family affair; the core of
the celebration is carried out within the family and takes place in the family home or at the family plot in the cemetery. Each household prepares its
offerings of food and drink for the dead, which traditionally consist of the
deceased person's favorite dishes. A temporary altar is set up on a table
where the food is served in clay dishes along with vases of marigold flowers, white candles, and photographs of the dead and of the saint to which
they were devoted. Small dishes of salt, glasses of water, and a plate of incense sanctifies the ceremony. Hollow skulls made with sugar paste display
the name of the dead person across the forehead.

November 1 is the day to celebrate children, particularly those who
died during the year. The ringing of church bells on October 31 at 8 P.M.
announces the arrival of the "spirits of the children."[6] By this time altars
have been set up where the food has been set out. This consists of Day of

Altar of the Dead in Oaxaca. Photo by Jorge Contreras Chacel/Banco Mexicano de Imágenes.

the Dead bread, sweet tamales, fruit, ears of corn, *atole*, milk, candied pumpkin, and fruit jams, accompanied by yellow marigolds and sugar skulls. Fast foods, such as potato chips, Doritos, Coca-Cola, candy, and cookies, as well as plastic toys may also be placed on the children's altar, demonstrating the change in the diet of Mexican children.

The main ceremony is held on November 2, when the souls of the adults are celebrated and given the most splendid offering the family can afford. Tamales are always included, as is a loaf of Day of the Dead bread and chicken or turkey in a mole sauce. Other dishes may include enchiladas and chalupas or other favored dishes. Beverages range from coffee, chocolate, and *atole* to whatever alcohol the deceased preferred. A bottle of beer or a shot glass of tequila or *mezcal* will form part of the offering, if the deceased enjoyed them. If the person was a smoker, a package of his favorite cigarettes will be included. There is an element of pride and status in providing an elaborate offering for relatives. Some people attempt to impress their neighbors through their ability to make an elaborate and expensive offering for their deceased.

The living delight in preparing the ceremony, and in this way honor their friends and relatives who have preceded them on their journey to another world. The souls are believed to be present as spirits who have returned from the other world. The spirits are not seen; however, their presence is sensed. They do not physically consume the food and drinks, but rather absorb their essence. When the souls have had their fill, it will be the turn of the living members of the family to take part in their share of the offering. Some of the food will be taken to the cemetery to be placed upon the graves of the deceased and consumed by family members on the gravesite. Sometimes a path is formed with marigold petals to lead the souls to their proper destination in the cemetery. The sight of thousands of candles lighting up the night cemetery on November 2 is indeed impressive.

In wealthy middle-class homes in Mexico City, there may be a tradition of presenting an offering consisting of a few photographs of the deceased, flowers, candles, and a special bread called *pan de muerto* (bread of the dead) without the rest of the food offerings. The special bread baked for this fiesta is generally a round, domed loaf with extra dough filleted on top of the loaf in the shape of a head and extremities, to symbolize death.

The fiesta provides folk artists with many subjects to work with around the theme of death. Artisans produce skulls, skeletons of papier-mâché, entire bands of musicians with their musical instruments, or small open coffins with a skeleton inside that pops up like a jack-in-the-box when a button is pushed. This is also a good time of the year to satirize local politicians and government officials by making effigies in compromising situations.

In rural areas, the preparation for the event is a major preoccupation for much of the year. Months earlier, pottery villages begin making large cooking vessels (*ollas*) and incense burners to be used in the ceremony. Rural markets bustle during the week or so before the fiesta and sell all the essential items for the celebration. Flowers of all kinds, candles, breads, fruits and vegetables, sweets, green pottery dishes, plastic toys, and different types of incense are placed on sale. Many farmers are willing to sell their crops and prized animals at a reduced price in order to obtain money for the fiesta. Indigenous people consider it an obligation to set up an altar to honor their dead and believe that some ill may come to them in the form of an illness or death in the family if they fail to fulfill their duties.

Federal and city governments and cultural organizations now promote the celebration of the Day of the Dead as a way for Mexicans to express their identity. Contests are organized by these groups to encourage the population to set up of altars in town squares, markets, or public buildings, and a prize is awarded the most well-made display. Banks, hotels, super-

Bread of the Dead (*pan de muertos*). Photo by Santiago Castillo/Banco Mexicano de Imágenes.

markets, public buildings, businesses, and cultural organizations have
begun to offer a display of the altar of the dead to stress their commitment
to this most Mexican of all customs. This celebration is not disappearing;
rather, it is becoming more and more important in Mexican cultural life.

In recent decades plastic Halloween pumpkins have made their appearance in the marketplace alongside the more traditional skulls and skeletons. Batmans, Draculas, and witches, more reminiscent of American
Halloween costumes, are now common in Mexico. Small children carrying orange pumpkins made of plastic are beginning to beg passersby for
their "Halloweeeeeen" candy.

DECEMBER FIESTAS

December 12 marks the beginning of the December celebrations.[7] This is
the Day of the Virgin of Guadalupe and marks the first appearance of the
Virgin, the patron saint of Mexico. On December 12, thousands of pilgrims
pay a visit to her shrine, the Basilica of Guadalupe, on the outskirts of Mexico City. Many come from long distances to pay her homage and approach
the shrine, walking painfully on their knees as a special type of penitence.
Native dances are performed in the atrium of the basilica. Gorditas, a tiny
corn-based snack about two inches in diameter and half an inch thick, are
wrapped in colorful pieces of tissue paper and sold by women who set up
their braziers to cook the gorditas in the atrium of the shrine. These represent the typical food associated with the December 12 celebration.

Christmas Festivities

Strictly speaking, Christmas fiestas begin with the *posadas*, the festivities held for the nine days from December 15 to 23. The word *posada* can be translated as an inn, a small hotel, or a place of refuge. The *posada* reenacts the biblical account of Mary and Joseph's search for lodging on the night Jesus was born in Bethlehem. Both children and adults participate in the fiesta. The guests are divided into two groups. The first group consists of the pilgrims who walk in procession, each one carrying a small lighted candle, and a designated couple who heads the procession and carries a replica of the nativity scene on a tray. They go from door to door, pleading for shelter by singing a request for admission. The innkeepers make up the group inside, who musically deny them admittance. The pilgrims are then obliged to continue on to the next station, where the ritual petition for shelter is repeated and rejected. Finally, at the last stop, the doors open wide, the weary couple is admitted, and the two groups joyously sing the final verse of the litany together. At this time a refreshment such as hot chocolate, *atole,* or a Christmas punch called *ponche navideño* may be offered. There are many recipes for this beverage, most of which include fruits such as crab apples, apples, pears, and guavas, as well as sugarcane sticks, brown sugar, and stick cinnamon. A shot of rum can be added to the punch served to an adult if it is requested. This is called *ponche con piquete,* or "punch with a sting."

The Piñata

Later, during the same fiesta, the piñata is broken. This is a clay pot covered with bits of brightly colored tissue paper and filled with Christmas fruit, candy, peanuts, and sticks of sugarcane, as well as whistles, noisemakers, and plastic toys.

The most traditional shape for a Christmas piñata is the star of Bethlehem, although many other shapes are used. After it is filled, the piñata is hung on a long rope, which is fixed on one end and held on the other end by someone standing on the roof, to enable him to swing the piñata out of the reach of the person trying to hit the pot. Small children are first in line to try their luck at breaking the pot. If they are very small, they are allowed to look at the piñata while they hit it; their eyes are not covered with a bandana. They whack the piñata a few times with a broomstick, then pass the stick on to the next child waiting in line. Older children and adults are blindfolded and turned around in a circle several times to disorient them and make it more difficult to hit the piñata. The contestant tentatively strikes the air until he finally touches the pot and knows in which direction to strike. By this time the piñata is pulled away, out of his reach, so he must blindly strike in every direction, hoping his broomstick will meet up with the piñata at some point. He is allowed only three strikes before he must relinquish the stick to the next person. The attempt to break the piñata is accompanied by the singing of special verses to encourage the striker. Finally, someone will give the pot a solid whack in the belly and it will break, spilling all the contents onto the ground. At this moment, everyone present, young and old alike, will scramble on top of the shattered piñata and gather as much booty as possible for himself, which he may share with others later.

Christmas Eve Dinner

The traditional Christmas dinner is served at 11 P.M. on December 24. This late hour allows many Catholics to attend Christmas Eve mass before dinner is served. Families with small children choose an earlier hour for dining to enable all the family to eat together. There are four traditional Christmas dishes, one or several of which may be served at the Christmas Eve dinner. These are a codfish stew, roast turkey, a fricassee of breaded shrimp in *revoltijo de romeritos*, and the traditional Mexican Christmas salad known as *la ensalada de Nochebuena*.[8]

A typical menu for this dinner might begin with a walnut soup, which is followed by a delicious codfish stew, the Mexican version of the original Spanish *bacalao a la vizcaína*. The Mexican dish is somewhat different, as it includes *chiles güeros*, raisins, and almonds. This is the most popular dish served for Christmas Eve dinner. Roast turkey stuffed with a dressing of almonds, raisins, stick cinnamon, and chopped pork loin is also popular. Sweet potatoes, pasta, or mashed potatoes are common accompaniments. The Mexican Christmas salad is an unusual medley of ingredients, including romaine lettuce, beets, *jícamas*, apples, oranges, lemons, peanuts, Christmas candy, sugar cane, cloves, brown sugar, and more, but it is in fact, very tasty. Dessert may consist of Spanish *turrones* (sweets) from Alicante or Jijona, made of almonds, sesame seeds, and egg yolks. *Buñuelos*, sugar-coated almonds, and dried fruits may also be served at the end of the meal.[9]

New Year's Eve Fiesta

Friends and families gather on New Year's Eve to bid farewell to the old year and welcome in the new one on December 31. Typical dishes for this celebration are similar to those served on Christmas Eve. The meal may consist of a fish soup with a main dish of roast turkey, *bacalao*, roast pig, or *revoltijo de romeritos*. The Christmas Eve beet salad may make its appearance again at the New Year's Eve table. Desserts may include a variety of Mexican sweets such as a ground peanut candy (*mazapan*), candied fruits, or *buñuelos*. Twelve grapes are provided for each guest from the fruit-bowl centerpiece on the table, which by tradition are supposed to be consumed, one by one, with each strike of the clock at midnight. This is difficult to do, and most guests end up with a mouthful of half-chewed grapes.

RITE-OF-PASSAGE FIESTAS

Christening

The first celebration to be offered a child in Mexico is the christening party following baptism in the Catholic Church. Mexico is predominantly a Catholic country, and many rituals and ceremonies involve the Church. Babies are baptized in white garments, which symbolizes the purity of their souls.[10] During the ceremony, the child is freed from original sin through the purifying action of the holy water. Babies are baptized with the name they will bear, often the name of one of their parents or the name of the saint on whose particular day they were born. Both boys and girls are given a first name, followed by the father's surname and then the mother's surname; thus he will have two last names throughout his life.

The choice of godparents is very important for people in lower income levels, as there are many responsibilities that go with the role. For example, they are not only expected to provide moral support throughout the child's life, but economic assistance as well. If the baby is a girl, godparents are expected to help with the 15th-birthday coming-out, called the *quinceañera fiesta*. The first immediate obligation of the godfather is to provide a handful of coins, called the *bolo*, which are tossed high in the air as the group leaves the church. This act symbolizes the fruits of fortune that it is hoped will accompany the child throughout his or her life. Neighborhood children keep a watchful eye for any baptism ceremony, as this will mean a few extra coins in their pockets. Godparents are also expected to give the baby a religious medal of a saint, which can be worn on a chain around the neck throughout his or her lifetime. Parents distribute printed notices of the child's baptism to friends and family.

Food served at christening festivities varies according to the social level and personal resources of those involved and even the region of the country. Both savory and sweet tamales of many varieties are favorites for bap-

tism fiestas throughout the country. They may be served with hot chocolate, fruit-flavored *atoles*, or coffee. More formal or elaborate christenings
may be offered in the form of a brunch, where a wide variety of dishes may
be served. Almost any morning dish, such as chicken with almond mole
sauce, Montezuma's pie, or *torta de elote* (sweet-corn cake), may be served.
Royal eggs, made with egg yolks, honey, and pine nuts, are also popular
and considered appropriate for the occasion.

First Communion Fiestas

Because the First Communion usually takes place at a midmorning mass
in the church, the fiesta is either a brunch at noon or a lunch. If it is a
large event, any of a variety of morning dishes may be served. For a small,
family-style event, a fruit plate and savory and sweet tamales would be
served, with hot chocolate, fruit *atoles*, or coffee. A basket filled with
small sweet breads and cookies is usually part of the table decoration.
Guests bring presents for the child being celebrated, and he is made to feel
special throughout the reception. Another set of godparents (*los padriños
de Primera Comunión*) is assigned the child by the parents or by his or her
own choice. They in turn give the godchild a medal of a saint. The event
usually ends with the serving of a white First Communion cake.

Birthday and Saint-Day Celebrations

Any festive or nonfiesta food is considered appropriate for a birthday or
saint-day fiesta. Often the two fiestas coincide, as babies may be named
after the saint on whose day they were born. Again, tamales, mole, barbecued meat, *pozole*, or any other dish would be acceptable. Hiring a mariachi band to wake the person with "Las Mañanitas" on the morning of his
birthday is becoming a thing of the past, due to the expense and tight
schedules most people are forced to keep.

Coming-Out Parties

In former times, most young Mexican girls were presented to society on
their 15th birthday. A celebration was prepared that included a mass followed by a reception for friends and family. This custom has lost importance in upper-class Mexico. Many young girls prefer a trip to Europe
rather than a *quinceañera fiesta*. The custom as it is practiced in Tláhuac,
a lower-income suburb of Mexico City, will be used as an example.

The young girl's baptismal godparents are expected to present her with the last toy she is to receive before becoming a young woman with more worldly interests. Baptismal godparents are also expected to pay for her dress as well as the Catholic mass and accompany her during the mass and the fiesta. New godparents are also chosen, who must provide the religious medal, the crown she will wear during the mass, the many-tiered cake, and her shoes and bear the cost of the video and photographs. The cost of the food at the banquet is assumed by her parents. The menu may consist of chicken with mole sauce, Mexican rice, deep-fried pork bits known as *carnitas*, barbecued lamb, chicken in maguey leaves called *mixiotes*, tamales, and beans. The 15th-birthday dessert is generally an elaborate, many-tiered cake, which is an important part of the fiesta. All godparents of the girl expect to take a small bag of leftovers called an *itacate* home with them at the end of the fiesta.

Weddings

Wedding fiestas can be as varied as the resources and pretensions of the bride's parents allow. Large events are usually catered. In upper-class Mexico City, one of many fine caterers may be called upon to provide the wedding banquet. The menu also depends upon the formality of the wedding. Informal weddings that take place on haciendas outside the city serve more rustic or popular food than those served in a hotel or banquet hall. A menu for a hacienda wedding may include snacks (*botanas*), a soup or consommé, mole poblano with turkey or roasted meats, Mexican rice, a cactus-paddle (*nopal*) salad, savory beans, and a variety of hot sauces. A wedding cake is generally served, which is sliced by the couple, who traditionally feed each other the first bite.

A more formal wedding menu may include cream-of-nut soup, tournedos with morels in a chile-cream sauce, fish in puff pastry, or perhaps confit of duck, with the appropriate garnishes, vegetables, and salads. By tradition, the wedding cake is generally served as dessert.

An interesting anecdote to wedding-food customs is *la correteada* or the "send-off," as practiced among the inhabitants of Tláhuac, a lower-income suburb of Mexico City. Wedding festivities may last for eight days after the wedding itself, and the parents of the bride are obliged to continue entertaining the guests with food and drink. On the eighth day, a dish called *mixmole* (a fish sauce) is served, which serves as a subtle reminder to the guests that the party is over, with the implication that they should not expect more food and drink and are expected to leave.[11]

FUNERALS

A funeral in a community with few resources will be described here, as food is more important in funerals at this social level than it is in more affluent areas. In Tláhuac, when a death occurs in a family, help is immediately solicited among the rest of the family to organize the wake and the burial. The body is generally mourned for a day and a night, depending upon the hour of death. Most of the people attending the wake bring some type of food, such as rice, beans, oil, sugar, and cookies or bread as a means of helping the bereaved family. Members of the family organize women to help prepare the food offered to all attending the wake and after the burial. No meat should be eaten on the day of the death. Fish dishes, such as *charales* with cactus-paddle leaves in a green sauce, eggs with potatoes in a green sauce, and Puebla-style *romeritos* with potatoes and shrimp patties, accompanied by tortillas, beans, and fruit-flavored drinks called *aguas frescas* are traditional dishes deemed appropriate for a funeral meal. Nine days later, the family again invites those who had accompanied them at the wake to share a meal with them. Typical dishes served are fried pork bits (*carnitas*), a pork and hominy dish (*pozole*), or other dishes, depending upon the family's finances. A mass is offered in the church a year after the death in memory of the deceased, and those who attend the mass are invited to a meal at the deceased person's home. On this occasion, *carnitas*, chicken in mole sauce, bean or water tamales, and cinnamon tea may be served. Death can be an expensive rite of passage.[12]

CIVIC FIESTAS

The Battle of Puebla, celebrated on May 5, is perhaps more important as a fiesta celebrated by Mexicans living in the United States than it is in Mexico, with the exception of the city of Puebla, where the event occurred.

According to history, in 1862 a small, badly equipped group of Mexican guerrillas drove a powerful army of 6,000 French invaders out of the city of Puebla and kept it from falling into French hands. The festivities on May 5 commemorate this victory. The city was later taken by the French, resulting in the Austrian prince Maximilian being installed by Napoléon on the throne as emperor of Mexico.

In the city of Puebla, schoolchildren celebrate the fiesta with parades of marching bands and neighborhood fairs with mechanical rides and food booths. Families gather to celebrate with games, cockfights, and Puebla-style food. Typical snacks may be one of the many tortilla-based *antojitos*, such as *chalupitas*, *sopes*, or tacos. In other parts of Mexico, the fiesta is not considered as important and is merely appreciated as a day without work.

RELIGIOUS AND HARVEST FIESTAS

Autumn-harvest festivals date from pre-Hispanic times, when the Aztecs celebrated the birth of the corn goddess, Xilonen, during the month of Ochpaniztli, which corresponds to the month of September on the Gregorian calendar. During this fiesta, people celebrated the "first fruits" of the season or the "first young ears of corn" in the goddess's honor.

This type of fiesta is still being celebrated in Highland Guerrero in a ceremony called *xilocruz*, also known as the "ceremony of the tender ears of corn."[13] This is a private ritual that each family carries out in their own cornfield. Before the ceremony, crosses are set up in each corner of the field, and incense is burned to clear the area of evil spirits. Náhuatl-speaking people call the ceremony *quitotoca mayantli*, or "the scaring away of hunger." It is a ritual performed to solicit the protection of the corn crop until it can be harvested. On this occasion, a special dish called *elopozole* is prepared with tender young corn, the herb epazote, *guajillo chile* pepper, diced squash, chunks of corn on the cob, and a bit of pork or chicken. This fiesta "of the first fruits" is carried out in many areas of rural Mexico.

Shortly after the Catholic religion was brought to Mexico, the Church assigned a patron saint to each town for the people to venerate and consider their protector. Mexicans soon found a way to honor the patron saint of the city, town, village, or neighborhood by holding a fiesta on the special day of the saint, although in reality they were honoring a pre-Columbian god of their choice. They merely accepted the Catholic custom of the fiesta in order to obtain permission from the priests to hold the celebration. It is not clear how effective the Church was initially in remolding native habits, as the people were very clever about hiding their forbidden pre-Columbian beliefs. In modern Indian society, beliefs of pagan origin often blend with Christian doctrine.

Harvest fiestas are common in rural Mexico, particularly in the southern states of Guerrero, Oaxaca, and Chiapas. These three states have a large Indian population, where pre-Hispanic traits survive in the rituals. Farmers seek the help and protection of their gods in a vain attempt to control the weather, on which their welfare depends.

A fiesta held every year on October 4 in San Francisco Olinalá, Guerrero, is both a harvest and a religious festival in honor of San Francisco, patron saint of the town.[14] Olinalá is well known for the fine lacquer crafts they produce. The fiesta is known by several names: "the fiesta of San

Harvest offering in the Fiesta of San Francisco, Olinalá, Guerrero. Photo by Janet
Long.

Francisco," "the fiesta of chile peppers," and "the fiesta of the *masúchiles*."
The reference to chile peppers and *masúchiles* comes from the colorful offerings the artisans of Olinalá make and carry to the church as an offering
to their saint. The word *masúchil* is a combination of two Náhuatl words,
ma from *maitl*, or "hand," and *súchil*, which comes from the word *xochitl*,
or "flower." The word can be translated as an offering of flowers.
Masúchiles are tall structures, profusely decorated with large red and green
poblano-style peppers, marigolds, and other autumn flowers. They are carried through the streets of the village during the procession and are finally
deposited at the altar of the church as an offering to San Francisco. Some
measure as much as seven feet tall, which makes them unwieldy objects to
carry in the procession.

This is the most important fiesta of the year for San Francisco Olinalá.
In many ways, it is a typical fall fiesta in rural Mexico, with a visiting saint
that accompanies San Francisco in leading the procession through the
town streets, allowing the artisans to display their *masúchiles*. Marching

bands, dances in the atrium of the church, firecrackers and rockets, and food and drink are common to all harvest fiestas. In this fiesta, young men and boys, their faces covered with jaguar (*tigre*) masks and costumes slink and dance through the streets of the town as they perform the "dance of the *tecuani*." This figure is associated with the destruction of the planted seeds. The dancers all profess to dance "for the crops," but it also evident that they clearly enjoy their feline role and the entertainment they provide. The jaguar has been a sacred symbol of power since pre-Hispanic times. The final event is a mass held in the church of San Francisco on October 4. The *masúchiles* are later distributed among the population, who use the seeds of the chile peppers and flowers for the next year's crop.

Huge barrels of *pozole* are prepared by the family members of the principal sponsor and organizer of the fiesta. He must collect a fee from each household to cover the expenses of the music, food, fireworks, dancers, flowers, and other expenses. All inhabitants of Olinalá as well as visitors are invited to partake of the *pozole*. Some households gain prestige by offering breakfasts in their homes to the musicians, dancers, and those who provide fireworks for the fiesta. This is indeed an elaborate festival, of which the inhabitants of Olinalá are justly proud. They state that offering a good fiesta for San Francisco will produce a better harvest in November. They have no explanation for the use of chile peppers in the offerings, and say that only God knows and that they are merely following the customs of their ancestors. They are not aware of the pre-Hispanic elements of their fiesta. The ideas they profess are part of the belief system typical of this part of the country, which helps to identify them as a cultural group and at the same time reinforces their patterns of traditional behavior.

COMMERCIAL FAIRS

It has become expensive to put on a fiesta. The younger generation often leaves the town to look for better work opportunities in cities or travels to the United States to work. The inhabitants of the town often do not have enough money to support the fiesta cycle. Some fiestas are becoming commercialized and have been turned into public fairs, rather than celebrated as fiestas.[15] Many of them continue to celebrate the patron saint of the town; however, municipal authorities help pay the expenses. Commercial fairs may be held to promote a particular product, such as silver, wine, or regional arts and crafts.

In October, a mole fair is held in San Pedro Actopan, Milpa Alta, on the outskirts of Mexico City. Dozens of restaurants and *fondas* (eateries) set up shop especially for the occasion. They serve different kinds of mole to the public and sell mole pastes and powders. This type of fair is sponsored by local authorities, who promote the town and the product for which it is famous and provide a festive atmosphere for visitors.

The fair honoring amaranth is traditionally held in Santiago Tulehualco, in the district of Xochimilco, the principal amaranth-producing area. During the first two weeks of February, some 60 stands are set up, offering traditional and new ways of utilizing amaranth in the daily diet. In this way they promote the commercialization of amaranth, which has a limited acceptance in the Mexican diet. In 2003, more than 50,000 people visited the amaranth fair, demonstrating a renewed interest in this high-protein product.

In January, the orange-producing town of Montemorelos, Nuevo León, celebrates its local harvest by filling the fountain in the central square with orange juice rather then water. January is the peak season of the orange harvest, when the fruit is at its lowest price and the town can afford to squander truckloads of oranges to fill the fountain.

Apan, Hidalgo, celebrates a pulque festival during the second week of April. Pulque is made from the sap or juice of the maguey cactus, or century plant. Pulque has been replaced by beer as the favorite beverage of many people. Beer has many advantages over pulque, as it can be bottled and easily transported to distant areas. Pulque must be consumed almost immediately. Attempts to bottle or can it have been unsuccessful.

Other commercial fairs include the sweet wine and liquor festival celebrated in Xicotepec, Puebla, in April. Many kinds of fruit are produced in the area, especially a native mulberry called *acachul*. The fruits are used to manufacture local wines and liquors.

In spite of the greater sophistication Mexico has gained in the past few decades, on its road to being considered an industrialized economy, the fiesta cycle has not fallen into disuse, nor has it lost its symbolic context. People continue to participate and search for meaning in the fiesta. A celebration serves as a unifying factor in a community, because it entails the participation of all members in the organization of the fiesta and may serve to improve daily relations among neighbors. Fiestas are becoming more complex and sophisticated. There have been occasions when some ceremonies have fallen into disuse only to be revived in recent years by the new generation. The festivities are flexible enough to adjust to changing social conditions in order to permit their continuance, and they play an important role in community life. Fiestas are one of the traits that identify the Mexican culture.

NOTES

1. Imelda de León, ed., *Calendario de Fiestas Populares* (Mexico City: Secretaría de Educación, Dirección General de Culturas Populares, 1988).

2. Octavio Paz, *El laberinto de la soledad* (Mexico City: Edtl. Planeta, 1959), 40–41.

3. "El niñopa," *Reforma*, 6 January 2004.

4. María Dolores Torres Yzabal and Shelton Wiseman, *The Mexican Gourmet* (San Diego, Calif.: Thunder Bay Press, 1995), 245–52.

5. Elizabeth Carmichael and Chlöe Sayer, *The Skeleton at the Feast: The Day of the Dead in Mexico* (Austin: University of Texas Press, 1992), 14–24.

6. E. Cortés Ruiz, B. Oliver, C. Rodríguez, D. Sierra, and P. Villanueva, *Los días de muertos: Una costumbre mexicana* (Mexico City: GV Editores, 1986), 7–18.

7. Patricia Quintana with Carol Haralson, *Mexico's Feasts of Life* (Tulsa, Okla.: Council Oak Books, 1989), 37–65.

8. Torres Yzabal and Wiseman, *The Mexican Gourmet*, 245–52.

9. Banco Nacional de México, *La cena de Navidad* (Mexico City: Organización Editorial Novaro, 1980), 12–40.

10. Quintana and Haralson, *Mexico's Feasts of Life*, 37–65.

11. Verónica Isabel Torres Cadena, "La alimentación en Tláhuac, Distrito Federal. Estudio de caso sobre cultura alimentaria en México" (master's thesis, Universidad Nacional Autónoma de México, 2003), 125.

12. Ibid., 204–5.

13. Janet Long-Solís, "Las ofrendas de San Francisco," *Estudios de Cultura Náhuatl* 20 (1990): 229–44.

14. Ibid.

15. México Desconocido, *Fiestas* (Mexico City: Guía México Desconocido, No. 9, 1993), 73–87.

8

Diet and Health

Mexico is a country of profound and often conflicting contrasts. At the same time as government and health officials attempt to cope with malnutrition and anemia in rural Mexico, one in every three adults in urban Mexico is overweight, making obesity the most serious health problem in the country today. During the past several decades, the federal government has designed and carried out many programs in an attempt to resolve the problem of inadequate nutrition. The programs are generally modified every six years, when a new government takes power, which often renders an efficient program powerless and ineffective. Solving the problems of malnutrition and anemia is proving to be easier to resolve than obesity, which has risen to epidemic levels during the past decade. This chapter will also attempt to explain why the Mexican diet, which was known to be healthy and nutritious and had served the Mexican people well for centuries, has now become ineffective and unable to solve the problems of health and nutrition. The efforts of the Mexican government to ameliorate these problems will also be outlined. However, first, some ancient Indian beliefs that still resonate and affect health are also discussed.

INDIAN PERCEPTION OF FOOD

A more thought-provoking approach to the Indian diet is to examine how Indians themselves perceive their food. It is a common belief in nearly all Mexican Indian cultures that food should be divided into groups, classified as "hot" or "cold." This theory is vaguely based upon the medical texts of the ancient Greek physicians Hippocrates and Galen. Of all the medical theories introduced into Mexico by the Spaniards, this has been the longest-lasting belief in Indian medicine. The system is based upon the belief that a human's health depends upon the balance of the four basic humors or fluids in the body. These consist of yellow bile, blood, black bile, and phlegm. If there is an alteration or imbalance in one of these humors, a person may be subject to illness. Food, illnesses, and their remedies are classified as "cold," "hot," "humid," or "dry." Cold maladies must be treated with hot foods and medicines. In the same way, the treatment of a hot illness must consist of a cold remedy or the consumption of cold foods. New World plants, animals, and minerals were easily incorporated into this system, because of the bipolar concept that existed in Nahua beliefs. Mexican scholars have shown that the same concept, but with a different explanation, was part of the Mesoamerican world view.

The custom of dividing food into hot and cold categories and limiting its consumption on this basis can sometimes be detrimental to nutrition. Some Indian groups do not allow children to eat fruits after having consumed milk or *atole* because of the belief that fruits are cold. For the same reason, they discourage children from eating fruit at night. Another perception related to food is the belief among the Ténuk Indians in San Luis Potosí that the only foods that give them a sensation of "having eaten" are corn and beans.[1]

The Mochó Indians in Chiapas believe that corn is the only food that is incorporated directly into the bloodstream. While beverages serve to lower or eliminate what one eats, the only beverages that nurture are those made of corn.[2]

The urban Zapotecs of San Pablo Mitla, Oaxaca, divide foods into those that are edible and those that are inedible under certain circumstances. This is a cultural construct based upon sensory and cultural determinants. Aroma, taste, texture, and appearance determine which foods can be eaten, and when.[3]

MALNUTRITION AND ANEMIA

The first national survey on nutrition in Mexico was carried out by the Health Department (Secretaría de Salud) in 1988.[4] The poll assessed the intake of micronutrients essential for growth and development and included body measurements such as height and weight. The survey took into consideration children under 5 years of age and women between the ages of 12 and 49, which represent the reproductive years of a woman's life. The country was divided into four regions: northern Mexico, central Mexico, Mexico City and surrounding areas, and southern Mexico. Dietary habits were analyzed on a regional basis. The most serious cases of malnutrition were detected in rural areas in southern Mexico, in states with large indigenous populations. Eleven years later, in 1999, another survey was carried out using the same geographical parameters and adding an additional category for children between the ages of 6 and 11.[5] The similarity in the design of the two polls allowed specialists to compare the statistics of the two surveys and judge the improvement or lack of it in different areas.

In the 1988 survey, on a national level, 14.2 percent of children under the age of five were found to be underweight. This figure was reduced to 7.5 percent in the 1999 survey, showing an improvement of nearly 50 percent. In the same age group, 22.8 percent of the children were discovered to be short for their age in the 1988 survey. This is an indicator of chronic malnutrition, a higher risk of disease, and a lower ability to carry out schoolwork efficiently. In the 1999 survey, this percentage had been reduced to 17.7 percent, which indicates a reduction of 22 percent in the prevalence of growth retardation. Low weight for height was 6 percent in 1988 and had been lowered to 2 percent in 1999, registering a decrease of 67 percent in 11 years. Half of the indigenous children surveyed were found to be shorter than average, due to an inadequate energy supply.

An abnormally low concentration of hemoglobin in the blood is known as anemia. The percentage of children under the age of five with this condition was 27.2 percent on a national level in 1999; thus, one out of every four children under the age of five was considered anemic, due to a poor iron intake in their diets. Among indigenous children polled, 36 percent were shown to have anemia. The prevalence of anemia is higher during the second year of life, reaching nearly 50 percent for children between 12 and 23 months of age and 33 percent in children between 24 and 35 months. According to the results of this survey, growth retardation and anemia, due to an iron deficiency, constitute the principal nutrition problems in children under five years of age.

The 1988 survey indicated that pregnant and lactating women between the ages of 12 and 49, considered the childbearing years, showed a degree of low weight and anemia, due to the lack of iron in the diet. In the 1999 survey, 26.4 percent of pregnant women between 12 and 49 years were found to be anemic, compared with 20 percent of those women who were not pregnant. Mexico City had the lowest rates, with higher rates registered for both the northern and southern sections of the country. This constitutes a serious health problem that could be corrected by providing iron-rich foods and food supplements of iron and folic acid to the diet of expectant mothers. The 1999 report found nutrition extremes over the last decade had polarized. The states with the poorest nutrition statistics got worse, while the best-performing states improved.

Mexican food habits have changed substantially in the past few years. Nutritionists have observed an increase in the consumption of wheat products, in substitution of corn, in the form of breads, cereals, pastas, cookies, and pastries. This is in part caused by the transition from a rural to an urban diet due to the heavy migration from the countryside to urban areas during the past few decades. The general availability of refined, high-fat, and high-sugar products in urban areas makes fast-food products convenient purchases. The new products available on the market, introduced by the North American Free Trade Agreement in 1994, often substitute rather than complement Mexican ingredients in the diet. The increased participation of women in the labor force results in less time for women to prepare family meals and forces them to rely on ready-made foods, which may be higher in fats and simple carbohydrates than home-made meals. There is also a tendency to accept the new food imports because of their higher status over the traditional diet, especially in middle and high income levels. The external influence is less dramatic on rural diets; however, the migration of undocumented Mexican labor to the United States, when workers return with a preference for diets high in animal fats and sugars, has proved detrimental to the rural diet as well. The frequency of obesity, diabetes, and cardiovascular problems as a result of changes to a more refined diet high in fats and sugars can be observed in both urban as well as rural Mexico.

GOVERNMENTAL PROGRAMS FOR NUTRITIONAL AID

For several decades, the Mexican government has carried out various programs in an attempt to improve the diet and nutrition of the Mexican population. These have included changes in economic policies, control of food prices, subsidies for the production of food, retail sale of government-subsidized foods, and programs of food distribution. These include free primary-school breakfasts in rural schools and food boxes or baskets containing products that make up the basic diet known as *la canasta básica*.

The results of the 1999 survey indicate that 28 percent of Mexican homes received some kind of food assistance. The four main food-aid programs active at the turn of the century, in terms of coverage for children under five years of age, were Liconsa, which distributes milk at subsidized prices; DIF (Desarrollo Integral de la Familia), with various health and nutrition activities, including the distribution of food baskets that contain basic foods and school breakfasts for children at the primary-school level; Progresa, an integral program directed toward combating poverty in rural areas, which includes the distribution of nutrient-enriched foods for poor women and children under two years of age; and Fidelist, which distributes corn tortillas at subsidized prices. The Liconsa program works mostly in urban areas, while the activities of Progresa are directed more toward poor rural areas. A program dedicated to enriching wheat flour and nixtamalized corn with extra micronutrients has been successfully implemented within the past decade.

The Progresa program is especially active in poor rural areas of most of the country. Under this plan, primary-school children receive a bimonthly stipend from state authorities, which their parents are obliged to spend on food, clothing, or school supplies for the child. Secondary-school children receive a larger donation every two months, and the same restrictions apply to its expenditure.[6] The receipts for the previous purchases are required in order to qualify for new donations. A monthly food basket is given to those over 60 years old and can be obtained at governmental offices (La Presidencia Municipal) in many towns in rural Mexico. The basket includes rice, oil, cornmeal, sugar, pasta, cookies, and two bars of soap for washing dishes and clothes for the minimal price of five Mexican pesos (about 40 U.S. cents). This program also falls under the control of Progresa.

Some private supermarkets offer biyearly government-sponsored programs (in December and during summer-vacation periods) to help lower-income families purchase food baskets, which include products calculated to make up the basic-food basket for people who earn a minimum wage at a savings of 25 percent. In reality, anyone who wishes can purchase these food baskets merely by requesting them at the supermarket. The contents of the basket include standard brands of cooking oil, canned pinto beans, sugar, rice, canned jalapeño chiles, pasta for making soup, lentils, canned tuna, coffee, *atole* powder, chicken consommé, chocolate powder, and oatmeal.

The Valle del Mezquital in Hidalgo is a semidesert area inhabited by Otomi Indian communities who live in extreme poverty. This is one of the most deprived areas of the country, where malnutrition is endemic. Some five years ago, physicians at the Federico Gómez Children's Hospital of Mexico City developed a formula called Him-Maíz to relieve malnutrition among Otomi babies and small children. The formula consists of corn-flour *atole* with added milk, sugar, and oil and is designed to serve as a food complement to be taken after meals three times a day. The reason for the failure of some aid programs can be traced to a lack of cooperation or understanding on the part of the needy. In one case, the mother of two severely malnourished children (ages three and six), modified the formula recommended by the coordinator of the program and reduced the amount of corn flour from 1/2 cup to three tablespoons and omitted the oil completely, explaining, "I don't add the oil, because we don't like it" ("No lo pongo el aceite porque no nos gusta").[7]

The program is sponsored by the Círculo Mexicano de Integración Educativa (CEMIE) and the Fundación Porvenir (Foundation for the Future). Parents are given the ingredients to make the formula at a community center every two months, at which time their children are weighed and measured to see their progress or lack of improvement. Children are at a higher risk of malnutrition between the ages of 8 and 20 months, when they no longer have access to their mother's breast milk. Children who suffer from malnutrition are shown to be at a higher risk of respiratory and gastrointestinal diseases. During the last 50 years, many similar programs aimed at providing food for the needy have been put into practice in Mexico. The most successful experiments have been those in which mothers receive instructions on how to prepare better-quality food and are organized as a group and provided with financial support. One of the major problems in government-supported food programs is the monotony of the foods offered.

NUTRIENT-ENRICHED FOODS

The process of adding external substances to a food product in order to render it more nutritious is not a novelty in Mexico. Part of the traditional technology of making tortillas since ancient times has included the addition of extra calcium and enhancing its vitamin content. The nixtamalization of corn in water has always been done with the addition of added limestone. The purpose of this ancient technique was to give greater flexibility and a more delicate flavor to the finished product. In addition, through this process the tortilla is converted into a rich source of calcium, and the alkaline treatment liberates the niacin present in corn.[8]

Another case in point is the addition of iodine to table salt. Iodine insufficiency is present in nearly five percent of the Mexican population, who do not have access to health services and do not consume foods rich in iodine, such as fish, milk, fruits, and grains. The lack of iodine in the diet can cause a reduction of thyroid hormones necessary for good health. This deficiency is characterized by retarded growth and associated with the appearance of goiter, which may cause a mental deficiency known as congenital hypothyroidism.

In 1970, a group of doctors discovered that in the states of Guerrero, Oaxaca, Chiapas, Yucatán, Puebla, Hidalgo, and southern Nuevo León, there were communities where approximately 20 percent of the population was suffering from goiter. The addition of iodine to table salt has diminished the severity of this deficiency. Between 1997 and 2000, the percentage of goiter cases in Mexico dropped from 12.8 percent to 1.3 percent.[9] In spite of these measures, the number of Mexicans who live in rural communities with few resources and still suffer from this deficiency remains at five percent. All salt that is manufactured in industrial facilities must contain iodine; however, some communities obtain locally produced salt, which is free of iodine. A program to be completed in 2005 will make the addition of iodine to table salt for human consumption mandatory. The program will be directed toward rural areas where indigenous communities, farmers, and mestizos reside, who still have a deficiency in this nutrient.

One of the most noted deficiencies in the Mexican diet in all social levels is iron, which reflects an inadequate diet. This has been shown to cause anemia in both children and expectant mothers, as well as retarded growth patterns in children. A baby can absorb half of the iron present in his mother's breast milk, but only 10 percent of the iron present in cow's milk.[10] Iron is a component of hemoglobin, which transports oxygen from the lungs to the body cells; this makes it an indispensable element for reaching an optimum state of nutrition. School-age children who are affected by an iron deficiency show less interest in learning, a reduced attention span, and chronic fatigue.

Anemia is more prevalent in rural Mexico than in urban communities. Available food sources rich in iron include spinach; greens (*quelites*); strawberries; potatoes; cooked beans; soybeans; whole milk; meat (veal, beef, and pork); chicken; liver; eggs; fish; sardines; oatmeal; cereals with added iron; cooked pasta; and dried fruits such as raisins, dates, and prunes.[11] There are many sources of iron available in the diet; however, the problem lies in the limited ability of the body to absorb it. Although it is preferable to consume iron in its natural state, it is a common additive in many industrialized food products, such as wheat and corn flour. The addition of ascorbic acid, which helps the absorption of iron already present in a foodstuff, may be more important than the addition of iron itself.

Nutrients have been added to industrialized food products in the form of vitamins and minerals in an effort to improve the Mexican diet since 1987. Some industrial processes destroy the natural nutrients in a product, and these substances need to be restored when the process is finished. Examples of this include the destruction of ascorbic acid during the bottling process of fruit juices; the process of grinding cereal grains to produce refined flour, which eliminates the husk of the grain along with the fiber and most of the thiamine; and the process to produce skimmed milk, which implies the separation of the fat content, with the customary loss of the vitamins A and D. The vitamins and minerals are reinstituted into the finished product.

The addition of vitamins and minerals to both wheat and corn flour plays an important role in the Mexican diet, as many products are made from these basic ingredients. Wheat flour has added iron, folic acid, protein, thiamine, riboflavin, niacin, and calcium. Corn flour is fortified with thiamine, riboflavin, niacin, folic acid, calcium, iron, and zinc. Some nutritionists do not approve of fortifying industrialized foods, using the argument that the sector of the population that usually purchases industrialized food products is not the sector that needs the extra vitamins or minerals in their diets.

OBESITY

Obesity represents the most serious health problem in Mexico today. One in every three adults in Mexico is overweight or obese, and the prediction is for these statistics to continue rising for both children and adults in the coming years.

The results of the 1988 nutritional survey showed that 4.7 percent of children under five years of age were overweight or obese. This figure increased to 5.4 percent in the 1999 survey, with a higher increase shown in northern Mexico and Mexico City and surrounding areas. Obesity in children is associated with a higher risk of obesity in adolescents and adults, with an increase in the risk of chronic illnesses.

The same 1988 survey indicated that 16.4 percent of women between 12 and 49 years of age, using a Body Mass Index (BMI) of between 25.0 and 29.9, were classified as overweight, while those with a BMI of 30, or 18.7 percent of the population, were considered obese.[12] The results of the 1999 poll showed that 30.8 percent of women were classified as overweight, while 21.7 percent were categorized as obese, again with higher incidences in northern Mexico, where there is greater consumption of food rich in animal fats. This is the area where greater obesity is registered in the population.

Changes in the diet noted for the 11-year period between surveys showed an increased number of calories in the diet. The fat content in the diet increased as well. In 1988, fats contributed approximately 23.5 percent of the total energy intake in adult women; this number increased to 30.3 percent in 1999. There was also a higher intake of sugar and refined . carbohydrates and a decrease in the purchase of fruits and vegetables.[13] The increase shown in overweight and obesity is parallel to the increase in the death rate from diabetes, hypertension, and cardiovascular diseases during that time period and is associated with an increase in high-energy density of diet and the consumption of refined carbohydrates and sugar, in a population whose physical activity is less than desirable. Less than 20 percent of the Mexican population participates in physical activities. The highest participation is shown in the 15–19 age group, where 27.8 percent of the population exercise. Only 3.5 percent of the population over 60 years old participate in a physical activity.

The increase in excessive weight and obesity is associated with chronic diseases such as type 2 diabetes mellitus; hypertension; atherosclerosis; high cholesterol; certain types of cancer; cardiovascular diseases; and orthopedic, respiratory, and psychological problems. Having to cope with high health costs as a consequence of obesity is a heavy burden for the Mexican health system to carry. Chronic anxiety, depression, a general lack of self-confidence, family conflicts, stress incapacity, social disorganization, and work problems caused by absenteeism are other problems known to affect obese people. In adolescents, the most serious danger of obesity appears to be the stigma that being obese carries among their peers.

Obesity is now accepted in the medical field as a chronic disease that can be controlled through long-term treatment, but it is very difficult to treat successfully. About 25 percent of the problem in Mexico is attributed to genetic factors. Inheritance may determine the distribution of the accumulation of fat in the body, and there is a clear tendency for members of the same family to have a similar BMI. The accumulation of fat in the upper body and abdomen increases the risk of heart disease independent of the degree of obesity. Thirty percent of obesity is attributed to cultural factors, such as the high-fat diet popular in Mexico and a general lack of discipline in food habits. Soft drinks, such as Coca-Cola and Pepsi, contribute heavily to obesity, because Mexicans drink on average more than a 12-ounce can of soda every day.[14] A soft drink of this size contains at least 30 grams of fructose, or 120 calories. Forty-five percent of the cases of obesity are attributed to nontransmissible environmental factors.

Obesity is known to be more common in women than in men, as they are the ones who have closer contact with food and food preparation. Also, women are less physically active than men. While 23.3 percent of the male population practices a sport, only 8 percent of women do. Obesity is more prevalent in the lower- and middle-income sectors of the population. Upper-class women are more aware of their appearance and have more resources to improve their figures through exercise and diet than do other levels of society. They also have access to more information on healthy diets and eat a higher percentage of fruits and vegetables. Women with a low education level show higher levels of obesity than more educated women, who may be better informed of the dangers of obesity and are more concerned with keeping a slim body, similar to that of their role models on television and in the movies.

It has been noted that persons afflicted with obesity eat fewer times a day than thin people, who may divide their food intake into five or more small meals throughout the day. Obese people, both young people and adults, tend to be less active physically than thinner people. A correlation can be seen between the number of years of schooling and physical activity. Both married men and women are shown to exercise more than single people. Those who eat a high-fat diet are known to eat for longer periods of time, because fat is thought to be less efficient in sending signals of satiety that are sent from the centers of appetite control in the gastrointestinal tract to the brain.[15] The National Consensus of Obesity has proposed that the BMI to classify obesity for the Mexican population be set at greater than or equal to 27 rather than 30, the number used in the United States.

Many factors must be considered when analyzing the recent upsurge in obesity in Mexico. The portion size of food has nearly doubled in the past few years; migration from the countryside to urban areas has changed the diet to one with higher calories and a more sedentary lifestyle; and people have begun to consume more calories than they expend, resulting in weight gain. The easy availability of high-sugar and high-fat snacks makes them easier to purchase than the preparation of a home-cooked meal. People are increasingly eating outside the home. The consumption of processed foods with a high content of oil and simple and refined carbohydrates with less fiber and complex carbohydrates plays a role in the surge in obesity.

The state of Yucatán has a double negative when it comes to weight control. Yucatecans are of short stature due to their Mayan heritage, and the local cuisine, while very good, is high in fried foods and in the use of pork in many dishes, which contributes to the obesity of the people.

The well-known dietary experience of the Papago Indians (of Pima Indian stock and language) may be used as a good example of the importance of cultural and environmental factors in obesity. The Papago live on both sides of the U.S.-Mexican border. The Mexican Papago live in Sonora, Mexico, while their fellow American Papago live in Arizona. When the political lines between the two countries were drawn after the purchase of Arizona, known as the Gasden Purchase, was ratified in 1854, the northern Papago ended up on the U.S. side of the border. In recent years, the Arizona Papago changed their name to the Tohono O'odham Nation, to differentiate themselves from the Sonora Papago. While the Arizona group live on the large Tohono O'odham Indian Reservation, which is heavily dependent upon the U.S. government for food, medicine, and housing, the Mexican Papago are farmers and day laborers and live in quite precarious conditions, with no help from the Mexican government. The two groups share the same genetic background and, like all Indian cultures, have genetic tendencies toward obesity and type 2 diabetes. Papago Indian families share the trait of a low metabolic rate, which is considered predictive of weight gain and the development of type 2 diabetes.[16]

The difference in obesity and type 2 diabetes between the two groups is striking and can be attributed to their differing lifestyles. While the Tohono O'odham live a sedentary life on the reservation, with their basic needs being taken care of by the U.S. government, the Sonora Papago survive through hard work and physical labor, with no assistance from the Mexican government. Some years ago a study compared the BMI and weight of men and women in the two populations and found a substantial difference in both indicators. Tohono women in Arizona have a BMI 10 points higher on average than their counterparts in Sonora. The BMI of Arizona Tohono men is six points higher than those in Sonora. Full-blooded Papago Indians are found to have the highest prevalence of type 2 diabetes, as compared with those of mixed heritage. The highest rates were found in children, whose parents developed diabetes at an early age. Ninety-five percent of those with diabetes are overweight or obese. The modern Tohono diet is higher in calories than the traditional Indian diet, and physical activity has decreased. Their food specialty is fried bread, which is not the ideal food for a population afflicted with diabetes. The food donated by the U.S. government is surplus food, often in the form of canned fruits in sweet syrups. Although the Tonoho O'odham wash the fruit, they are never completely successful in removing the sugar, and this must raise the glucose in their blood to high levels. The changes in diet and physical activity are associated with the increased prevalence of type 2 diabetes.

Papago Indians living in Sonora who consume a more traditional diet and one with less animal fat and more complex carbohydrates have a lower prevalence of type 2 diabetes. They also expend more calories through physical activity, which contrasts with the sedentary lifestyles of the Tohono O'odham.[17] The latter are said to have the highest rate of obesity and type 2 diabetes mellitus in the world.

Obesity is a public health problem that the Mexican Health Department is trying to address through strategies of prevention, the education of the public through the media, and therapeutic strategies that take into consideration the regional causes of the problem.

DIABETES MELLITUS

Recent statistics indicate that 10.75 percent of the Mexican population between the ages of 20 and 69 are afflicted by some type of diabetes mellitus, which is equivalent to more than 5.5 million persons.[18] Almost 23 percent of those affected with diabetes are unaware they have the illness. This is equivalent to more than 1 million people who have not yet been diagnosed. Sixty-five percent of those affected are women, who in general have a higher rate of obesity than men and are less active physically. Urban areas register a higher rate of diabetes than do rural zones. It is one of the principal causes of death in Mexico, along with cardiovascular problems and cancer. In 2002, close to 50,000 Mexicans died of causes related to diabetes mellitus.

Obesity has become one of the major factors in the risk of acquiring the disease. An excess of more than 20 percent in weight is a clear indication of the danger of becoming a diabetic. It has been calculated that 8 of every 10 people suffering from type 2 diabetes are overweight or obese. Thirteen and a half percent of obese or overweight people develop type 2 diabetes, compared with 3.5 percent of the population who maintain a normal, healthy weight. A program of balanced nutrition and an increase in physical activity can prevent type 2 diabetes, even among those who have high risk factors for contracting the disease. According to Public Health calculations, by the year 2025, over 20 percent of the population will have developed type 2 diabetes. Either the disease has increased by 25 percent in the past 10 years, or the techniques for detecting it have become more refined. Ninety percent of the cases of diabetes in Mexico are type 2 diabetes. A diet high in carbohydrates, lack of exercise, excess weight, chronic stress, and inheritance all play a role in the disease. Other factors that complicate type 2 diabetes are high levels of triglycerides in the blood, a high level of LDL cholesterol, high blood pressure, and insulin resistance. Mexicans, especially those from an Indian background, are more prone to contracting diabetes than those of European descent, because American Indians in general have a high tendency toward diabetes.

The use of fructose as a substitute for sugar in soft drinks, juices, and other industrialized foods is suspected by some researchers to be a cause in the increase of diabetes and obesity. Some poor families spend more on soft drinks than they do on food, erroneously believing that soft drinks are a good source of nutrition. The increase in type 2 diabetes among the Chiapas Indian population, who live a lifestyle with ample physical activity and who do not have automobiles, computers, or other modern facilities, is alarming.[19] This causes field anthropologists to question whether perhaps fructose is the underlying cause of increased type 2 diabetes in Chiapas and in general throughout Mexico. It is interesting to note that soft drinks are more expensive than equivalent amounts of milk.

ANOREXIA AND BULIMIA

Hip young girls in Mexico are called by the name of "strawberries," or *niñas fresa*. They are very worried about projecting a "good image" of their bodies on the social scene and in the way their clothes fit. They use their body as an introduction to society, to be accepted or rejected. Identity problems linked to their body images are similar to those found in young people in more developed countries.

Anorexia is a growing problem in Mexico and has increased considerably in the past five years. It is more prevalent among young women than in young men and affects mostly young people between the ages of 11 and 25. There are approximately 10 young women to every young man in Mexico afflicted by this problem.[20] In Mexico, around 0.5 percent of anorexics are young women, with a mortality rate of 10 percent in patients that have had treatment. There are several symptoms to identify anorexia: (1) a loss of body weight (at least 15 percent below normal weight in relation to stature), (2) an exaggerated fear of gaining weight, (3) an erroneous perception of the body, (4) amenorrhea, (5) fragile fingernails, (6) lack of warmth in the extremities, (7) the appearance of fine hair, (8) recurrent feelings of sadness and depression, (9) fatigue brought on by hyperactivity, and (10) isolation from friends and family. These symptoms are a type of symbolic language that young people use when they cannot directly express their emotions or fears related to growth; separation; sexuality; and the sensations of anguish, vulnerability, or resentment.

Bulimia nervosa is present in between 1 and 3 percent of women, though symptoms of bulimia exist in 19 percent of the adolescent population.[21] A continuum that leads from anorexia to bulimia has been noted that is known by the term *bulimarexia*, in reference to young girls who experiment with a combination of the two disorders.

Anorexia is defined as a rejection of food, due to an obsession with maintaining a low weight and an exaggerated fixation upon weight, figure, and food. In bulimia nervosa, the patient consumes large quantities of food and later eliminates it through vomiting or self-administered laxatives, in the belief that he or she will not gain weight. These are the two food disorders that appear most frequently in adolescents and young adults. Young girls afflicted with anorexia are continually trying to lose weight and will go to any extreme to achieve this goal. Strenuous exercise, diets, and self-medication are all used to avoid gaining weight. Anorexic young women have a distorted image of their bodies and are constantly looking at their figures in a mirror; prolong their meals for hours; and often hide food, especially carbohydrates. With time, they seek isolation and avoid the company of others, who may become aware of how little they eat. Young women with these characteristics have severe malnutrition and project sadness, a lack of interest, isolation, and a lack of communication with others. They easily become irritated and impulsive when they are told that they are doing grave damage to their health.

Food deprivation is not a novelty in Mexico. It was common behavior in Catholic convents, where food was considered a spiritual element that converted eating into a ritual act. The convent dining room was a space of penitence and purification, where food was transformed into something sacred through which the nuns could expunge their sins and purify their spirits.[22] Fasting and penitence were methods by which they attempted to attain purification of their bodies and souls. Partial fasting or total abstention of food and drink represented a form of personal humiliation, which was thought to make praying more effective. There was a complex schedule for penitence. In some of the convents, they ate only one meal a day, except on Sundays and on Christmas Eve. On some days, during Lent, nuns ate only bread and water. To leave a morsel of their favorite dish on their plate for the guardian angel was considered a manifestation of high spirituality.

THE PLATE OF GOOD EATING

The Mexican food guide, called *The Plate of Good Eating* (*El plato del bien comer*, or simply *El plato*) was designed to transmit as much food-orientation information as possible in a visual manner and to be used as a tool for educating the public about good food habits. The guide was prepared by a panel of nutritional experts using the most up-to-date information available while taking into consideration the cultural needs of the public. Food symbols are incorporated into the design to be more easily understood by the illiterate population. The design chosen is that of a large dinner plate divided into three basic food groups: (1) vegetables and fruits (vegetables are mentioned and illustrated first to emphasize their greater importance in the diet), (2) cereals, and (3) legumes and products of animal origin. *El plato* is accompanied by cutlery to emphasize its relation to eating. This presentation was well accepted by women from both rural and urban areas.[23]

The three groups are allotted the same amount of space on the chart, because it was found that some of the people surveyed were confused about graphic proportions and may not understand the proper use of the guide.[24] Two of the sections are subdivided into two departments, which at first glance may give the impression that the chart is divided into five categories instead of only three. The classification of vegetables and fruits is divided equally, with vegetables illustrated first, to convey a message of their greater importance in the diet. The group labeled "legumes and foods of animal origin" is separated into two parts; 2/3 of the area is allotted to legumes, while the remaining 1/3 is designated for animal products. The chart sends an implicit message that consumers should follow the same scheme when choosing their diet. No category was established for sugars, fats, and oils, under the philosophy that they are not primary foods, many industrialized foods contain these ingredients, and they are used in the preparation of many dishes. Also, the abuse of these ingredients contributes to nutritional problems such as the growing obesity situation in Mexico. Some specialists working on the design felt that including a specific category for these ingredients may convey the impression that their consumption was recommended by the committee.[25]

Without being specific about the number of daily rations that should be selected from each food group, a vague indication is given with the key words *muchos* (a lot) when referring to vegetables and fruits, *suficientes* (enough) when alluding to cereals and grains, and *pocos* (little) when mentioning meat and dairy products. The word *combina* is placed between the divisions of cereals and legumes, because the combination of these two food groups can produce a complete protein and is an important concept in the Mexican diet, as with the combination of corn and beans.

When working with children or illiterate groups, it is convenient to make use of colors to facilitate food recognition. A yellow background was chosen to identify cereals, green was the color selected to designate vegetables and fruits, and varying shades of red were used to symbolize legumes and meat products. The use of bright red was avoided as a background color so that it would not be interpreted as a signal of danger nor as a symbol of great importance. Great care was taken to develop a chart with which the Mexican public could easily relate to and recognize the ingredients represented. For example, squash flowers and *nopales* appear in the vegetable section of *El plato*, and tiny animal crackers and a bread roll (*bolillo*) are included in the division of cereals. This conveys a message to the public through products they are familiar with.

El plato del bien comer has specific purposes. The main one is to serve as a visual aid in food-orientation activities, where it is important to show corresponding food groups. In order to teach the public how to choose a balanced diet and a healthy regime, it is important to encourage combination and variation in food selection. With this in mind, one of the important messages conveyed is that in each meal, at least one food from each of the three food groups should be chosen, and that from one meal to another, or from one day to another, they should choose a different item from the group in order to promote a balanced and varied diet. The public is encouraged to substitute foods within the same food group.

When possible, it is suggested that *El plato* be accompanied by a list of recommendations to reinforce good nutritional information. The list ends with the wise advice "Enjoy your food." The list is presented here in an abbreviated form:

1. Include at least one item from each of the three food groups in the three main meals of the day.
2. Eat a variety of foods, including several uncooked and unpeeled vegetables and fruits. Combine legumes and cereals. Limit the consumption of meat. Choose fish or skinless chicken in preference to beef, pork, mutton, or kid.
3. Eat in moderation.
4. Restrict the consumption of fats, oils, and sugars. Use oil instead of lard, butter, or margarine. Cook with small amounts of salt and sugar. Do not place a

salt shaker or a sugar bowl on the table as a temptation to add more of these condiments. Eat salty and sweet foods in moderation.

5. Drink plenty of water.

6. Practice strict sanitary habits in the storage, preparation and consumption of food. Drink only boiled or disinfected water. Clean and disinfect vegetables and fruits. Wash hands with soap and water before eating and after going to the bathroom. Eat fish and shellfish only when well cooked.

7. Participate in a physical activity for 30 minutes each day. Include aerobic exercise to increase the heart rate; begin with 5 or 10 minute intervals and slowly build up good physical condition.

8. Maintain a healthy weight.

9. Be vigilant of children's growth and development. Keep the waistline smaller than the circumference of the hips.

10. Do not drink more than two alcoholic beverages a day, and only as an accompaniment for food. Do not smoke.

11. Enjoy good food, preferably in the company of the family. Enjoy your food![26]

NOTES

1. Margarita M. Ávila Uribe and María de la Luz Suárez Soto, "Hábitos alimentarios de los Tének o Huastecos de San Luis Potosí," *Cuadernos de Nutrición* 18, no. 5 (1995): 10.

2. María de la Luz del Valle, "Rituales alimentarios y ciclo de vida en Villa Milpa Alta, D. F." (master's thesis, Universidad Nacional Autónoma de México, 2003), 114.

3. Ellen Messer, "Plantas alimenticias zapotecas: Transformación de dos culturas," in *Conquista y comida: Consecuencias del encuentro de dos mundos*, ed. Janet Long (Mexico City: Universidad Nacional Autónoma de México, 1996), 320.

4. J. Sepúlveda-Amor, M. Lezana, R. Tapia-Conyer, J. Valdespino, H. Madrigal, and J. Kumate, "Estado nutricional de preescolares y mujeres en México: Resultados de una encuesta probabilística nacional," *Gaceta Médica de México* 126 (1990): 207–24.

5. J.R. Dommarco, T.S. Levy, S. Villalpando, T. González de Cossío, B. Hernández, and J. Sepúlveda-Amor, *Encuesta nacional de nutrición 1999* (Cuernavaca, Mexico: Instituto Nacional de Salud Pública, 2001).

6. Modesta Vázquez Gaspar, conversation with the author, 1 April 2004.

7. Sonia del Valle, "Apuestan a papillas en Hidalgo," *Reforma*, 21 March 2004, 12A.

8. Hector Bourges, "Bases para una política de adición de nutrimentos," *Cuadernos de Nutrición* 11, no. 4 (1988): 17–32.

9. Yolanda Rojas, "Bocio endémico: enfermedad milenario," *Cuadernos de Nutrición* 27, no. 2 (2004): 63–66.

10. Leopoldo Vega Franco, "El hierro en la infancia," *Cuadernos de Nutrición* 12, no. 4 (1989): 33–37.

11. Ana Bertha Pérez de Gallo, "El hierro en la dieta habitual," *Cuadernos de Nutrición* 10, no. 5 (1987): 42–43.

12. J. Sepúlveda-Amor and J. R. Dommarco, supplement to *Encuesta Nacional de Nutricion 1999* (Mexico City: Secretaria de Salud, Instituto Nacional de Salud Pública, and Instituto Nacional de Estadística, Geografía e Informativa 2001), 13.

13. Dommarco et al., *Encuesta nacional de nutrición, 1999*, 7–224.

14. Ronald Nigh, "Globalización y salud: El síndrome metabólico de Chiapas," *Chan Tecolotl* 14, no. 163 (March 2004): 4–5.

15. "Etiología y fisiopatogenia de la obesidad," in *Obesidad en México*, ed. L. Vargas Ancona, R. Bastarrachea, H. Laviada, J. González, and H. Ávila Rosas (Mexico City: McGraw Hill Interamericana, 2002), 11–24.

16. National Institute of Diabetes and Digestive and Kidney Diseases, "The Pima Indians: Pathfinders for Health," NIH Publication 95–3821 (Washington, D.C.: U.S. Government Printing Office, 1995).

17. S. S. Carter, J. Pugh, and A. Monterrosa, "Non-Insulin-Dependent Diabetes Mellitus in Minorities in the United States," *Annals of Internal Medicine* 125, no. 3 (1996): 221–32.

18. Datos de la Encuesta Nacional de Salud, ENSA, 2000.

19. Nigh, "Globalización y salud," 4–5.

20. Karine Tinat, "La anorexia y la feminidad en México," *Ichan Tecolotl* 4, no. 163 (2004): 5–6.

21. Armando Barriguete, "Anorexia y bulimia nervosa: el control del miedo," *Cuadernos de Nutrición* 26, no. 6 (2003): 282–84.

22. Rosalía Loreto López, "Prácticas alimenticias en los conventos de mujeres en la Puebla del siglo XVIII," in *Conquista y comida: Consecuencias del encuentro de dos mundos*, ed. Janet Long (Mexico City: Universidad Nacional Autónoma de México, 1996), 481–503.

23. H. Bourges, M. Kaufer Horowitz, E. Casanueva, and M. Plazas, "Los condimentos de El Plato del Bien Comer," *Cuadernos de Nutrición* 26, no. 6 (2003), 269–73.

24. E. Casanueva, E. Durán, M. Kaufer Horowitz, M. Plazas, E. Polo, G. Toussaint, H. Bourges, and R. Camacho, "Fundamentos de El Plato del Bien Comer," *Cuadernos de Nutrición* 25, no. 1 (2002): 21–28.

25. M. Kaufer Horowitz, R. Valdés-Ramos, W. Willett, A. Anderson, and N. Solomons, "Análisis comparativo de los mensajes de las representaciones visuales de siete guías alimentarias nacionales," *Cuadernos de Nutrición* 26, no. 6 (2003): 261–68.

26. Bourges et al., "Los condimentos," 273.

Glossary

achiote   seasoning paste made with ground annatto seeds, herbs, and bitter oranges

adobo   thick cooking sauce made with tomatoes, vinegar, and spices

almuerzo   brunch

antojito   appetizer

atole   corn-based beverage

bitter orange   Seville orange

bolillo   hard roll bread

botana   an appetizer

buñuelo   deep-fried wheat tortilla, served with molasses syrup

cantina   bar

capirotada   Lenten dessert made with slices of wheat-flour rolls, fried, and served with syrup, raisins, cinnamon, and shredded cheese

cazuela   clay pot

cena   supper

cenaduría   small restaurant, mostly found in provincial Mexico, that specializes in serving suppers

champurrado   chocolate-flavored *atole* drink

chinampas   deeply rooted artificial islands composed of reeds and water lilies and covered by silt

cocina   kitchen

comal   clay grill for cooking tortillas and spices

comedor   dining room

comida   main meal of the day

desayuno   breakfast

doblada   tortilla spread with sauce or other ingredients and folded in half

enchilada   tortilla dipped in a sauce, filled, and rolled

enchilado   dish with hot, spicy sauce

fonda   small restaurant

garnacha   thick corn tortilla stuffed with beans and topped with a variety of ingredients

gordita   a tiny corn-based snack wrapped in colored pieces of tissue paper and sold in the Basilica of Guadalupe, especially on December 12, the day of the Virgin of Guadalupe

guisado   stew

hacienda   ranch or plantation

huarache   corn-based snack in the shape of the sole of a sandal

huitlacoche   corn fungus; also called *cuitlacoche*

limas   key limes

lonchería   small restaurant that specializes in midday meals

maguey   century plant

maíz   corn

mano   muller used with the *metate*

masa   dough made with corn flour and water

masa harina   corn flour

mazapan   ground-peanut candy

mestizo   a person of mixed Indian and European heritage

metate   grinding stone

mezcal   distilled alcohol made from the agave plant

milpa   cornfield where beans and squash are also grown and wild quelites are tolerated

molcajete   basalt mortar for grinding seeds and sauces

molote   masa fritter stuffed with chorizo sausages and potatoes

Náhuatl   language spoken by the Aztecs

ocote   small sticks of resinous pine used to kindle a fire

olla   a round clay pot

pambazo   hard-roll sandwich filled with fried potatoes, chorizo, lettuce, and chipotle chiles

pan   bread

panadería   bread store

panucho   Yucatecan snack made with bean-filled tortillas

papa-dzul   Yucatecan enchilada made with toasted pumpkin seeds

pib   Yucatecan pit barbecue

picadita   snack similar to *sope*

picante   spicy or hot

pinole   toasted corn flour dissolved in water

platillo   dish of a specific food

plato   plate

plaza   market or square

postre   dessert

pozol agrio   fermented corn and water

pozole   pork and hominy stew

puesto   a street or market stand

pulque   fermented drink made from the century plant

quelites   greens

quesadilla   a turnover of tortilla dough, usually (but not always) filled with cheese (queso)

recado   seasoning for Yucatecan cooking

salbutes   fried tortillas covered with shredded turkey, pickled onions, and additional toppings

sopa   soup

sope   a small, round snack made with tortilla dough

taco   tortilla wrapped around a filling; may be fried

tamalada   party where the principal food served is tamales

tamale   corn dough beaten with lard, filled, and steamed in a corn husk or a banana leaf

taquiza   taco party

tejolote   pestle for the *molcajete*

tentempie   between-meal snack

tesgüino   alcoholic beverage made from corn

tomatillo   green husk tomato

torreja   wheat-flour roll dessert dipped into beaten egg before frying and
served with a cinnamon-flavored syrup and shredded lime peel

torta   sandwich made with a hard roll

tortilla   thin, unleavened pancake, made with ground dried corn

tostada   small tortilla fried and topped with a variety of ingredients

totopo   a small triangular piece of fried tortilla

trigo   wheat

Resource Guide

GENERAL REFERENCE WORKS

Carrasco, David. *The Oxford Encyclopedia of Mesoamerican Cultures*. New York: Oxford University Press, 2001.

Farb, Peter, and George Armelagos. *Consuming Passions: The Anthropology of Eating*. Boston: Houghton Mifflin, 1980.

Katz, Solomon H., ed. *The Encyclopedia of Food and Culture*. New York: Charles Scribner's Sons, 2003.

Kiple, Kenneth F., and Kriemhold Coneè Ornelas. *The Cambridge World History of Food*. 2 vols. Cambridge: Cambridge University Press, 2000.

MacClancy, Jeremy. *Consuming Culture: Why You Eat What You Eat*. New York: Henry Holt, 1992.

Pelto, G., and L. A. Vargas, eds. "Introduction: Dietary Change and Nutrition." *Ecology of Food and Nutrition* 27, no. 3–4 (1992): 159–61.

CHAPTER 1

Byers, Douglas S., ed. *The Prehistory of the Tehuacán Valley*. Vol. 1, *Environment and Subsistence*. Austin: University of Texas Press, 1967.

Carrasco, David. *Daily Life of the Aztecs*. Westport, Conn.: Greenwood Press, 1998.

Coe, Sophie. *America's First Cuisines*. Austin: University of Texas Press, 1994.

Díaz del Castillo, Bernal. *The Discovery and Conquest of Mexico*. New York: Grove Press, 1956.

Long, Janet, ed. *Conquista y comida: Consecuencias del encuentro de dos mundos*. Mexico City: Universidad Nacional Autónoma de México, 1996.

Ortiz de Montellano, Bernard. *Aztec Medicine, Health, and Nutrition.* New Brunswick, N.J.: Rutgers University Press, 1990.

Pilcher, Jeffrey. *¡Que Vivan los Tamales! Food and the Making of Mexican Identity.* Albuquerque: University of New Mexico Press, 1998.

Sahagún, Bernardino de. *General History of the Things of New Spain: Florentine Codex.* 12 vols. Ed. and Trans. C. E. Dibble and A.J.O. Anderson. Santa Fe, N.M.: School of American Research, 1950–82.

Vargas, Luis Alberto, and Leticia Casillas. "La alimentación en México durante los primeros años de la Colonia." In *Historia general de la medicina en México: Medicina Novohispana, siglo XVI,* ed. Fernando Martinez Cortés, 85–111. Mexico City: Academia Nacional de Medicina-Facultad de Medicina de la Universidad Nacional Autónoma de México, tomo II, 1990.

CHAPTER 2

Andrews, Jean. *Peppers: The Domesticated Capsicums.* Austin: University of Texas Press, 1984.

Coe, Sophie, and Michael Coe. *The True History of Chocolate.* London: Thames and Hudson, 1996.

Crosby, Alfred W., Jr. *The Columbian Exchange: Biological and Cultural Consequences of 1492.* Westport, Conn.: Greenwood Press, 1972.

Foster, N., and Linda S. Cordell, eds. *Chilies to Chocolate: Foods the Americas Gave to the World.* Tucson: University of Arizona Press, 1992.

García Acosta, Virginia. *Las panaderías, sus dueños y trabajadores. Ciudad de México. Siglo XVIII.* Mexico City: Ediciones de la Casa Chata, 1989.

Kaplan, Lawrence. "What Is the Origin of the Common Bean?" *Economic Botany* 35 (1981): 201–12.

Long, Janet. "The Mexican Contribution to the Mediterranean World." *Diogenes* 159 (winter 1992): 37–49.

Long-Solís, Janet. *Cápsicum y cultura: La historia del chilli.* Mexico City: Fondo de Cultura Económica, 1986.

Mintz, Sidney. *Sweetness and Power.* New York: Viking Penguin Books, 1985.

Olaya, Clara Inés. *Frutas de América: Tropical y subtropical: Historia y usos.* Santa Fé de Bogotá, Colombia: Grupo Editorial Normal, 1991.

Sokolov, Raymond. *Why We Eat What We Eat.* New York: Summit, 1991.

Super, John C. *Food, Conquest, and Colonization in Sixteenth-Century Spanish America.* Albuquerque: University of New Mexico Press, 1988.

Whitaker, T. W. "The Origin of the Cultivated *Cucurbita.*" *American Naturalist* 90 (1956): 171–76.

CHAPTER 3

Benitez, Fernando. *The Century after Cortés.* Chicago: University of Chicago Press, 1965.

Corcuera, Sonia. *Entre gula y templanza*. Mexico City: Universidad Nacional Autónoma de México, 1981.

Gero, J.M., and M. Conkey. *Engendering Archaeology: Women and Prehistory*. Oxford, England: Basil Blackwell, 1991.

Gibson, Charles. *The Aztecs under Spanish Rule*. Stanford, Calif.: Stanford University Press, 1964.

Liss, Peggy. *Mexico under Spain, 1521–1556*. Chicago: University of Chicago Press, 1975.

Long-Solís, Janet. *El sabor de la Nueva España*. Mexico City: Instituto Mora, 1995.

CHAPTER 4

Foster, George C. *Tzintzuntzan: Mexican Peasants in a Changing World: A Late Pre-Hispanic Cultural System*. Boston: Little, Brown, 1967.

Kennedy, John G. *Tarahumara of the Sierra Madre*. Pacific Grove, Calif.: Asilomar Press, 1978.

Messer, Ellen. *Zapotec Plant Knowledge: Classification, Uses, and Communication about Plants in the Valley of Oaxaca*. Memoirs of the University of Michigan Museum of Anthropology, no. 10, part 2, 1978.

Rozin, Elizabeth. "The Structure of Cuisine." In *The Psychobiology of Human Food Selection*, ed. L.M. Barker. Westport, Conn.: Avi Press, 1982.

Tausend, Marilyn. *Savoring Mexico*. San Francisco, Calif.: Williams-Sonoma, 2001.

CHAPTER 5

Ávila, D., J.R. Bastarrechea, A. Díaz, K. Flechsig, G. Moedano, O. Norman, G. Pérez San Vicente, G. Salinas, M.C. Suárez, and L.A. Vargas. *Atlas Cultural de México: Gastronomía*. Mexico City: Grupo Editorial Planeta, 1988.

Bayless, R. *Mexican Kitchen*. New York: Simon & Schuster, 1996.

Kennedy, Diana. *The Cuisines of Mexico*. New York: Harper & Row, 1972.

Morales de León, Josefina, "Introducción a la cocina mexicana." *Cuadernos de Nutrición* 12, no. 4 (1989): 17–32.

Palazuelos, Susana. *México: The Beautiful Cookbook*. Hong Kong: Weldon Owen, 1991.

Quintana, Patricia. *The Taste of Mexico*. New York: Stewart, Tabori and Chang, 1986.

Stoopen, M., and A.L. Delgado. *La cocina veracruzana*. Veracruz, Mexico: Gobierno del Estado de Veracruz, 1992.

Tausend, Marilyn. *Savoring Mexico*. San Francisco, Calif.: Williams-Sonoma, 2001.

Torres Yzabal, María Dolores, and Shelton Wiseman. *The Mexican Gourmet*. San Diego, Calif.: Thunder Bay Press, 1995.

CHAPTER 6

Guía de Restaurantes, Ciudad de México. 23rd ed. Editorial Reforma, 2004.

Long, Janet. Fondas y Fogones. Mexico City: Banco Nacional de México, 1996.

Sabio Busquets, Monserrat. "Servicios de alimentación." Cuadernos de Nutrición 17, no. 5 (1994): 9–12.

Tinker, I. Street Foods: Urban Employment in Developing Countries. New York: Oxford University Press, 1997.

Vargas, L. A., and L. Casillas. "Diet and Foodways in Mexico City." Ecology of Food and Nutrition 27, no. 3–4 (1992): 235–48.

CHAPTER 7

Carmichael, Elizabeth, and Chloë Sayer. The Skeleton at the Feast: The Day of the Dead in Mexico. Austin: University of Texas Press, 1992.

Cortés Ruiz, E., B. Oliver, C. Rodríguez, D. Sierra, and P. Villanueva. Los días de muertos: Una costumbre mexicana. Mexico City: GV Editores, 1986.

Iglesias, Sonia. Navidades mexicanas. Mexico City: Consejo Nacional para la Cultura y Las Artes, 2001.

León, Imelda de. Calendario de Fiestas Populares. Mexico City: Secretaría de Educación, Dirección General de Culturas Populares, 1988.

Pomar, María Teresa. Fiestas en México. Mexico City: México Desconocido, 2000.

Quintana, Patricia, with Carol Haralson. Mexico's Feasts of Life. Tulsa, Okla.: Council Oak Books, 1989.

Tausend, Marilyn. Savoring Mexico. San Francisco, Calif.: Williams-Sonoma, 2001.

Torres Yzabal, María Dolores, and Shelton Wiseman. The Mexican Gourmet. San Diego, Calif.: Thunder Bay Press, 1995.

CHAPTER 8

Carter, J. S., J. A. Pugh, and A. Monterrosa. "Non-insulin Diabetes Mellitus in Minorities in the United States." Annals of Internal Medicine 125, no. 3 (1996): 221–32.

Gohdes, D., S. Kaufman, and S. Valway. "Diabetes in American Indians." Diabetes Care 16, suppl. 1 (1993): 239–43.

Rivera, J. T. Shamah, S. Villalpando, T. González, B. Hernández, and J. Sepúlveda-Amor. Encuesta Nacional de Nutrición: Estado nutricio de niños y mujeres en Mexico. Mexico City: Instituto Nacional de Salud Pública, 2001.

Vargas, L., R. Bastarrachea, H. Laviada, J. González, and H. Ávila. Obesidad: Consenso. Mexico City: McGraw-Hill Interamericana, 2002.

MEXICAN COOKBOOKS IN ENGLISH

Bayless, Rick. *Rick Bayless's Mexican Kitchen*. New York: Scribner, 1996.

Bayless, Rick, and Deann Bayless. *Authentic Mexican: Regional Cooking from the Heart of Mexico*. New York: William Morrow, 1987.

Gerlach, N., and J. Gerlach. *Foods of the Maya: A Taste of the Yucatan*. Freedom, Calif.: Crossing Press, 1994.

Kennedy, Diana. *The Cuisines of Mexico*. New York: Harper & Row, 1972.

———. *Recipes from the Regional Cooks of Mexico*. New York: Harper & Row, 1978.

Palazuelos, Susana. *México: The Beautiful Cookbook*. Hong Kong: Weldon Owen, 1991.

Quintana, Patricia. *The Taste of Mexico*. New York: Stewart, Tabori and Chang, 1986.

Quintana, Patricia, with Carol Haralson. *Mexico's Feasts of Life*. Tulsa, Okla.: Council Oak Books, 1989.

Tausend, Marilyn. *Savoring Mexico*. San Francisco, Calif.: Williams-Sonoma, 2001.

Torres Yzabal, María Dolores, and Shelton Wiseman. *The Mexican Gourmet*. San Diego, Calif.: Thunder Bay Press, 1995.

Index

Achiote, 11, 120
Agave, 8, 112. *See also Pulque*
Algae, 7
Amaranth, 3, 4, 5, 6, 8, 41
Annals of Cuautitlán, 9
Anorexia and bulimia, 175–77
Atole, 6, 8, 11, 35, 125
Avocados, 4, 41–42, 83
Aztecs, 3; agricultural calendar of, 5–6; agricultural fiestas of, 6; ceremony of the first fruit and, 7; diet and, 2–9; famine and, 9; fiestas and, 7, 8; flower wars and, 3; fruit and, 7–8; gatherers and, 4; gods and, 5–7; protein and, 7, 8–9

Balché. See Drinks
Banquets, Aztec, 8; Independent Mexico and, 26; New Spain and, 14–15, 20, 21, 22
Basic diet, 4, 7, 83
Beans, 3, 4, 7, 10, 22, 32, 38–39, 83, 88, 100
Biznagas. See Cactus fruit

Cacao. *See* Chocolate
Cactus fruit: *biznagas*, 83; *tunas*, 83
Cactus paddles, 42, 83, 88, 113
Catholic Church: fiestas and, 18–19; food of convents and, 17–19; food of monasteries and, 19–20; influence of food and, 17–20
Chayote, 42–43, 83. *See also* squash
Chilam Balam of Chumayel, Books of, 12
Chile peppers, 3, 4, 7, 22, 46, 47, 48, 103, 104, 106; Oaxacan, 116
Chinampas, 3
Chocolate, 8, 11, 43–45
Citrus fruit, 52–53
Comal, 70, 77
Cooking utensils: of Independent Mexico, 77; of New Spain, 70–74; pre-Hispanic, 68–70; of twentieth century, 78–81
Cooks: contemporary, 80–81; of Independent Mexico, 76–77; of New Spain, 74–75; pre-Hispanic, 63–65; of twentieth century, 79–80

Corn, 32–38; and beverages, 35, 45; and *huitlacoche*, 35–36; and tamales, 36–37; and tortillas, 37–38
Criollos, 18, 22, 23

Diabetes mellitus, 174–75
Díaz del Castillo, Bernal, 9, 14, 52
Drinks: *aguas frescas*, 88, 106; *atole*, 8, 11 35; *atolechampurrado*, 45; chocolate, 43–45; *chocolateatole*, 45; *horchata*, 59; *pozol*, 45; *tascalate*, 45; *tejate*, 45
Drinks, alcoholic: *balché*, 11; beer, 92, 100, 112; *mezcal*, 116; *pulque*, 8, 24; tequila, 104; *tesgüino*, 100

Epazote, 11
European domestic animals, 55–58

Famine: of New Spain, 23, 24; pre-Hispanic, 9, 12, 23–24
Fiestas, 139–62; Candlemas, 142–44; Carnival, 144–45; Civic fiestas, 157–58; Commercial fairs, 160–61; Days of the Dead, 148–51; December fiestas, 151–53; Independence Day, 146–48; Lent and Holy Week, 145–46; National, 141–54; New Year's Eve, 153–54; Religious and harvest fiestas, 158–60; Rite-of-Passage, 154–57; Santa Cruz, 146
Fondas, 124, 127–31
Food preparation: of Independent Mexico, 77; of New Spain, 70–74; of Twentieth century, 77–81; pre-Hispanic, 66–68
Fruit: citrus, 52–53; European, 53–55; pre-Hispanic, 7–8

Gage, Thomas, 19–20
Governmental-aid nutrition programs, 166–68
Greens, 83, 88

Honey, 11
Huitlacoche, 35–36
Hunters and gatherers, 1–2, 3, 4

Iguanas, 11
Independent Mexico, 24–26; foreign influence and, 24–25; new food products of, 25–26
Indian diet, 84–88
Indian perception of food, 163–164
Insects: as food, 7, 9, 83, 108–9; eggs of, 112; *gusanos de maguey*, 112, *jumiles*, 108–9

Jícama, 5, 45, 83, 84, 104

Kitchens: of Independent Mexico, 76–77; of New Spain, 70–74; of twentieth century, 77–81; pre-Hispanic, 65–66

Landa, Diego de, 10, 11, 12

Maize. *See* Corn.
Malnutrition and anemia, 164–66
Mangoes, 54–55
Manila Galleon, 21, 54
Market food, 131–32
Marqués de Croix, 21
Maximilian and Carlota, 26
Maya: banquets of, 10; beans and, 11; bloodletting ceremony and, 10; cooking methods of, 64, 120; corn and, 9; culture of, 2; diet of, 9–12; famine and, 12; fruit and, 11; greens and, 10, 11, 12; honey and, 11; protein and, 10–11; root crops and, 11; seafood and, 11
Meat, 55–58
Mesoamerica, 2
Metate, 64, 68, 77, 78
Mexica. *See* Aztec
Middle-class diet, 89–95; of children and adolescents, 95; of Jalisco, 93;

of Mexico City, 94; of northern
Mexico, 92; of Oaxaca, 93; of
Tlaxcala, 94; of Yucatán, 90
Molcajete, 68, 69, 78
Montezuma Ilhuicamina, 9
Montezuma II, 8
Mortar and pestle, 27

Nao de China. See Manila Galleon
New Spain: banquets of, 14, 18–19,
20, 21–22; famine of 23–24; fiestas
of, 23; food distribution of, 15–17;
food of, 13–24; food syncretism of,
22–23; markets of, 15–17; religion
and food of, 17–20; tribute of,15
Nixtamalización, 27, 67–68
Nopales. See Cactus paddles
North American Free Trade Agree-
ment (NAFTA), 29
Nutrient-enriched foods, 168–70
Nutrition of Indian groups, 84–88;
Huichol, 86; Mixtec, 85; Nahua
(Morelos), 85; Tarahumara, 84–86;
Tzotzil, 84; Yucatecan Maya, 84,
87; Zapotecs 84, 86
Nutritional surveys, 164–66

Obesity, 170–74

Papago Indians, 173–74
Papaya, 49
Philippines, gastronomic influence
from, 21
Pibs, 64, 120
Pineapples, 49
Plantains, 47, 117
Plant domestication, 4–5
Plate of Good Eating, 177–79
Pozol, 9, 10, 84, 86, 105, 106
Pre-Hispanic cuisine, 2–3
Pulque. See Drinks, alcoholic

Regional diets: of Baja, California,
101; of central Mexico, 106–15; of

Isthmus of Tehuantepec, 115–19;
of Maya area, 119–21; of northern
Mexico, 98–100; of Pacific coast,
101–4; of Sonora, 101; of Tamaulipas, 101; of western Mexico,
104–6
Relaciones de las cosas de Yucatán,
10–12,
Restaurants, 136–38
Rice, 58–59
Root crops, 11

Seafood, Mayan, 11
Soft drinks, 28
Spices, 60, 118, 119
Squash, 3, 4, 7, 12, 32, 39–41, 42–43,
83
Street food, 28, 123–27
Sugar, 60–61
Sweet potato, 5, 84

Tamales, 9, 36–37, 84, 125
Taquerías, 123, 132–35
Tehuacán valley, 33, 111
Tenochtitlán, 3
Teotihuacán, 2–3
Toltecs, 3
Tomatoes and *tomatillos*, 3, 47–49, 83
Torterías, 123, 135
Tortillas, 9, 10, 27, 37–38, 77, 83;
blue corn, 108
Tropical fruit, 49–50: *cherimoya*, 50;
guanábana, 50; guava, 50; *mamey*,
50; papaya, 49; pineapple, 49;
pitahaya, 50; *sapodilla*, 50; soursop,
50; *tuna*, 50; *zapote*, 50
Tudela Codex, 65
Tunas. See Cactus fruit
Turkey, 5, 7, 10, 11, 50–52
Twentieth century: food changes of,
26–29; North American Free
Trade Agreement and, 29; techno-
logical improvement of, 27;
transnational companies of, 28

Typical Mexican meals, 83–84

Viceregal Palace, 20, 21, 22,
   111
Von Humboldt, Alexander, 23

Wheat, 22, 24, 61–62, 99

Yucca, 5, 84

Zapotes, 4, 5, 8
Zea mays. See Corn

About the Authors

JANET LONG-SOLÍS is a Research Associate at the Institute of Historical Studies, Universidad Nacional Autónoma de Mexico.

LUIS ALBERTO VARGAS is a researcher at the Institute of Historical Studies, Universidad Nacional Autónoma de Mexico.

Recent Titles in
Food Culture around the World

Food Culture in Japan
Michael Ashkenazi and Jeanne Jacob

Food Culture in India
Colleen Taylor Sen

Food Culture in China
Jacqueline M. Newman

Food Culture in Great Britain
Laura Mason

Food Culture in Italy
Fabio Parasecoli

Food Culture in Spain
Xavier F. Medina

Food Culture in the Near East, Middle East, and North Africa
Peter Heine

Lightning Source UK Ltd.
Milton Keynes UK
UKOW03n1237220913

217617UK00011B/125/P